PLUTONA

JEFF LEMIRE   EMI LENOX   JORDIE BELLAIRE

STORY **EMI LENOX** & **JEFF LEMIRE**
SCRIPT **JEFF LEMIRE**
ART **EMI LENOX**
COLORS **JORDIE BELLAIRE**
LETTERS **STEVE WANDS**
BOOK DESIGN **SASHA HEAD**

PLUTONA created by **EMI LENOX**
PLUTONA'S LAST ADVENTURE by **JEFF LEMIRE**

IMAGE COMICS, INC.
Robert Kirkman - Chief Operating Officer
Erik Larsen - Chief Financial Officer
Todd McFarlane - President
Marc Silvestri - Chief Executive Officer
Jim Valentino - Vice-President

Eric Stephenson - Publisher
Corey Murphy - Director of Sales
Jeff Boison - Director of Publishing Planning & Book Trade Sales
Jeremy Sullivan - Director of Digital Sales
Kat Salazar - Director of PR & Marketing
Emily Miller - Director of Operations
Branwyn Bigglestone - Senior Accounts Manager
Sarah Mello - Accounts Manager
Drew Gill - Art Director
Jonathan Chan - Production Manager
Meredith Wallace - Print Manager
Briah Skelly - Publicist
Sasha Head - Sales & Marketing Production Designer
Randy Okamura - Digital Production Designer
David Brothers - Branding Manager
Addison Duke - Production Artist
Vincent Kukua - Production Artist
Tricia Ramos - Production Artist
Jeff Stang - Direct Market Sales Representative
Emilio Bautista - Digital Sales Associate
Leanna Caunter - Accounting Assistant
Chloe Ramos-Peterson - Administrative Assistant

IMAGECOMICS.COM

PLUTONA TP. JULY 2016. FIRST PRINTING.
TRADE PAPERBACK ISBN: 978-1-63215-601-3
HARDCOVER ISBN: 978-1-5343-0013-2

CHAPTER

1

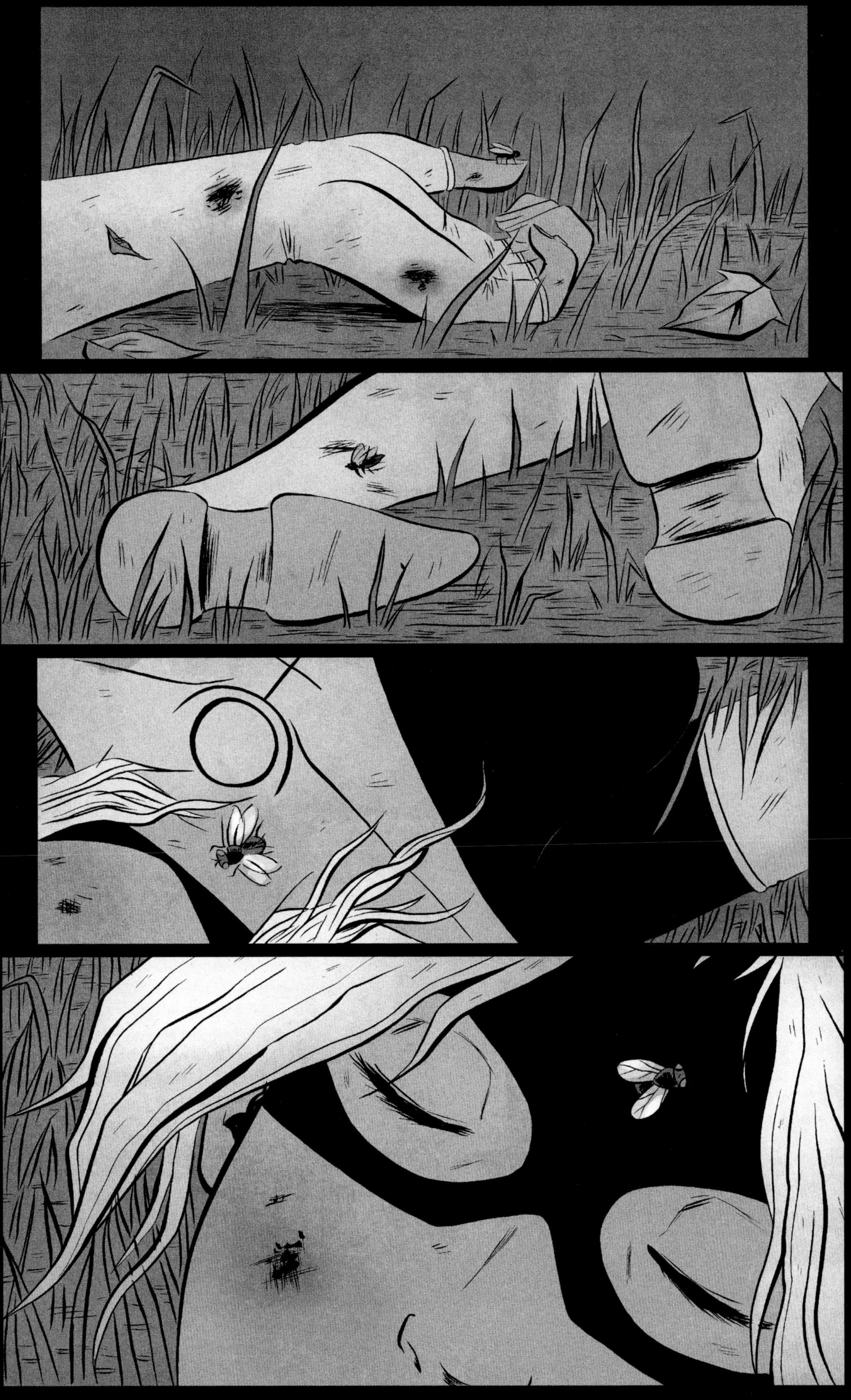

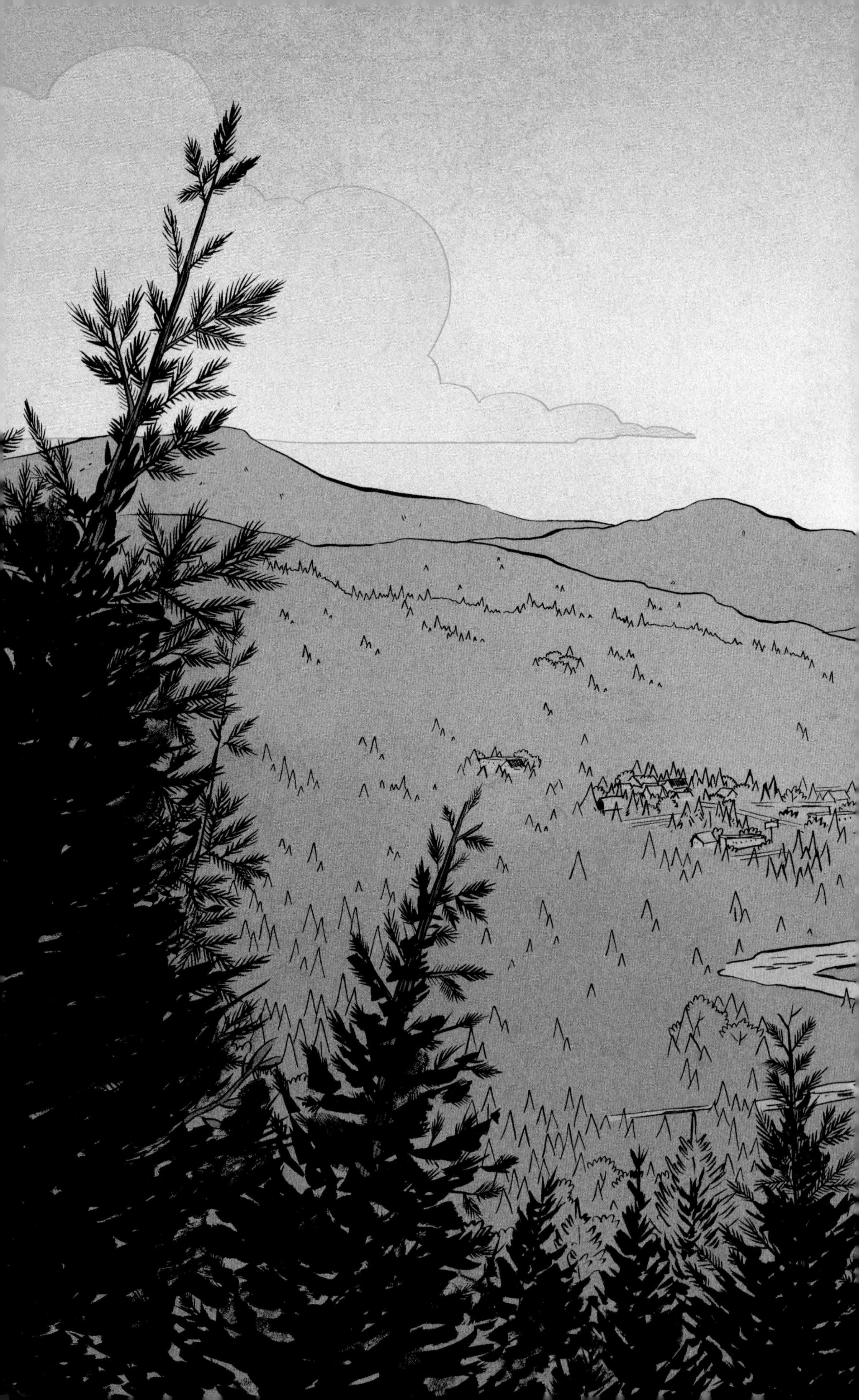

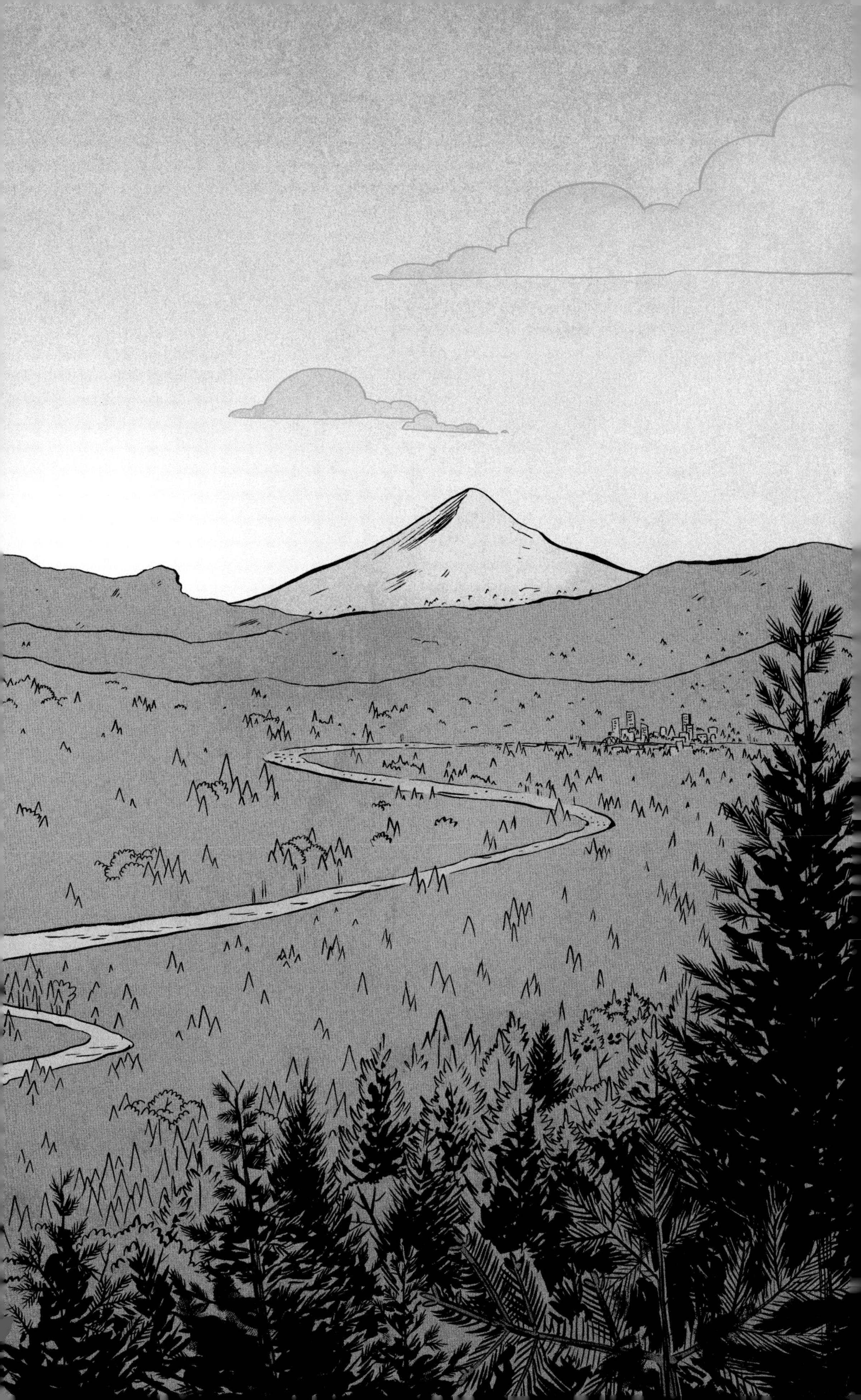

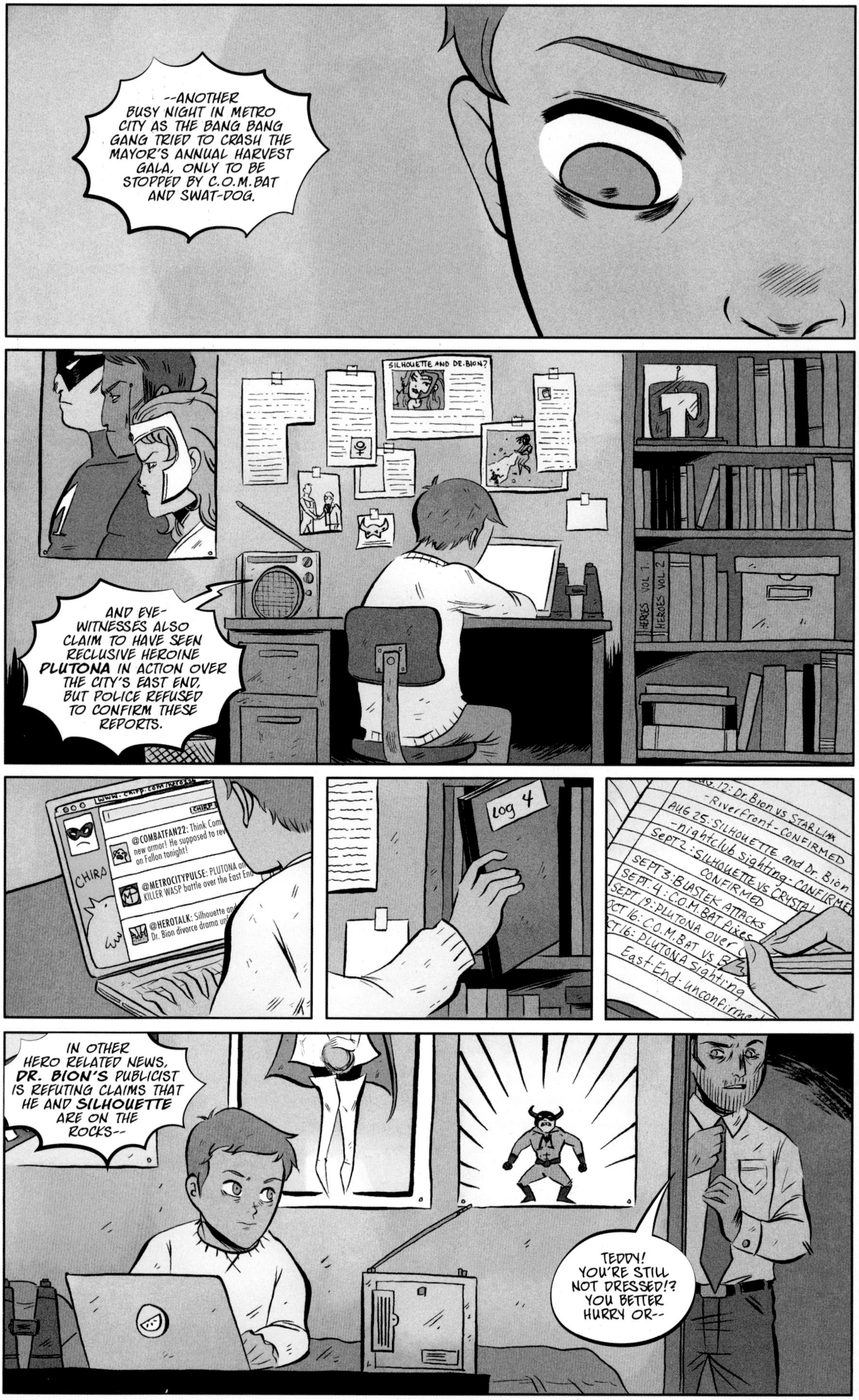
--ANOTHER BUSY NIGHT IN METRO CITY AS THE BANG BANG GANG TRIED TO CRASH THE MAYOR'S ANNUAL HARVEST GALA, ONLY TO BE STOPPED BY C.O.M.BAT AND SWAT-DOG.
SILHOUETTE AND DR. BION?
HEROES VOL. 1
HEROES VOL. 2
AND EYE-WITNESSES ALSO CLAIM TO HAVE SEEN RECLUSIVE HEROINE **PLUTONA** IN ACTION OVER THE CITY'S EAST END, BUT POLICE REFUSED TO CONFIRM THESE REPORTS.
CHIRP
@COMBATFAN22: Think
new armor! He supposed to
on Fallon tonight!
@METROCITYPULSE: PLUTONA
KILLER WASP battle over the East End
@HEROTALK: Silhouette
Dr. Bion divorce drama
LOG 4
Dr. Bion vs
-Riverfront-CONFIRMED
AUG 25: SILHOUETTE and Dr. Bion
-nightclub sighting-
SEPT 2: SILHOUETTE VS
CONFIRMED
SEPT 3: BLASTEK ATTACKS
SEPT. 4: C.O.M.BAT fixes
SEPT 19: PLUTONA over
OCT 16: C.O.M.BAT VS
PLUTONA sighting
East-End-
IN OTHER HERO RELATED NEWS, **DR. BION'S** PUBLICIST IS REFUTING CLAIMS THAT HE AND **SILHOUETTE** ARE ON THE ROCKS--
TEDDY! YOU'RE STILL NOT DRESSED!? YOU BETTER HURRY OR--

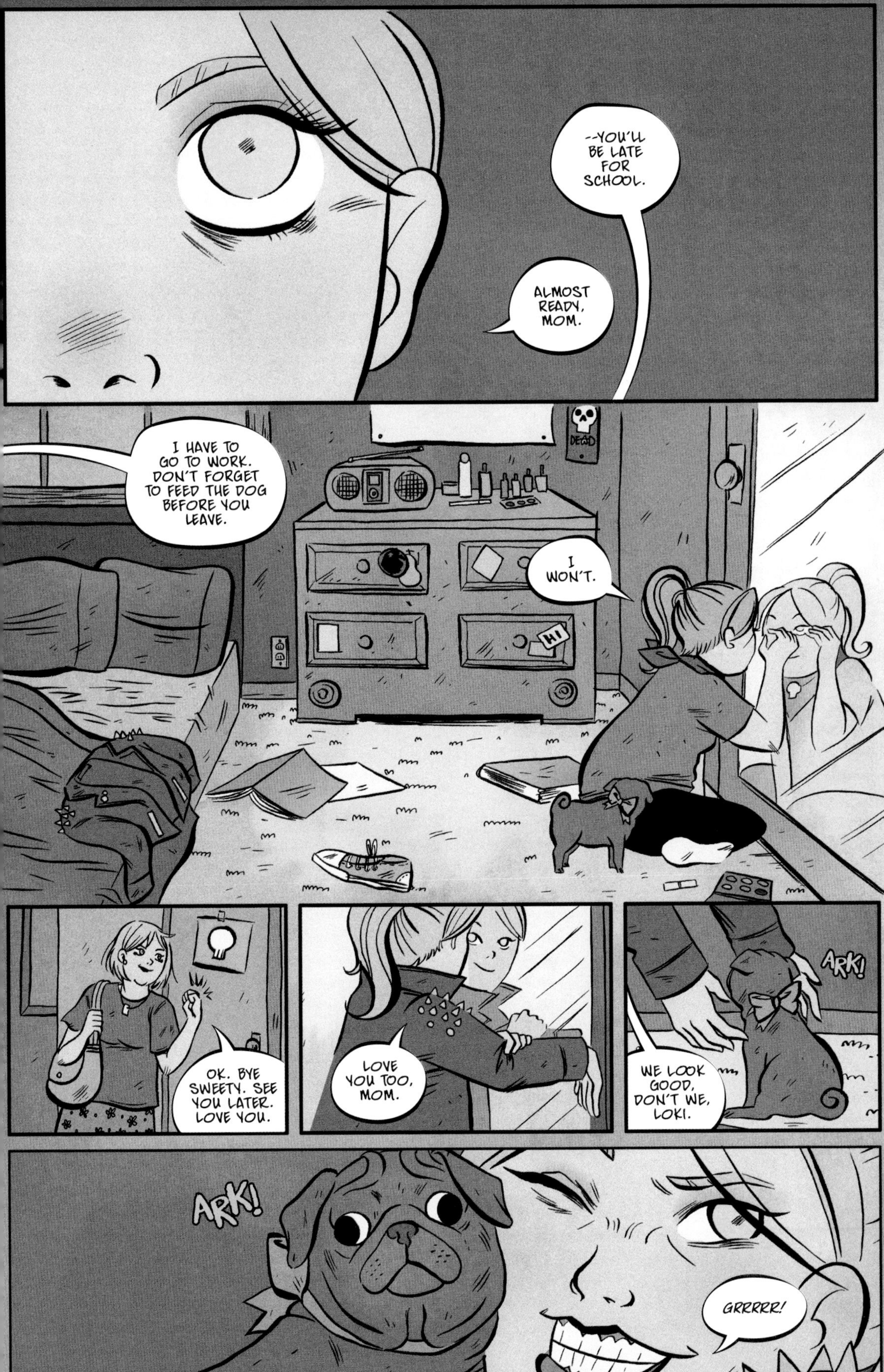
--YOU'LL BE LATE FOR SCHOOL.
ALMOST READY, MOM.
I HAVE TO GO TO WORK. DON'T FORGET TO FEED THE DOG BEFORE YOU LEAVE.
DEAD
I WON'T.
HI
OK. BYE SWEETY. SEE YOU LATER. LOVE YOU.
LOVE YOU TOO, MOM.
ARK!
WE LOOK GOOD, DON'T WE, LOKI.
ARK!
GRRRRR!

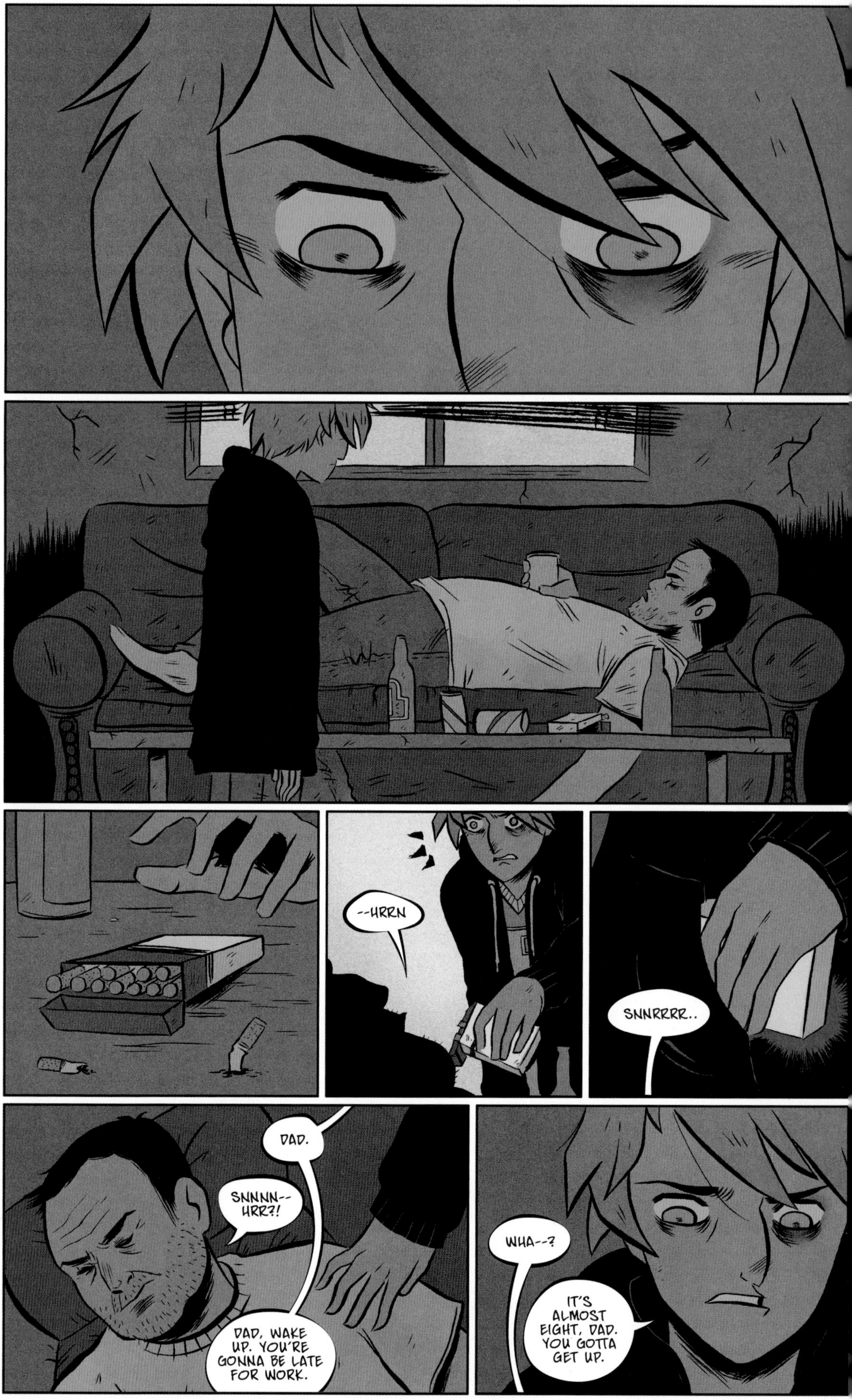
--HRRN
SNNRRRR..
DAD.
SNNNN--HRR?!
DAD, WAKE UP. YOU'RE GONNA BE LATE FOR WORK.
WHA--?
IT'S ALMOST EIGHT, DAD. YOU GOTTA GET UP.

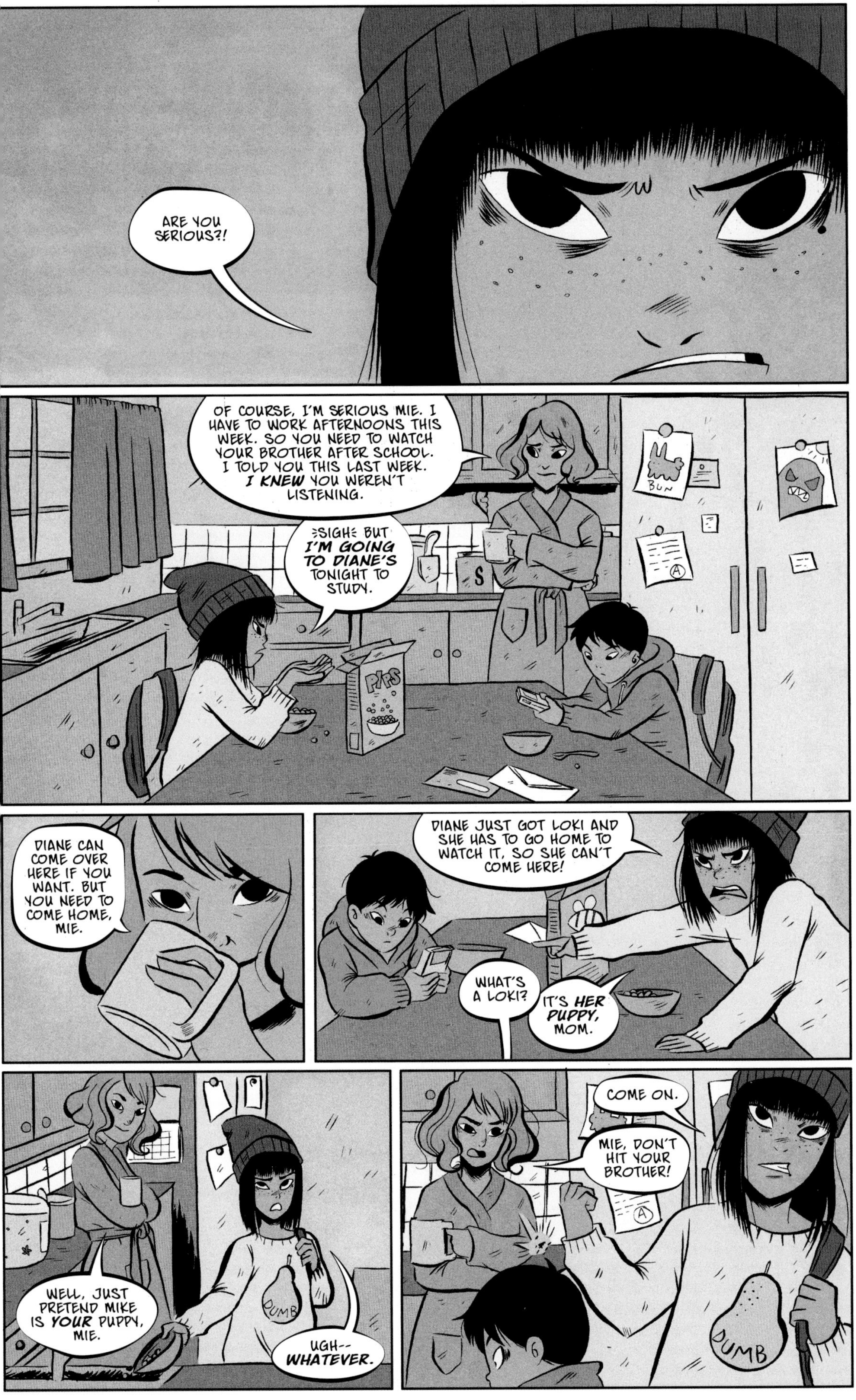
ARE YOU SERIOUS?!
OF COURSE, I'M SERIOUS MIE. I HAVE TO WORK AFTERNOONS THIS WEEK. SO YOU NEED TO WATCH YOUR BROTHER AFTER SCHOOL. I TOLD YOU THIS LAST WEEK. I KNEW YOU WEREN'T LISTENING.
SIGH BUT I'M GOING TO DIANE'S TONIGHT TO STUDY.
BUN
PIPS
S
DIANE CAN COME OVER HERE IF YOU WANT. BUT YOU NEED TO COME HOME, MIE.
DIANE JUST GOT LOKI AND SHE HAS TO GO HOME TO WATCH IT, SO SHE CAN'T COME HERE!
WHAT'S A LOKI?
IT'S HER PUPPY, MOM.
WELL, JUST PRETEND MIKE IS YOUR PUPPY, MIE.
DUMB
UGH-- WHATEVER.
COME ON.
MIE, DON'T HIT YOUR BROTHER!
DUMB

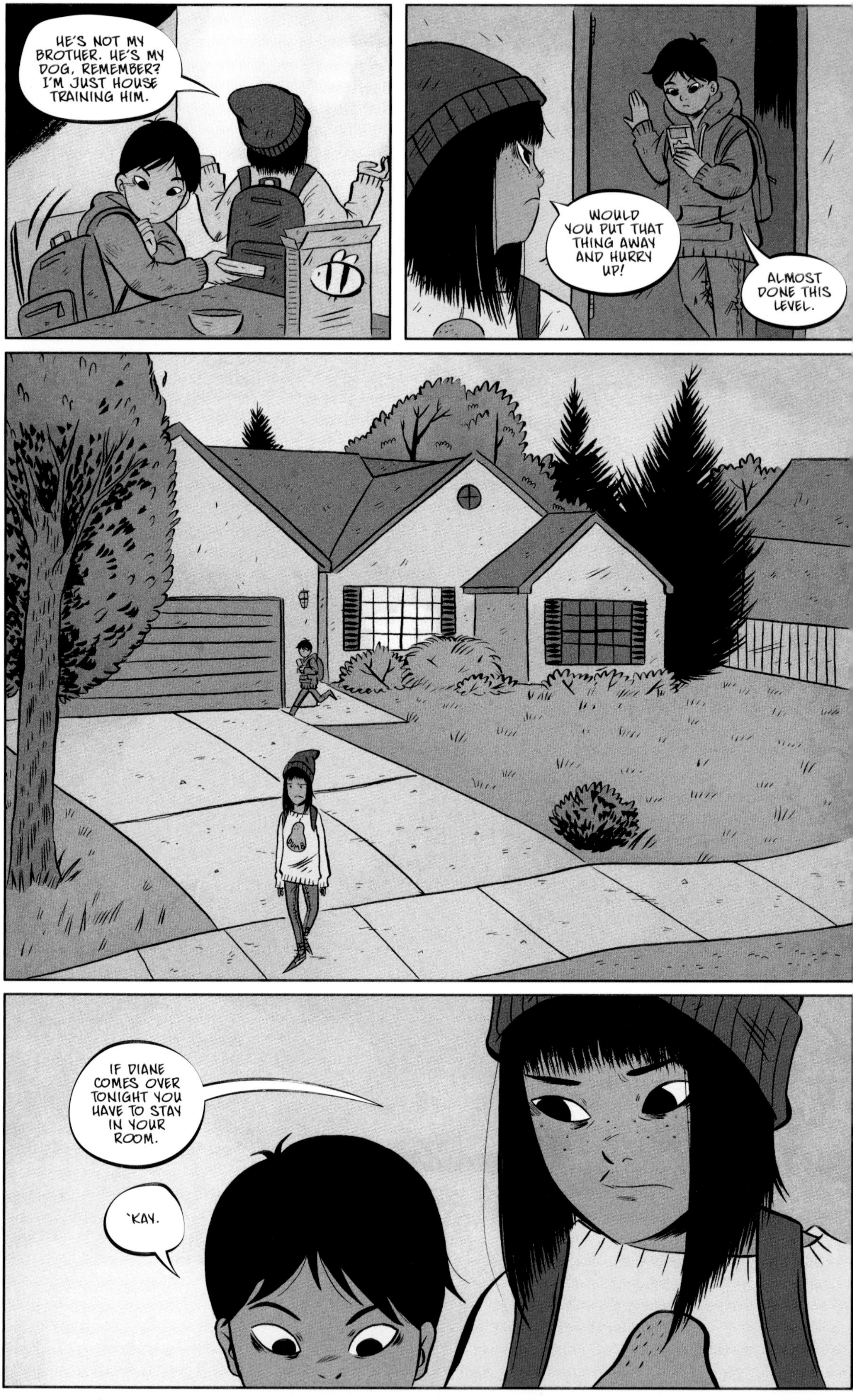
HE'S NOT MY BROTHER. HE'S MY DOG, REMEMBER? I'M JUST HOUSE TRAINING HIM.
WOULD YOU PUT THAT THING AWAY AND HURRY UP!
ALMOST DONE THIS LEVEL.
DUMB
IF DIANE COMES OVER TONIGHT YOU HAVE TO STAY IN YOUR ROOM.
'KAY.

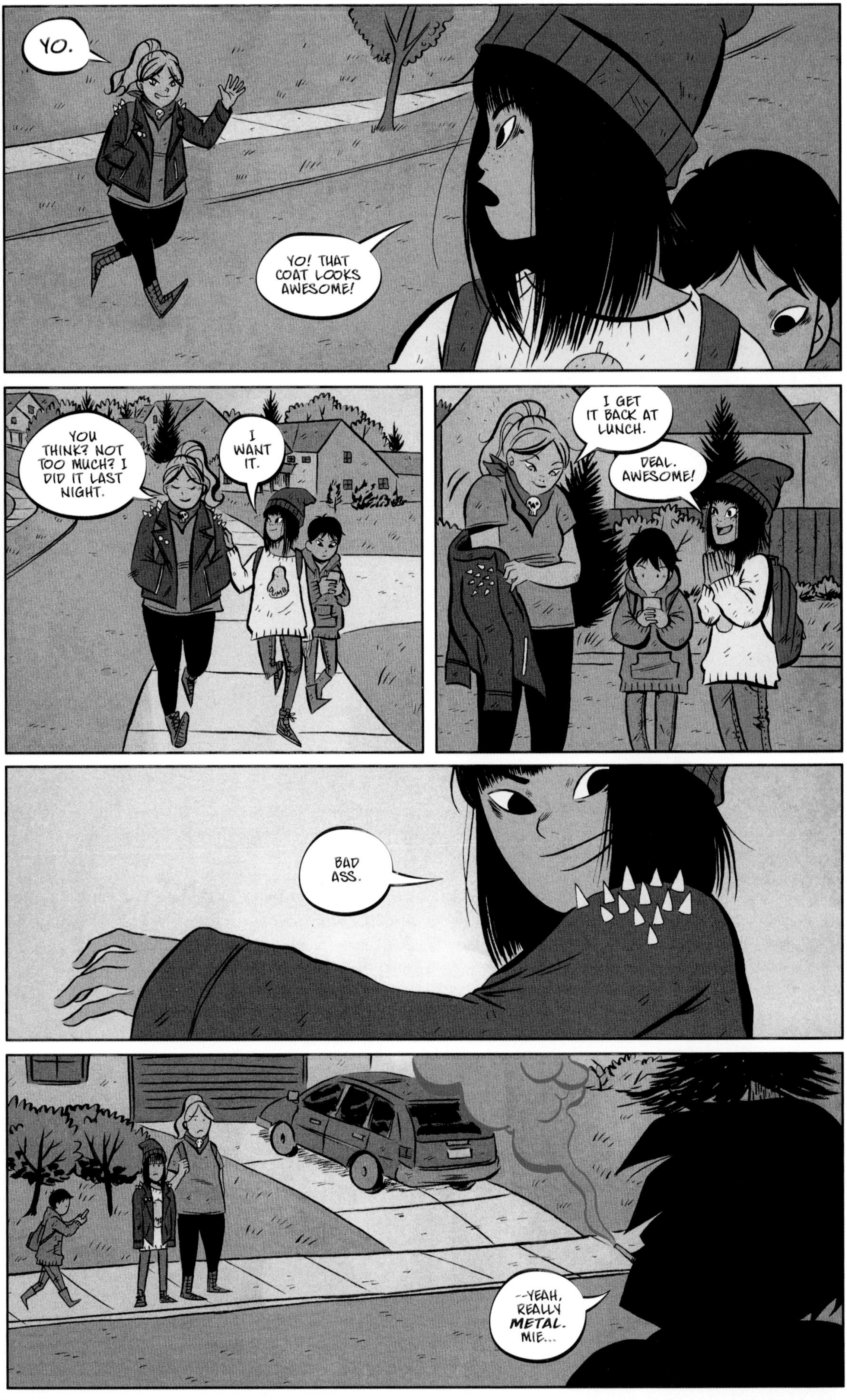
YO.
YO! THAT COAT LOOKS AWESOME!
YOU THINK? NOT TOO MUCH? I DID IT LAST NIGHT.
I WANT IT.
DUMB
I GET IT BACK AT LUNCH.
DEAL. AWESOME!
BAD ASS.
--YEAH, REALLY **METAL.** MIE...

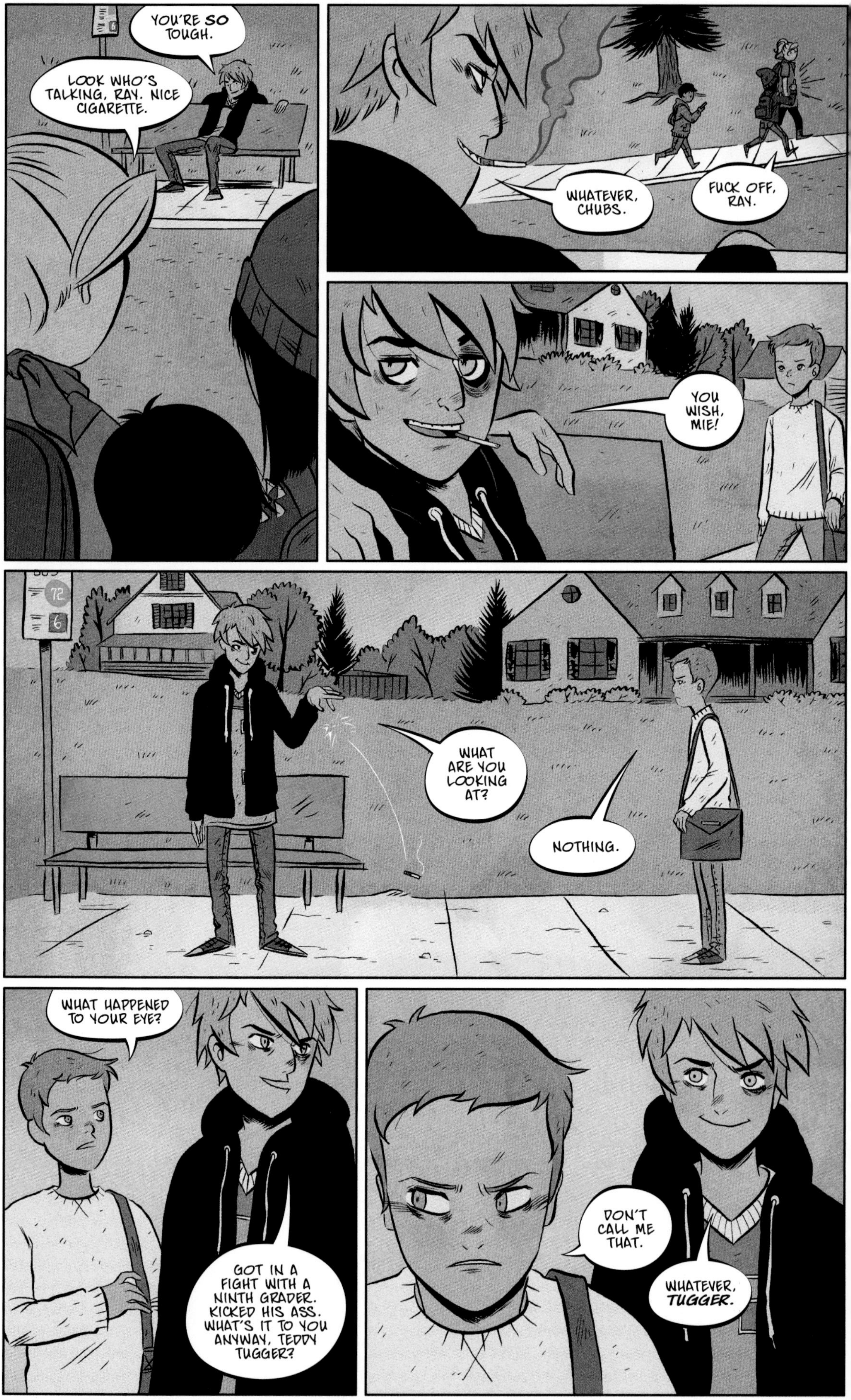
YOU'RE SO TOUGH.
LOOK WHO'S TALKING, RAY. NICE CIGARETTE.
WHATEVER, CHUBS.
FUCK OFF, RAY.
YOU WISH, MIE!
WHAT ARE YOU LOOKING AT?
NOTHING.
WHAT HAPPENED TO YOUR EYE?
GOT IN A FIGHT WITH A NINTH GRADER. KICKED HIS ASS. WHAT'S IT TO YOU ANYWAY, TEDDY TUGGER?
DON'T CALL ME THAT.
WHATEVER, TUGGER.

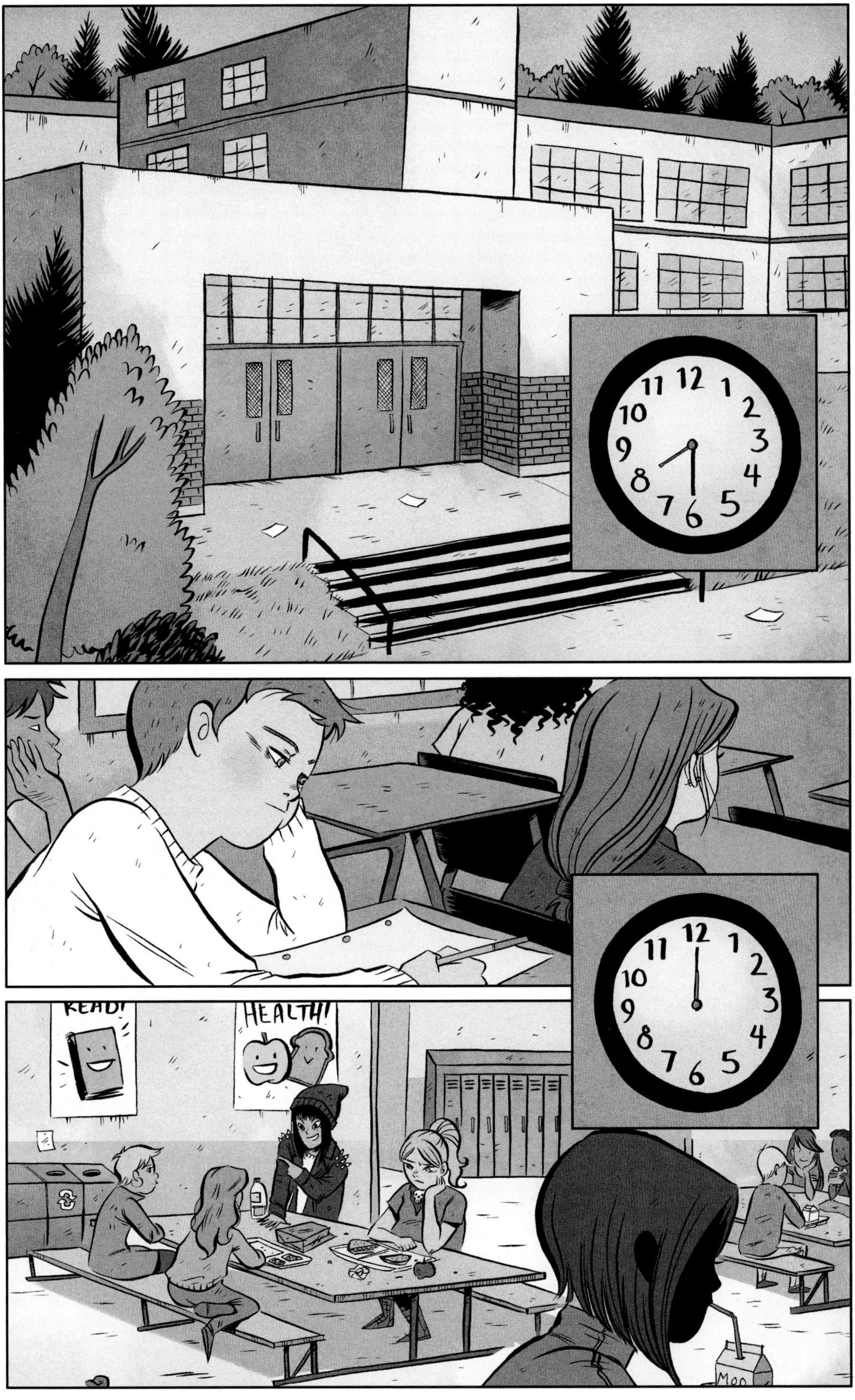
HEALTH!

RRRRRRRNNNNNNNGGGG

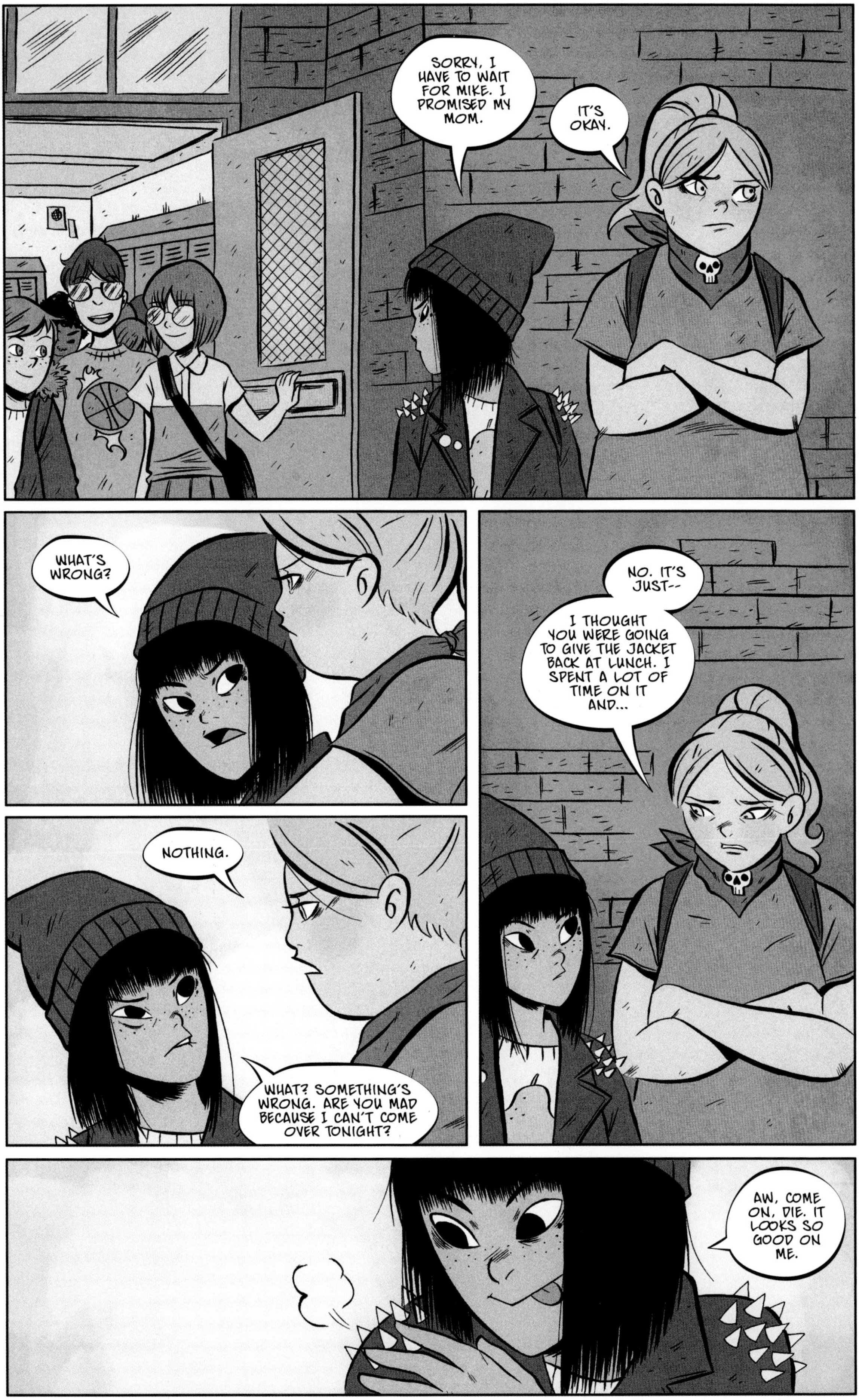
SORRY, I HAVE TO WAIT FOR MIKE. I PROMISED MY MOM.
IT'S OKAY.
WHAT'S WRONG?
NOTHING.
WHAT? SOMETHING'S WRONG. ARE YOU MAD BECAUSE I CAN'T COME OVER TONIGHT?
NO. IT'S JUST--
I THOUGHT YOU WERE GOING TO GIVE THE JACKET BACK AT LUNCH. I SPENT A LOT OF TIME ON IT AND...
AW, COME ON, DIE. IT LOOKS SO GOOD ON ME.

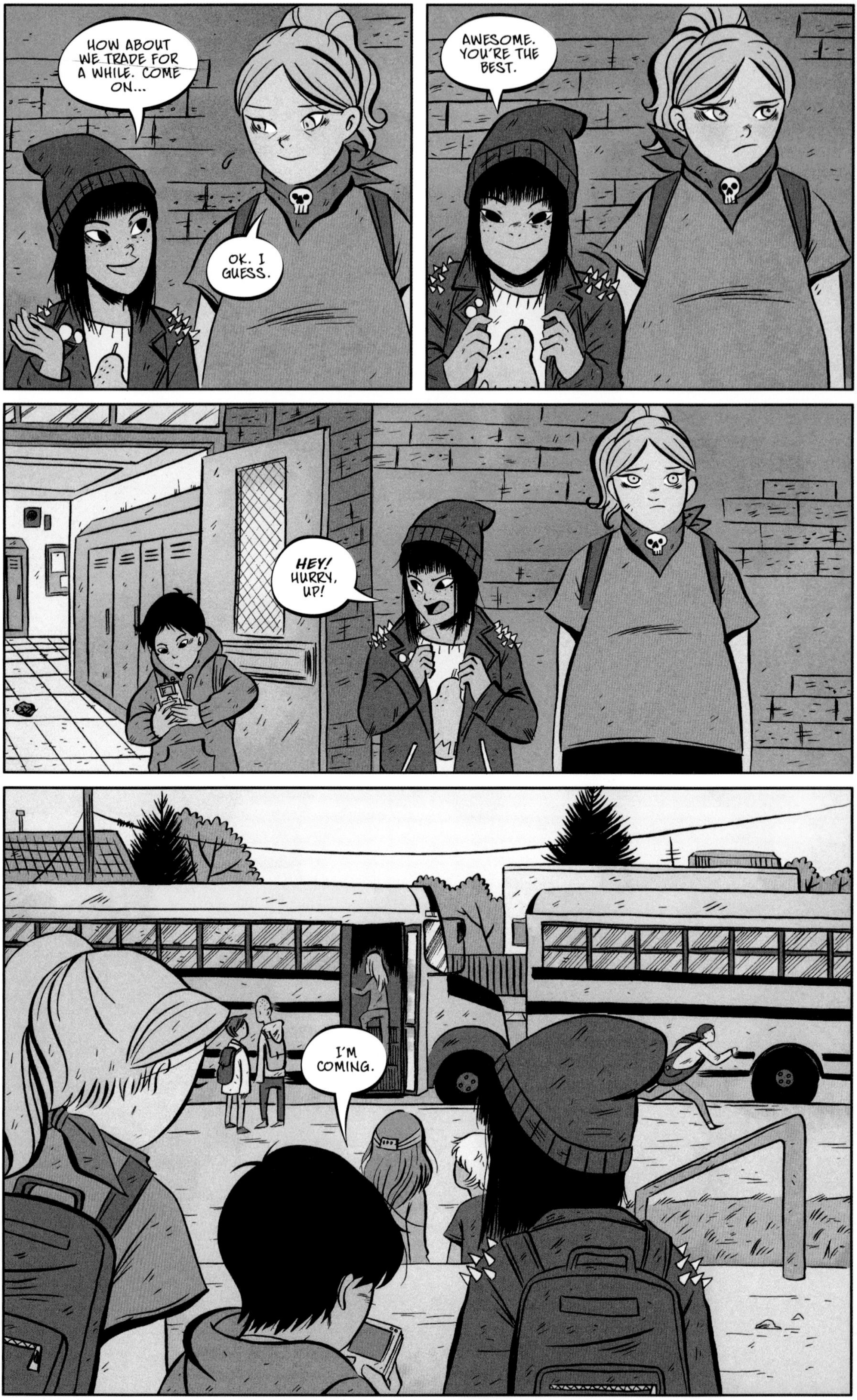
HOW ABOUT WE TRADE FOR A WHILE. COME ON...
OK. I GUESS.
AWESOME. YOU'RE THE BEST.
HEY! HURRY, UP!
I'M COMING.

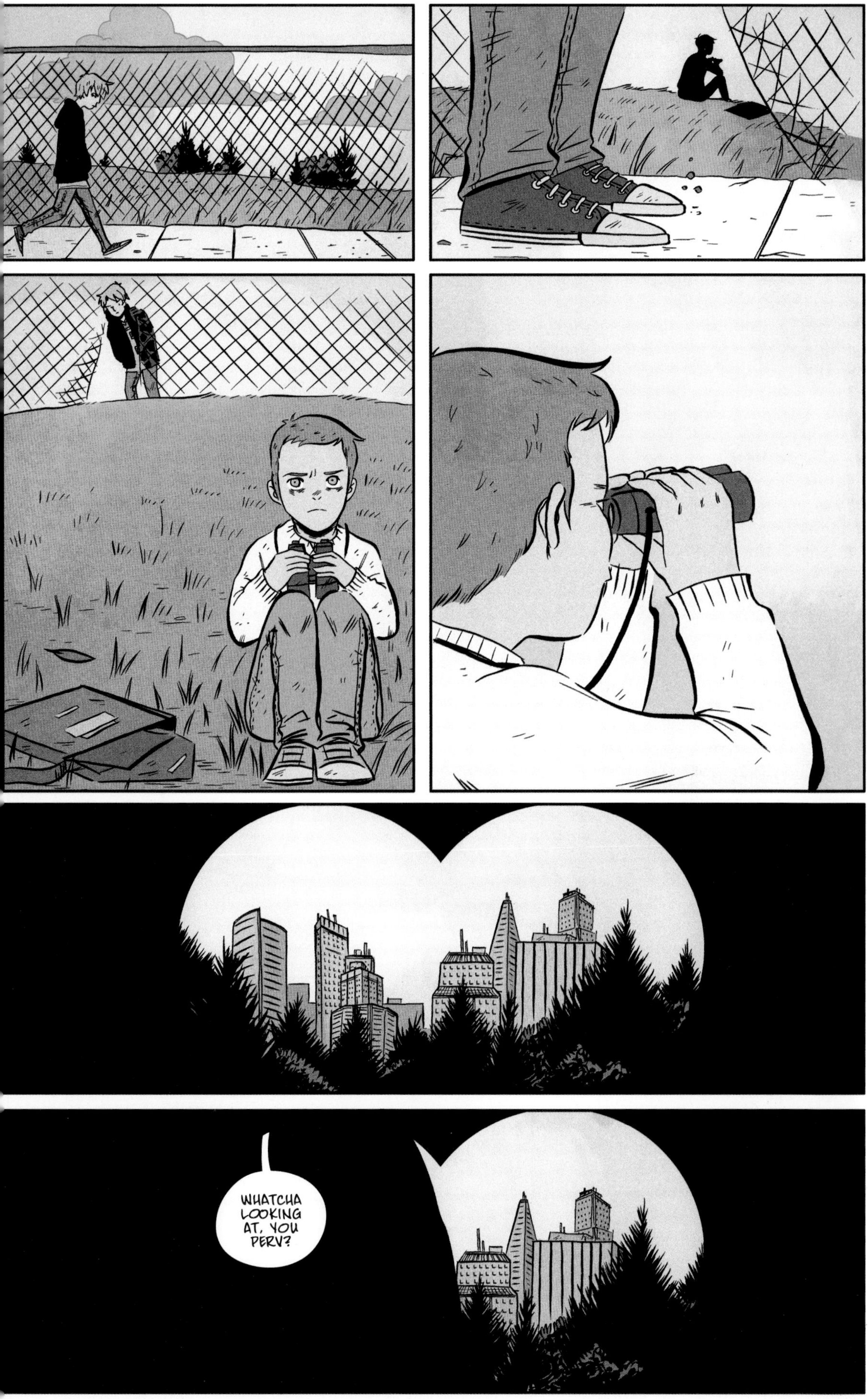
WHATCHA LOOKING AT, YOU PERV?

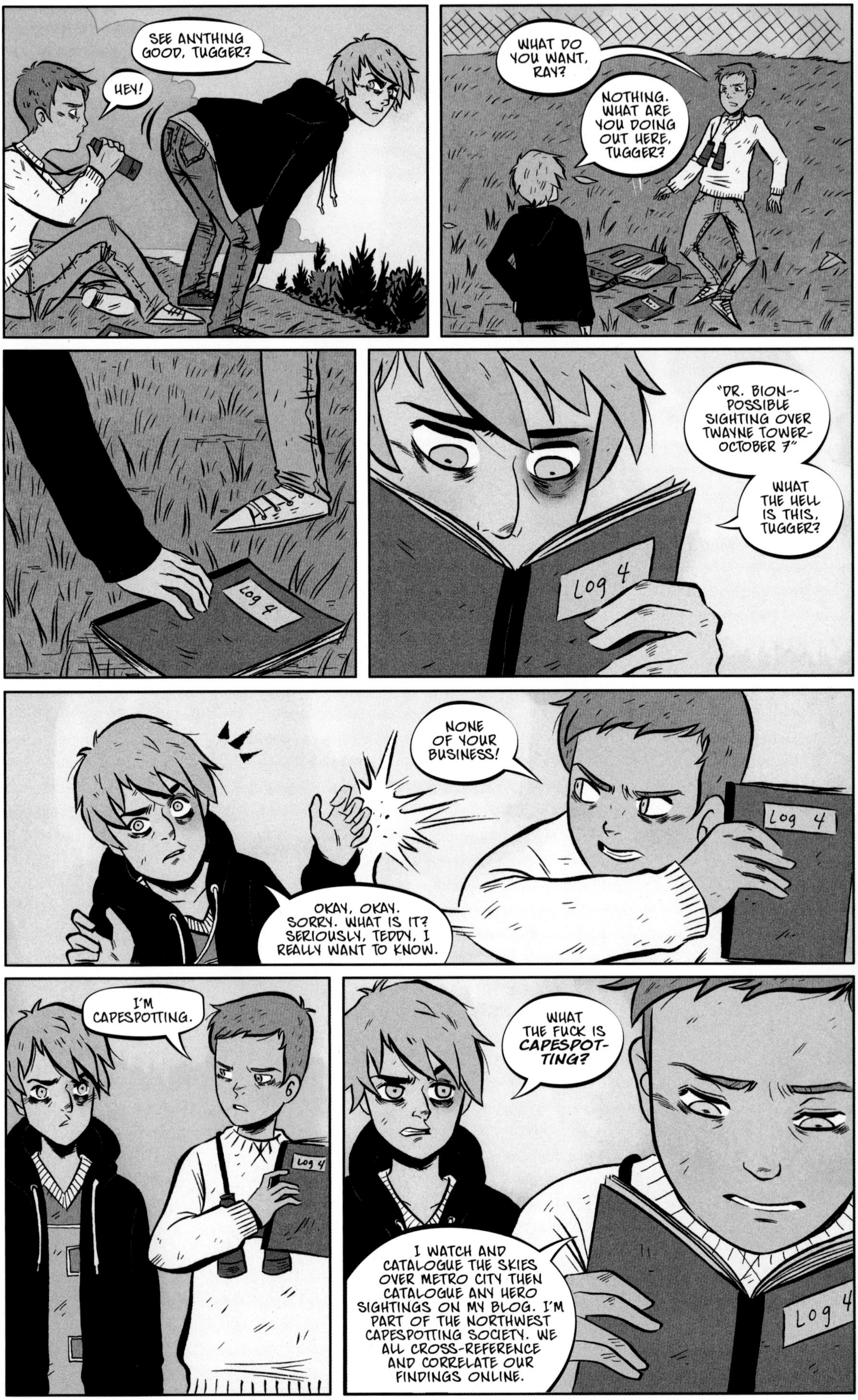
SEE ANYTHING GOOD, TUGGER?
HEY!
WHAT DO YOU WANT, RAY?
NOTHING. WHAT ARE YOU DOING OUT HERE, TUGGER?
Log 4
"DR. BION--POSSIBLE SIGHTING OVER TWAYNE TOWER-OCTOBER 7"
WHAT THE HELL IS THIS, TUGGER?
Log 4
NONE OF YOUR BUSINESS!
Log 4
OKAY, OKAY. SORRY. WHAT IS IT? SERIOUSLY, TEDDY, I REALLY WANT TO KNOW.
I'M CAPESPOTTING.
Log 4
WHAT THE FUCK IS *CAPESPOTTING?*
I WATCH AND CATALOGUE THE SKIES OVER METRO CITY THEN CATALOGUE ANY HERO SIGHTINGS ON MY BLOG. I'M PART OF THE NORTHWEST CAPESPOTTING SOCIETY. WE ALL CROSS-REFERENCE AND CORRELATE OUR FINDINGS ONLINE.
Log 4

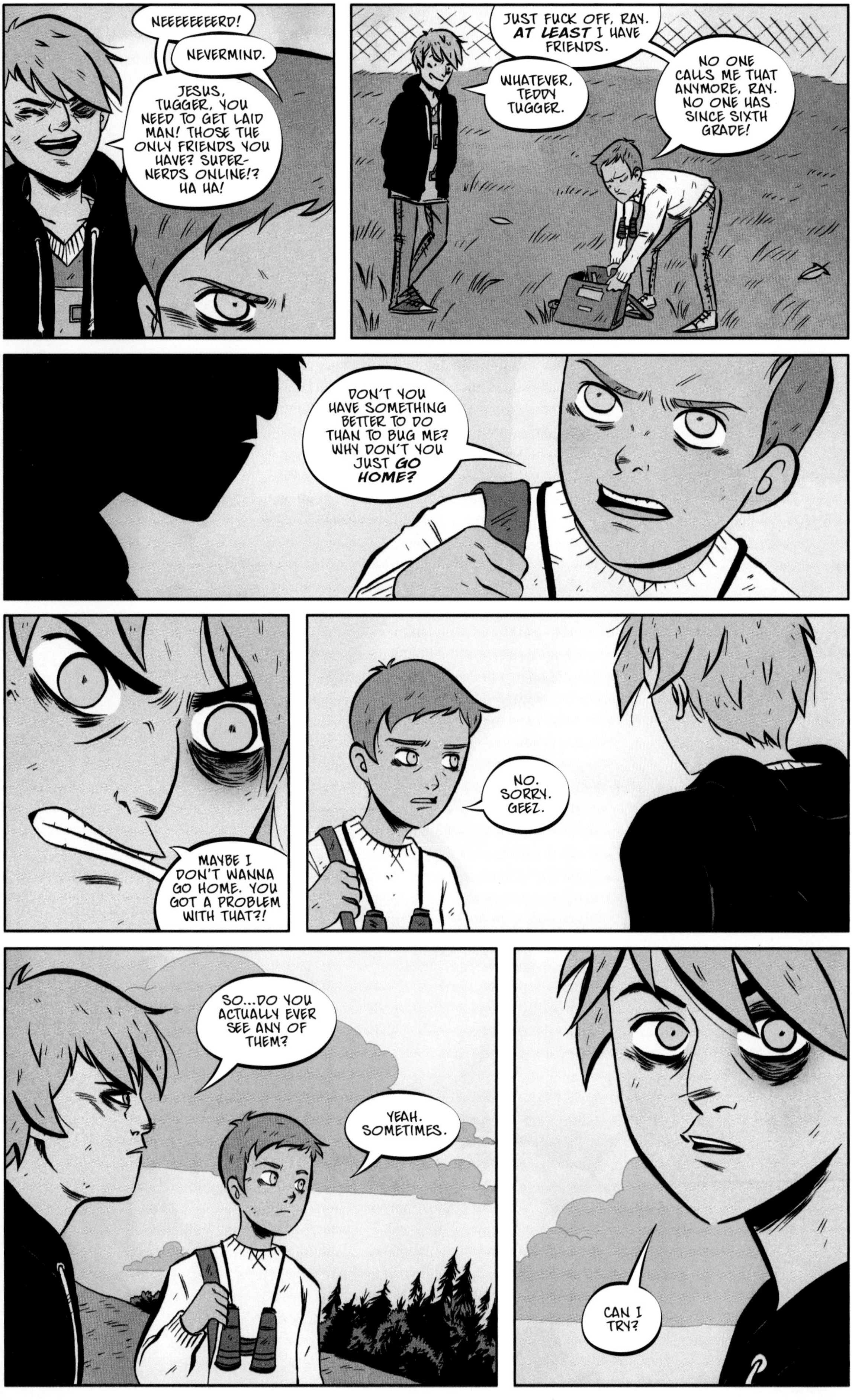
NEEEEEEEERD!
NEVERMIND.
JESUS, TUGGER, YOU NEED TO GET LAID MAN! THOSE THE ONLY FRIENDS YOU HAVE? SUPER-NERDS ONLINE!? HA HA!
JUST FUCK OFF, RAY. AT LEAST I HAVE FRIENDS.
WHATEVER, TEDDY TUGGER.
NO ONE CALLS ME THAT ANYMORE, RAY. NO ONE HAS SINCE SIXTH GRADE!
DON'T YOU HAVE SOMETHING BETTER TO DO THAN TO BUG ME? WHY DON'T YOU JUST GO HOME?
MAYBE I DON'T WANNA GO HOME. YOU GOT A PROBLEM WITH THAT?!
NO. SORRY. GEEZ.
SO...DO YOU ACTUALLY EVER SEE ANY OF THEM?
YEAH. SOMETIMES.
CAN I TRY?

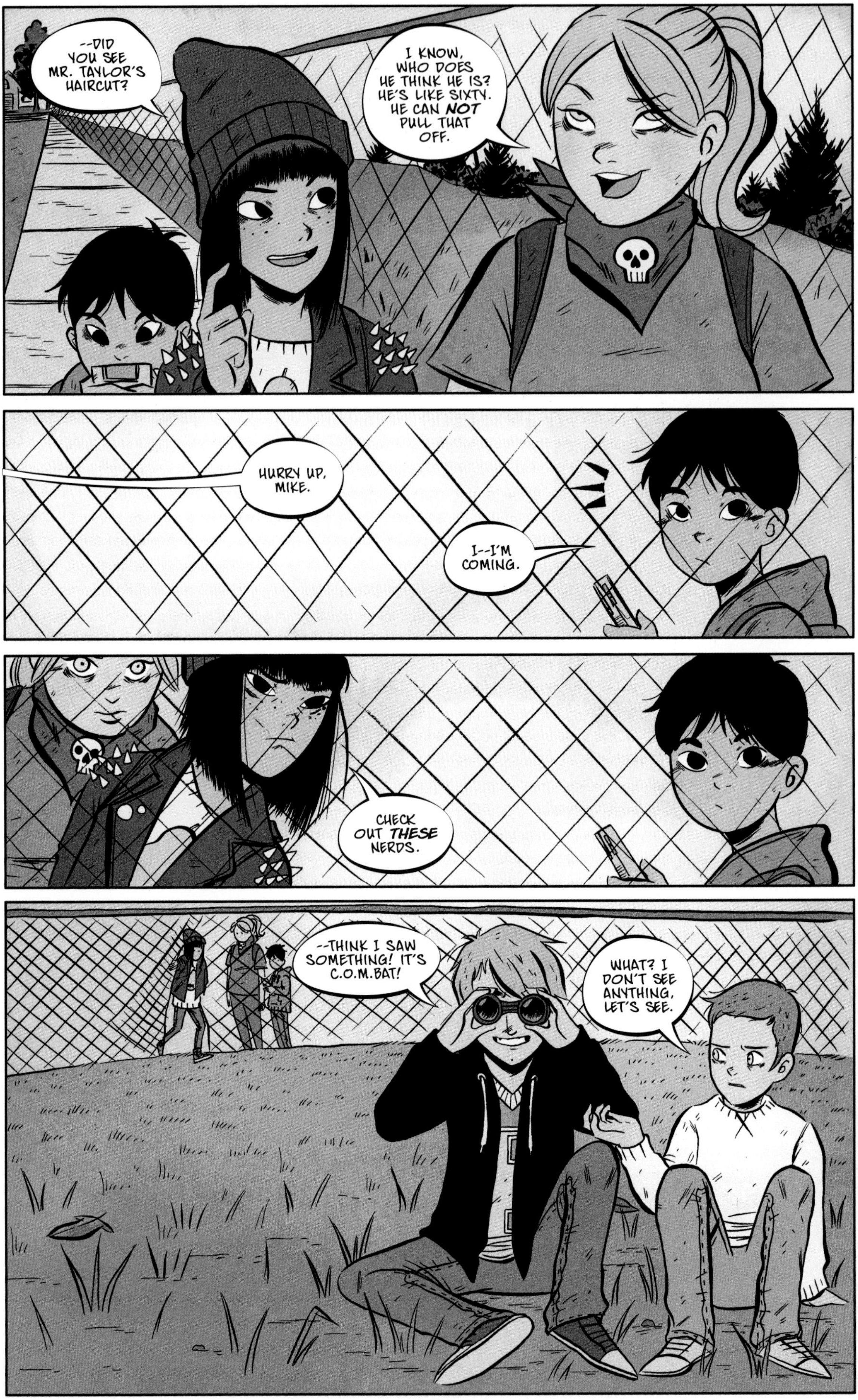
--DID YOU SEE MR. TAYLOR'S HAIRCUT?
I KNOW, WHO DOES HE THINK HE IS? HE'S LIKE SIXTY. HE CAN ***NOT*** PULL THAT OFF.
HURRY UP, MIKE.
I--I'M COMING.
CHECK OUT ***THESE*** NERDS.
--THINK I SAW SOMETHING! IT'S C.O.M.BAT!
WHAT? I DON'T SEE ANYTHING, LET'S SEE.

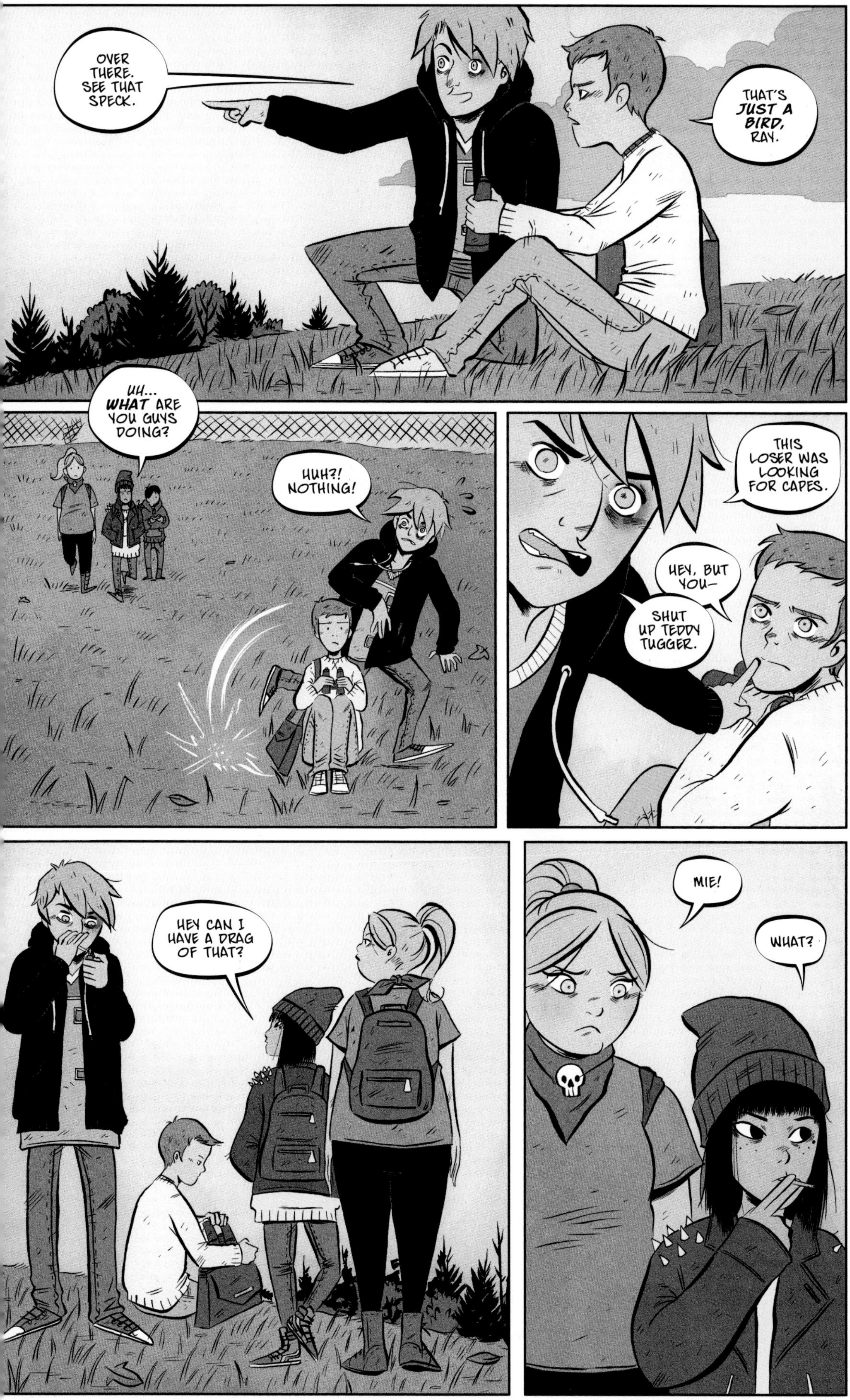
OVER THERE. SEE THAT SPECK.
THAT'S JUST A BIRD, RAY.
UH... WHAT ARE YOU GUYS DOING?
HUH?! NOTHING!
THIS LOSER WAS LOOKING FOR CAPES.
HEY, BUT YOU–
SHUT UP TEDDY TUGGER.
HEY CAN I HAVE A DRAG OF THAT?
MIE!
WHAT?

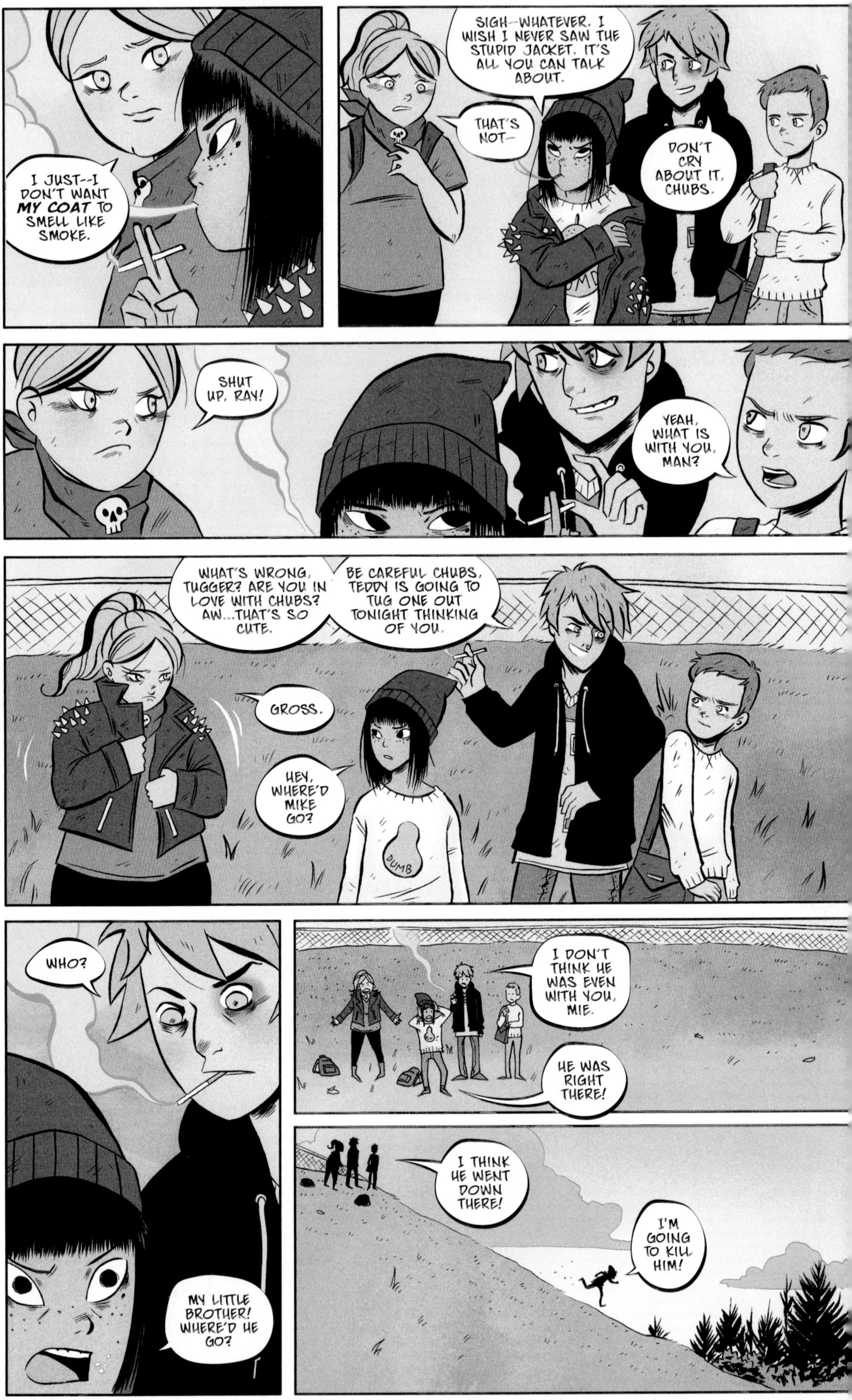
I JUST--I DON'T WANT **MY COAT** TO SMELL LIKE SMOKE.
SIGH--WHATEVER. I WISH I NEVER SAW THE STUPID JACKET. IT'S ALL YOU CAN TALK ABOUT.
THAT'S NOT--
DON'T CRY ABOUT IT, CHUBS.
SHUT UP, RAY!
YEAH, WHAT IS WITH YOU, MAN?
WHAT'S WRONG, TUGGER? ARE YOU IN LOVE WITH CHUBS? AW...THAT'S SO CUTE.
BE CAREFUL CHUBS, TEDDY IS GOING TO TUG ONE OUT TONIGHT THINKING OF YOU.
GROSS.
HEY, WHERE'D MIKE GO?
DUMB
WHO?
MY LITTLE BROTHER! WHERE'D HE GO?
I DON'T THINK HE WAS EVEN WITH YOU, MIE.
HE WAS RIGHT THERE!
I THINK HE WENT DOWN THERE!
I'M GOING TO KILL HIM!

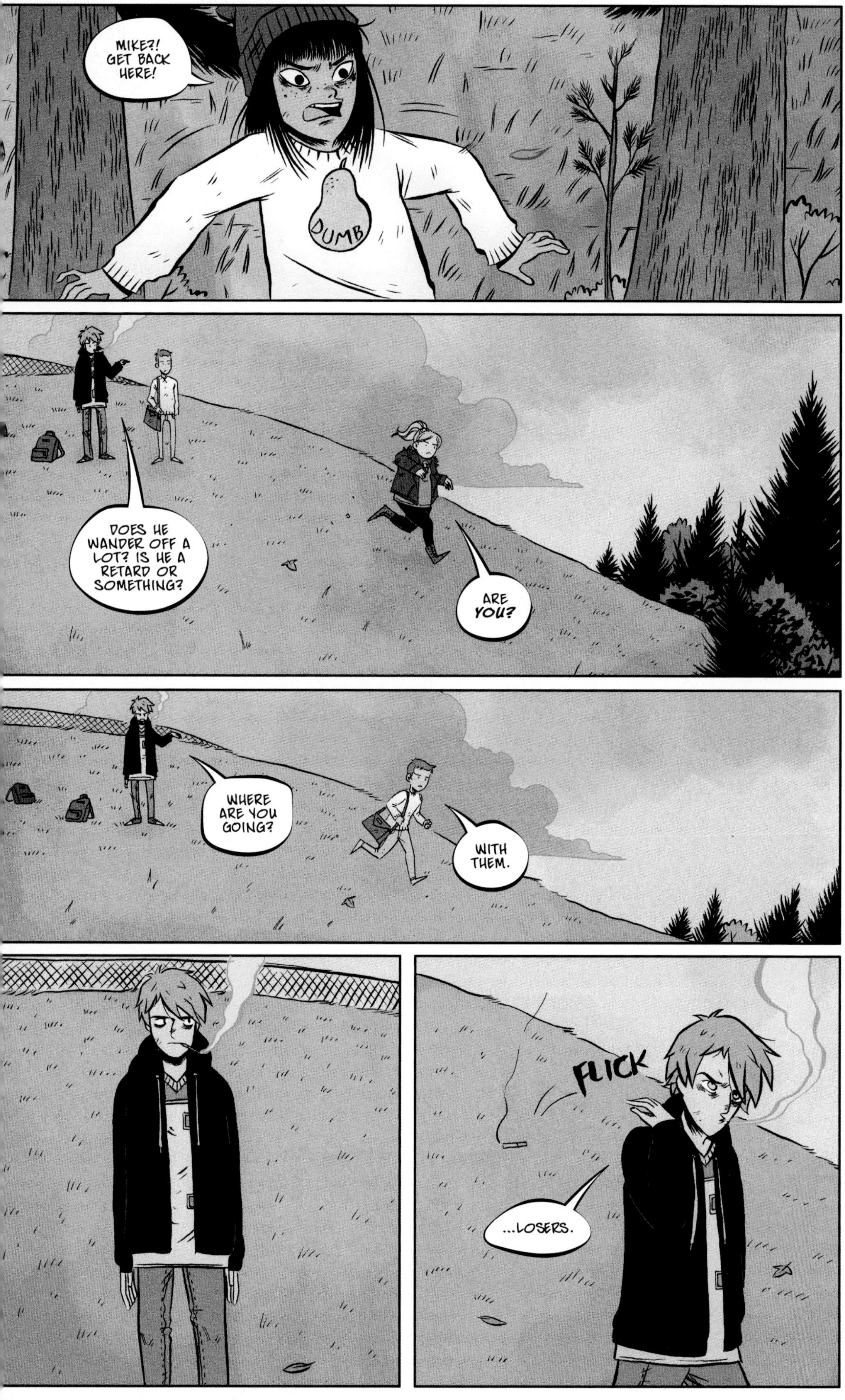
MIKE?! GET BACK HERE!
DUMB
DOES HE WANDER OFF A LOT? IS HE A RETARD OR SOMETHING?
ARE YOU?
WHERE ARE YOU GOING?
WITH THEM.
FLICK
...LOSERS.

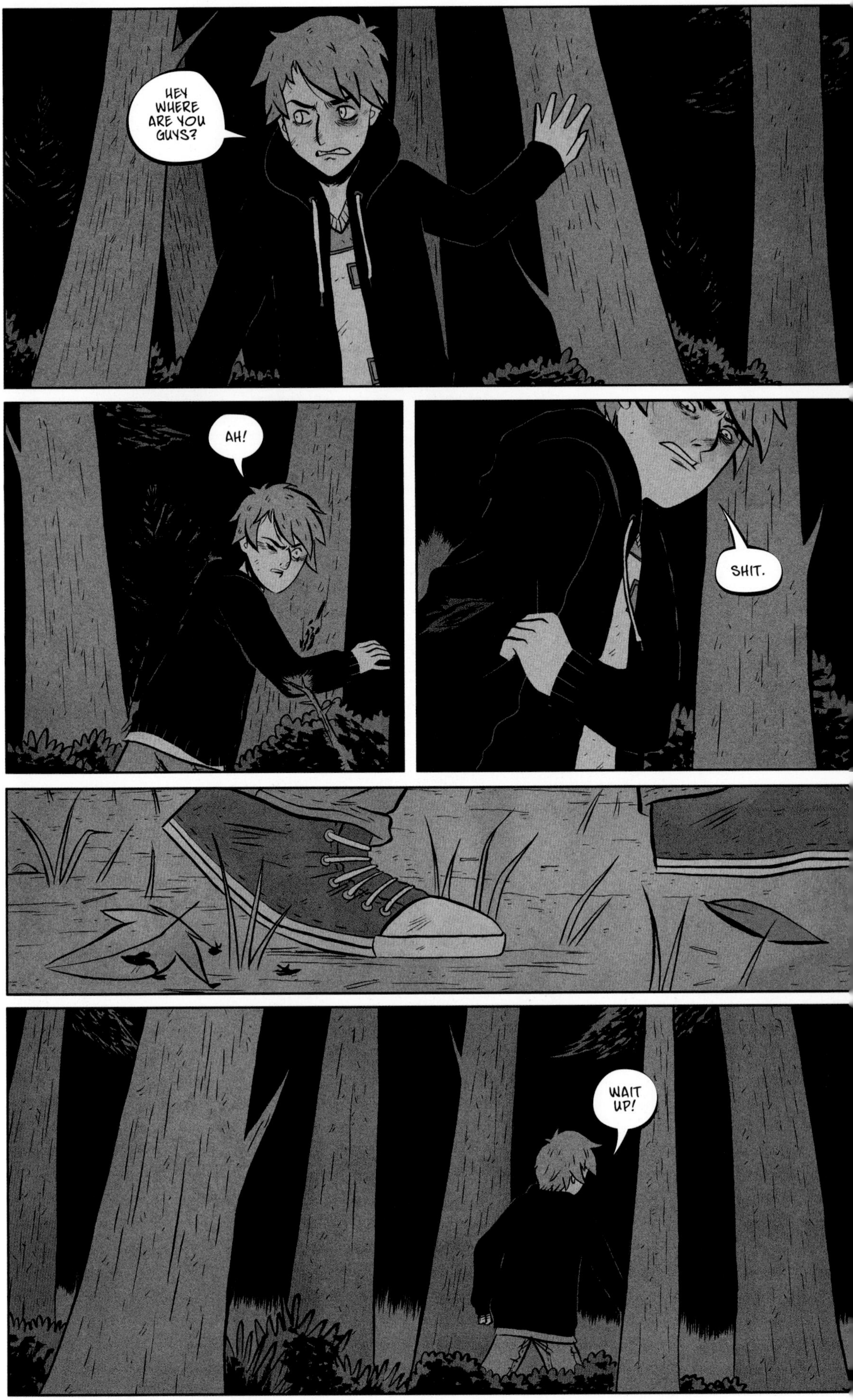
HEY WHERE ARE YOU GUYS?
AH!
SHIT.
WAIT UP!

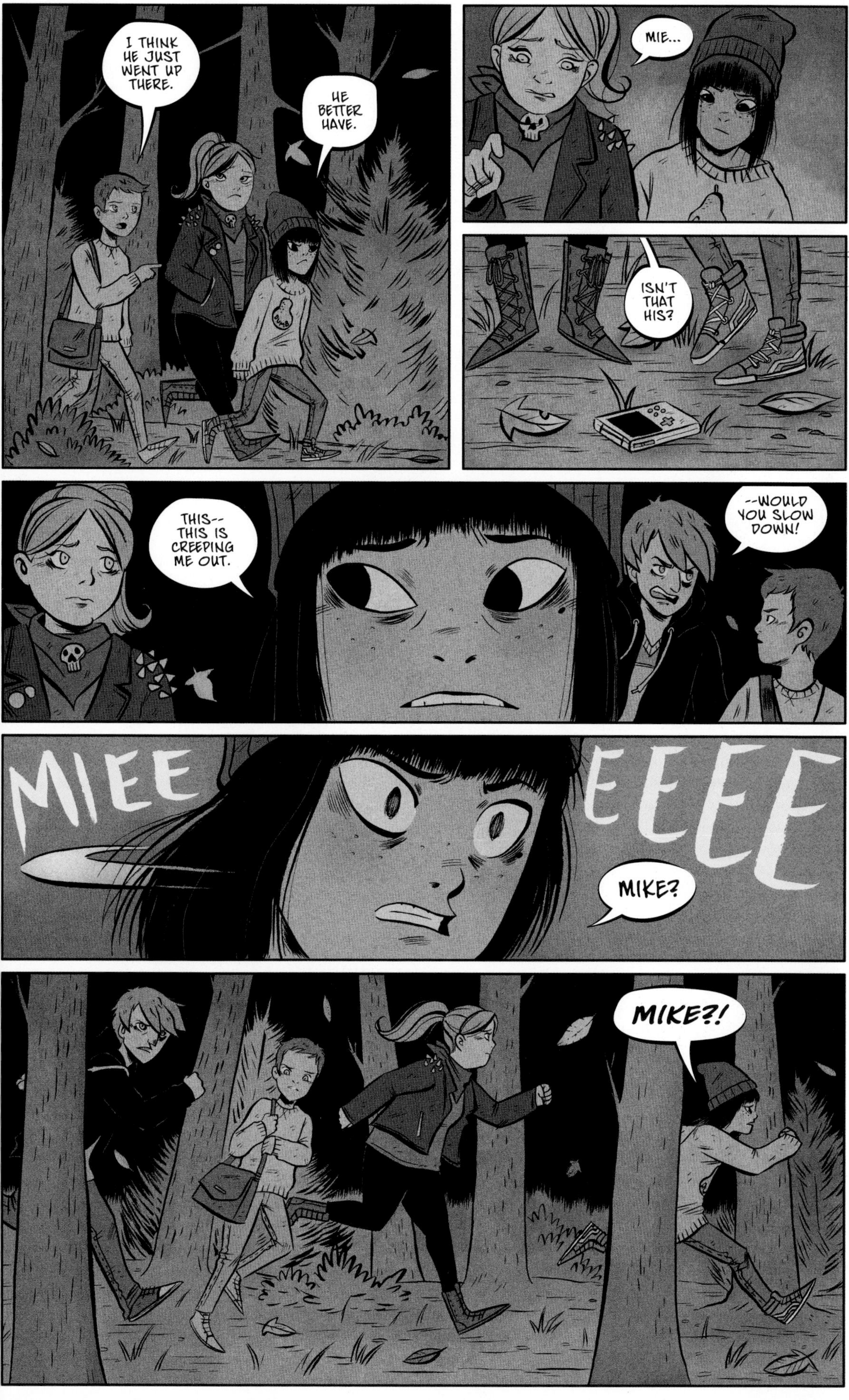
I THINK HE JUST WENT UP THERE.
HE BETTER HAVE.
MIE...
ISN'T THAT HIS?
THIS-- THIS IS CREEPING ME OUT.
--WOULD YOU SLOW DOWN!
MIEE
EEEE
MIKE?
MIKE?!

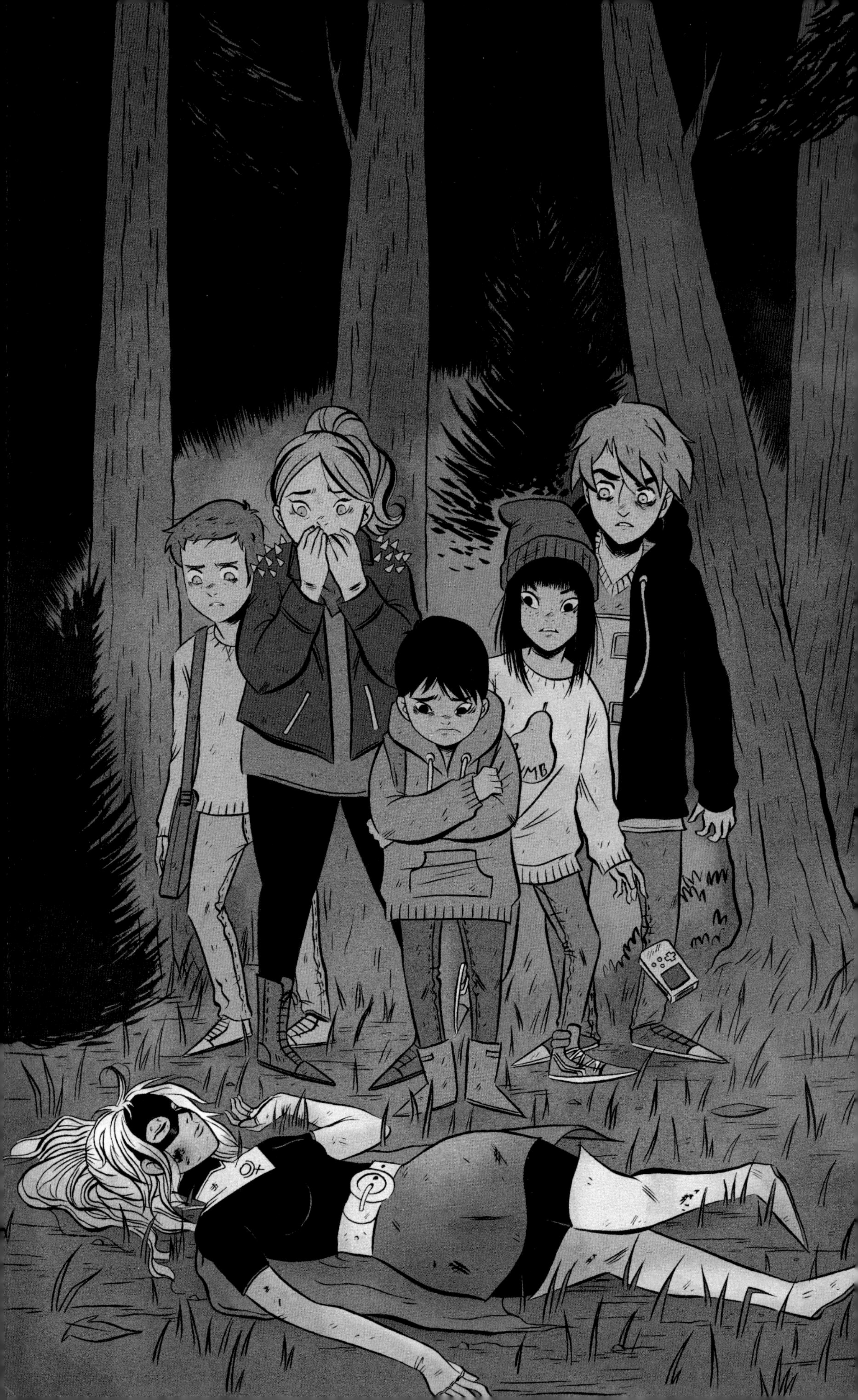

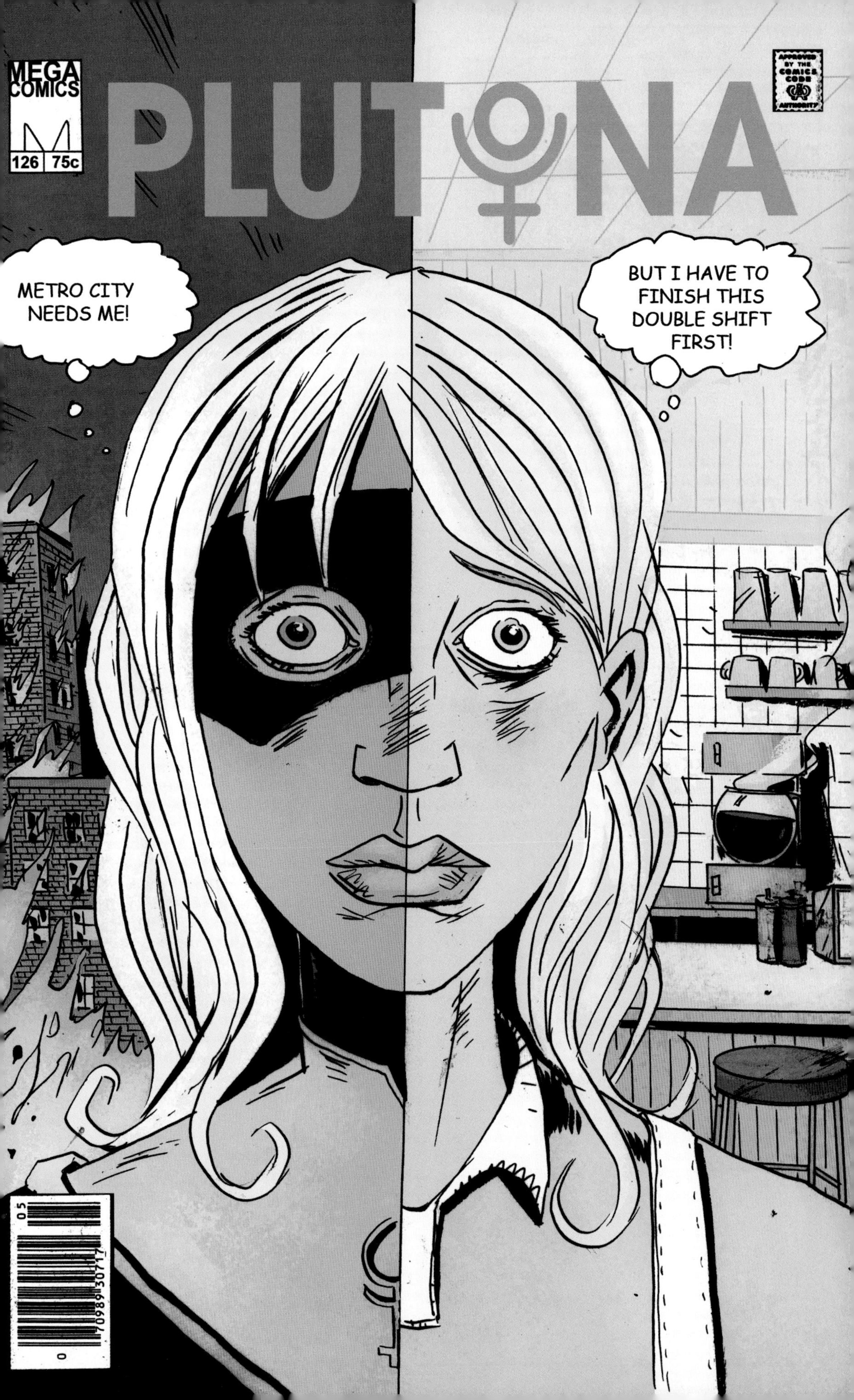
MEGA COMICS
126 75c
PLUTONA
APPROVED BY THE COMICS CODE AUTHORITY
METRO CITY NEEDS ME!
BUT I HAVE TO FINISH THIS DOUBLE SHIFT FIRST!

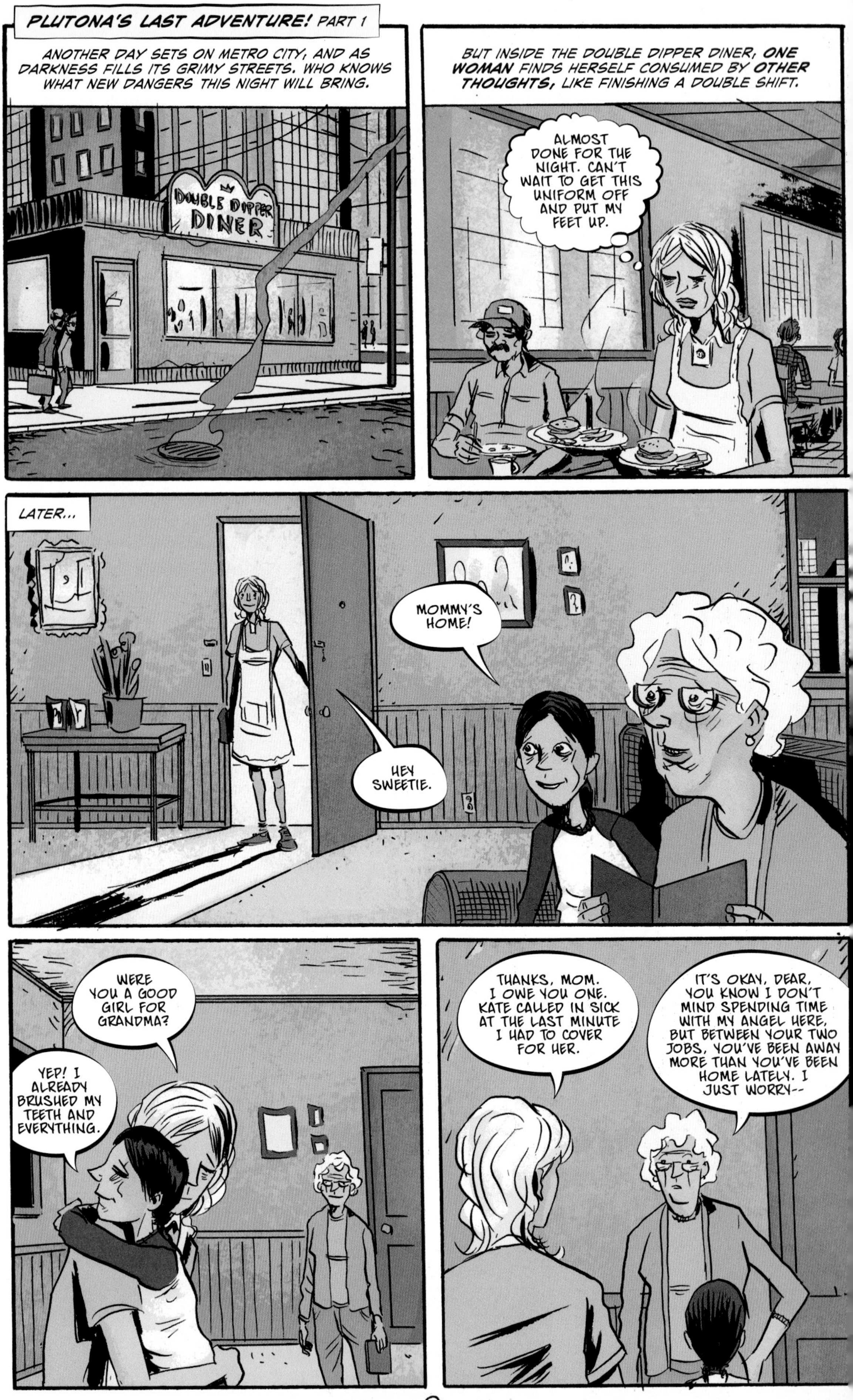
PLUTONA'S LAST ADVENTURE! PART 1
ANOTHER DAY SETS ON METRO CITY, AND AS DARKNESS FILLS ITS GRIMY STREETS. WHO KNOWS WHAT NEW DANGERS THIS NIGHT WILL BRING.
DOUBLE DIPPER DINER
BUT INSIDE THE DOUBLE DIPPER DINER, ONE WOMAN FINDS HERSELF CONSUMED BY OTHER THOUGHTS, LIKE FINISHING A DOUBLE SHIFT.
ALMOST DONE FOR THE NIGHT. CAN'T WAIT TO GET THIS UNIFORM OFF AND PUT MY FEET UP.
LATER...
MOMMY'S HOME!
HEY SWEETIE.
WERE YOU A GOOD GIRL FOR GRANDMA?
YEP! I ALREADY BRUSHED MY TEETH AND EVERYTHING.
THANKS, MOM. I OWE YOU ONE. KATE CALLED IN SICK AT THE LAST MINUTE I HAD TO COVER FOR HER.
IT'S OKAY, DEAR, YOU KNOW I DON'T MIND SPENDING TIME WITH MY ANGEL HERE, BUT BETWEEN YOUR TWO JOBS, YOU'VE BEEN AWAY MORE THAN YOU'VE BEEN HOME LATELY. I JUST WORRY--

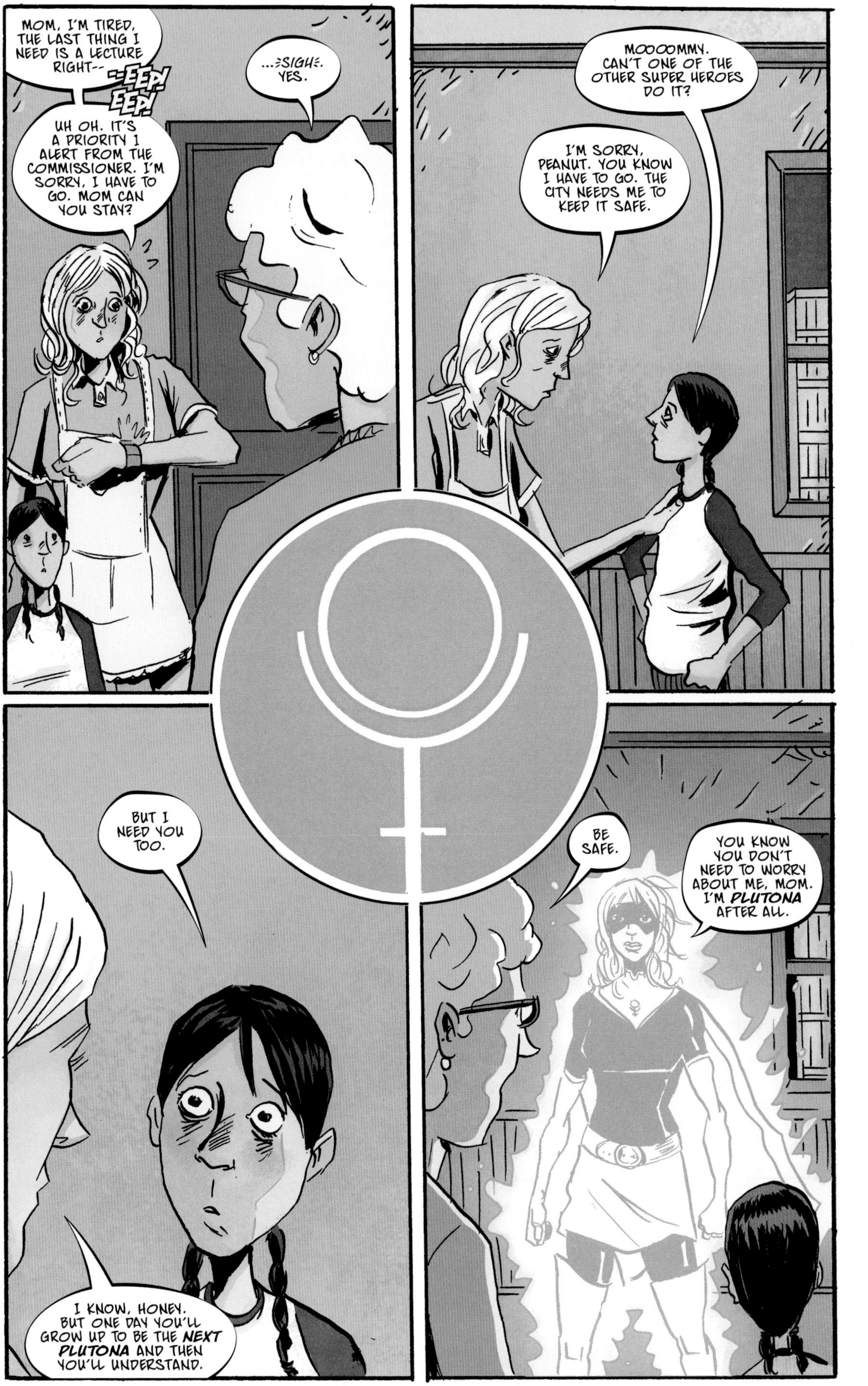
MOM, I'M TIRED, THE LAST THING I NEED IS A LECTURE RIGHT--
EEP! EEP!
UH OH. IT'S A PRIORITY 1 ALERT FROM THE COMMISSIONER. I'M SORRY, I HAVE TO GO. MOM CAN YOU STAY?
...SIGH. YES.
MOOOOMMY. CAN'T ONE OF THE OTHER SUPER HEROES DO IT?
I'M SORRY, PEANUT. YOU KNOW I HAVE TO GO. THE CITY NEEDS ME TO KEEP IT SAFE.
BUT I NEED YOU TOO.
I KNOW, HONEY. BUT ONE DAY YOU'LL GROW UP TO BE THE **NEXT PLUTONA** AND THEN YOU'LL UNDERSTAND.
BE SAFE.
YOU KNOW YOU DON'T NEED TO WORRY ABOUT ME, MOM. I'M **PLUTONA** AFTER ALL.

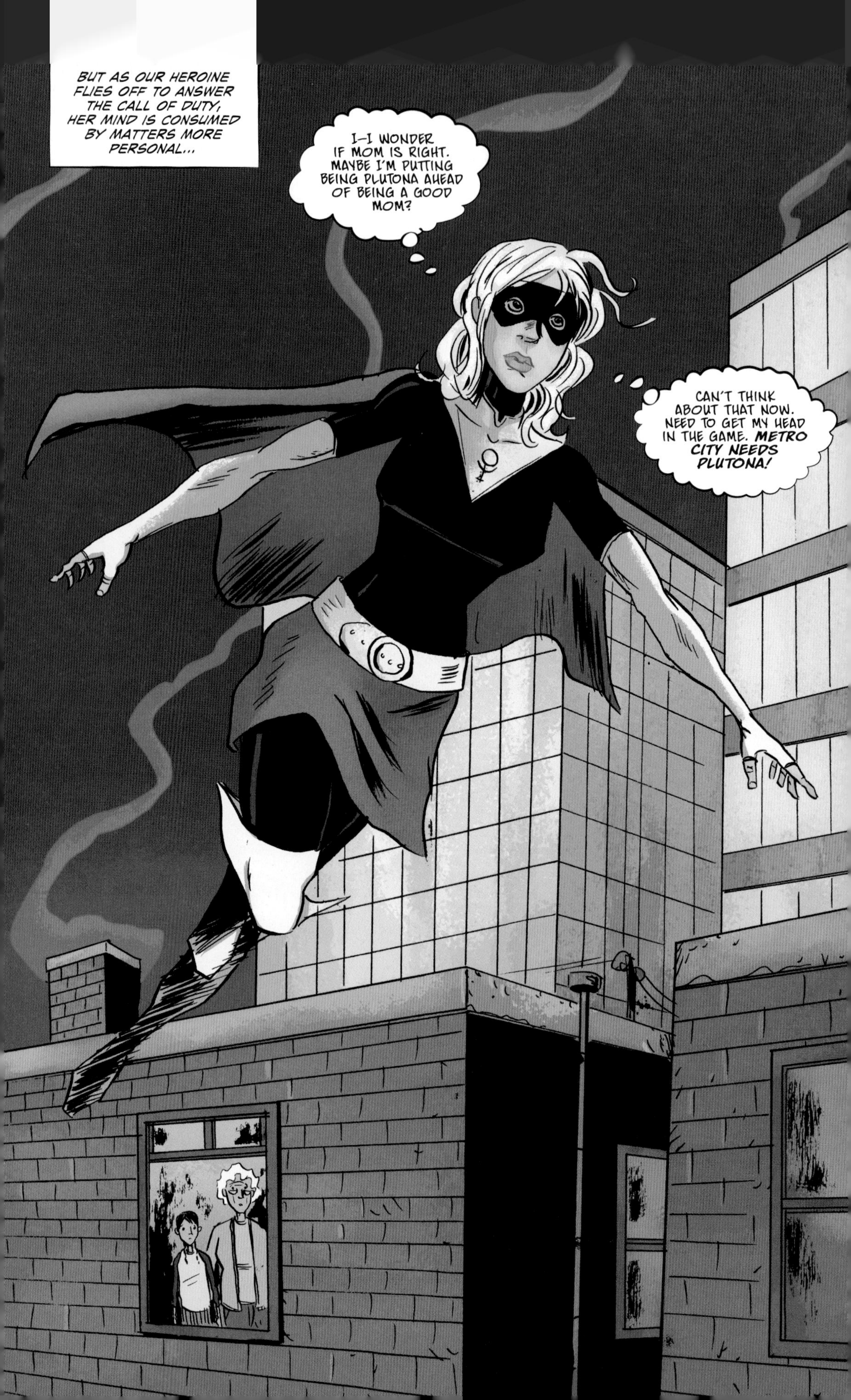
BUT AS OUR HEROINE FLIES OFF TO ANSWER THE CALL OF DUTY, HER MIND IS CONSUMED BY MATTERS MORE PERSONAL...
I-I WONDER IF MOM IS RIGHT. MAYBE I'M PUTTING BEING PLUTONA AHEAD OF BEING A GOOD MOM?
CAN'T THINK ABOUT THAT NOW. NEED TO GET MY HEAD IN THE GAME. METRO CITY NEEDS PLUTONA!

CHAPTER

2

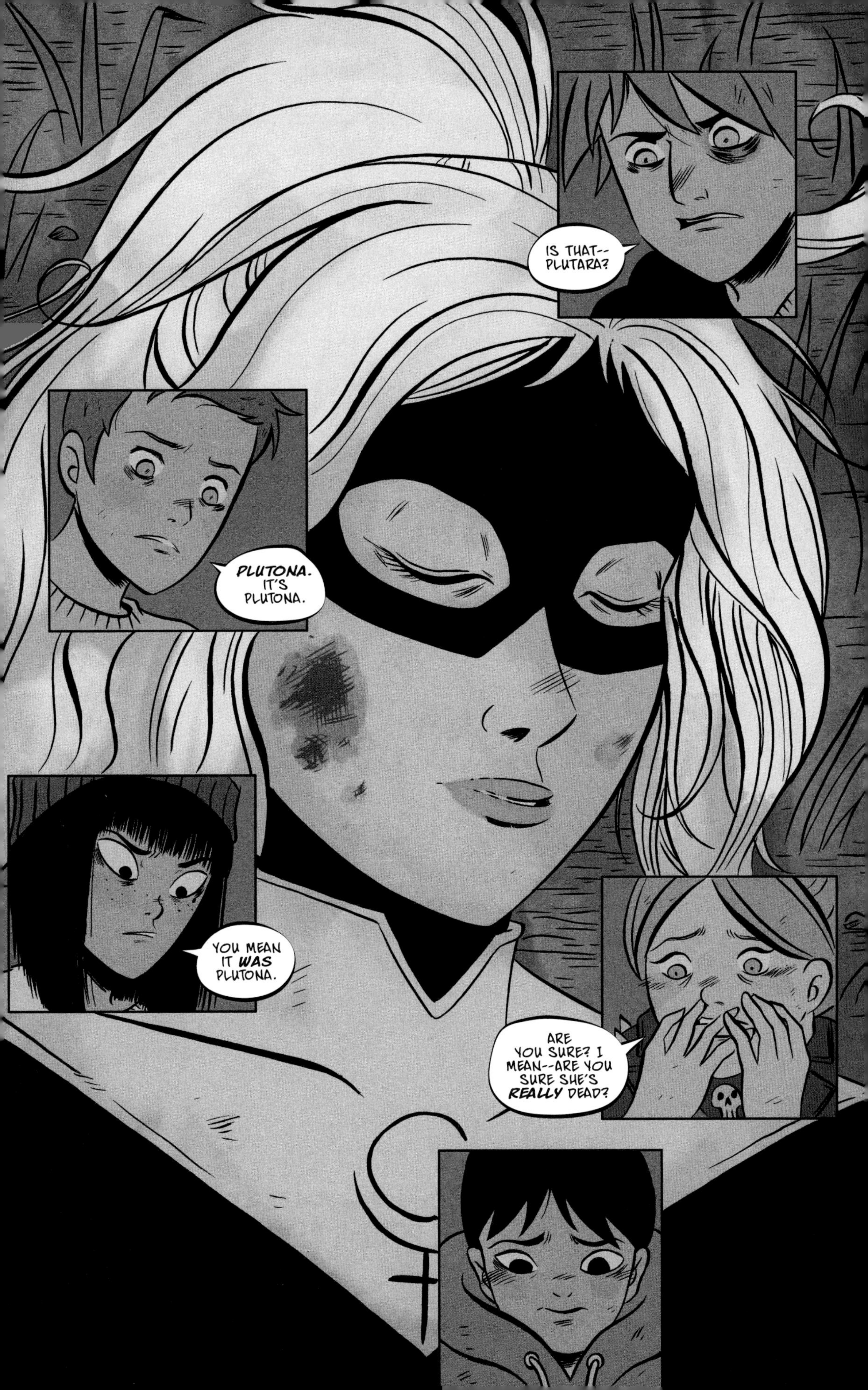

IS THAT-- PLUTARA?
PLUTONA. IT'S PLUTONA.
YOU MEAN IT **WAS** PLUTONA.
ARE YOU SURE? I MEAN--ARE YOU SURE SHE'S **REALLY** DEAD?

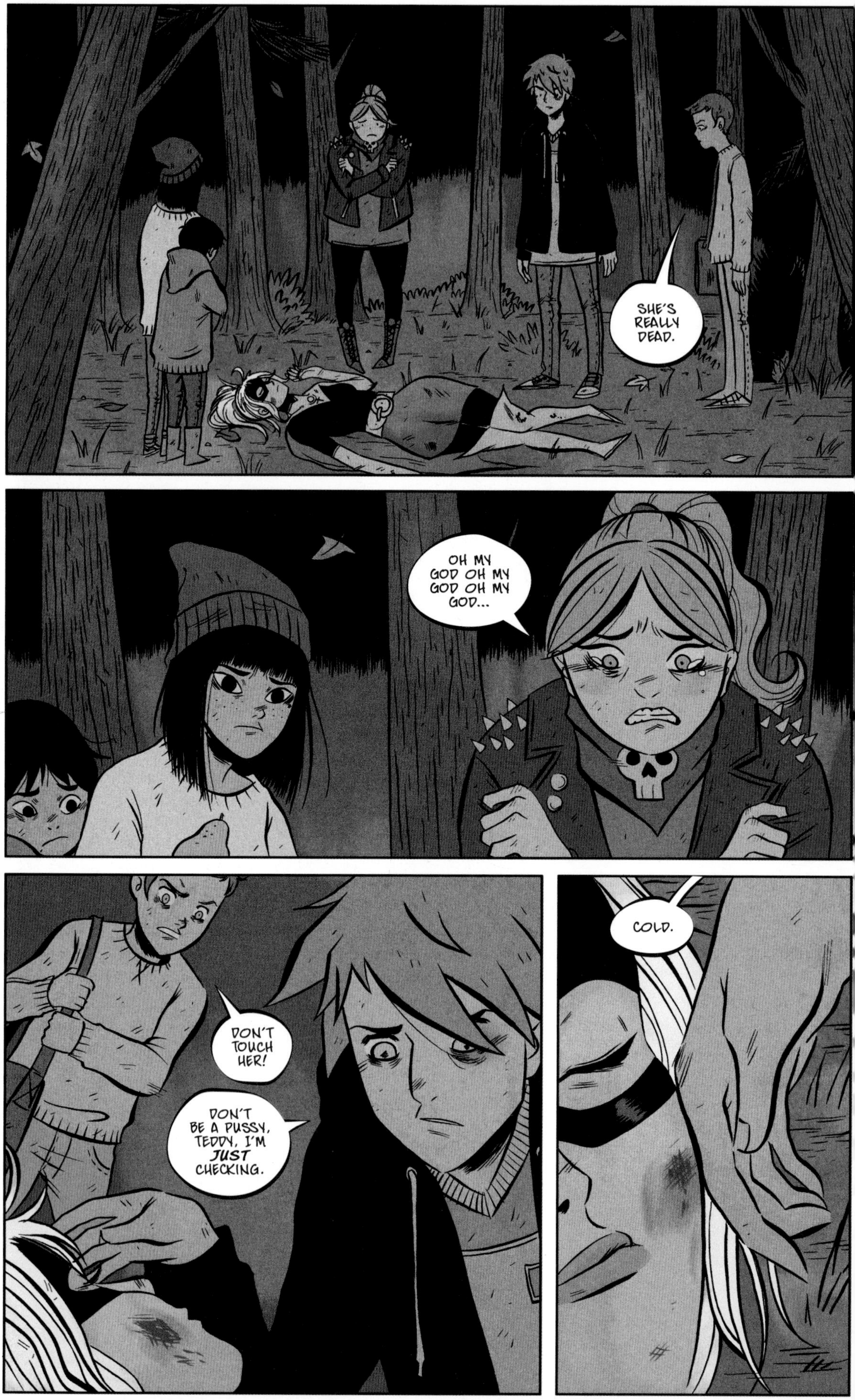
SHE'S REALLY DEAD.
OH MY GOD OH MY GOD OH MY GOD...
DON'T TOUCH HER!
DON'T BE A PUSSY, TEDDY, I'M *JUST* CHECKING.
COLD.

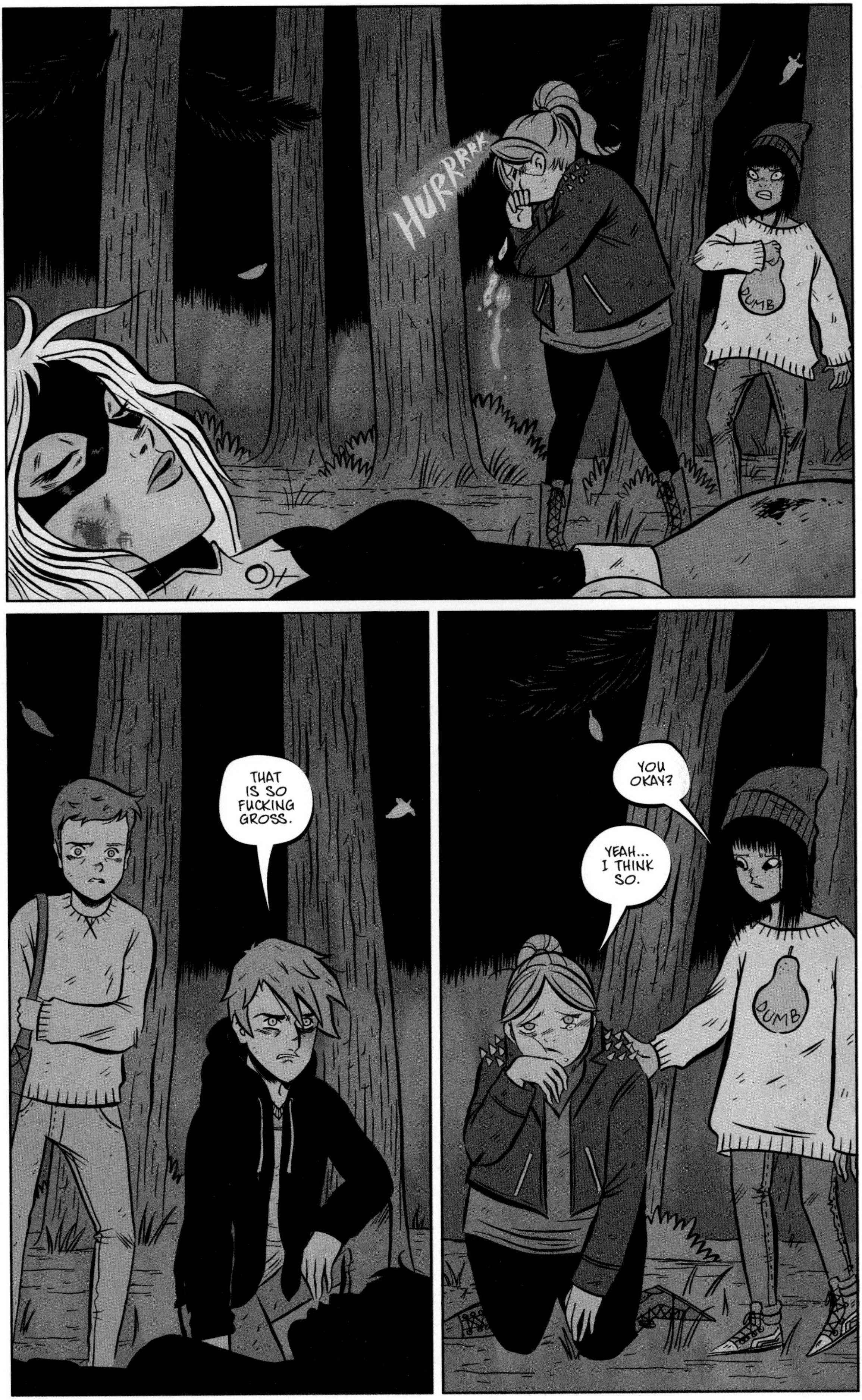
HURRRRK
THAT IS SO FUCKING GROSS.
YOU OKAY?
YEAH... I THINK SO.
DUMB

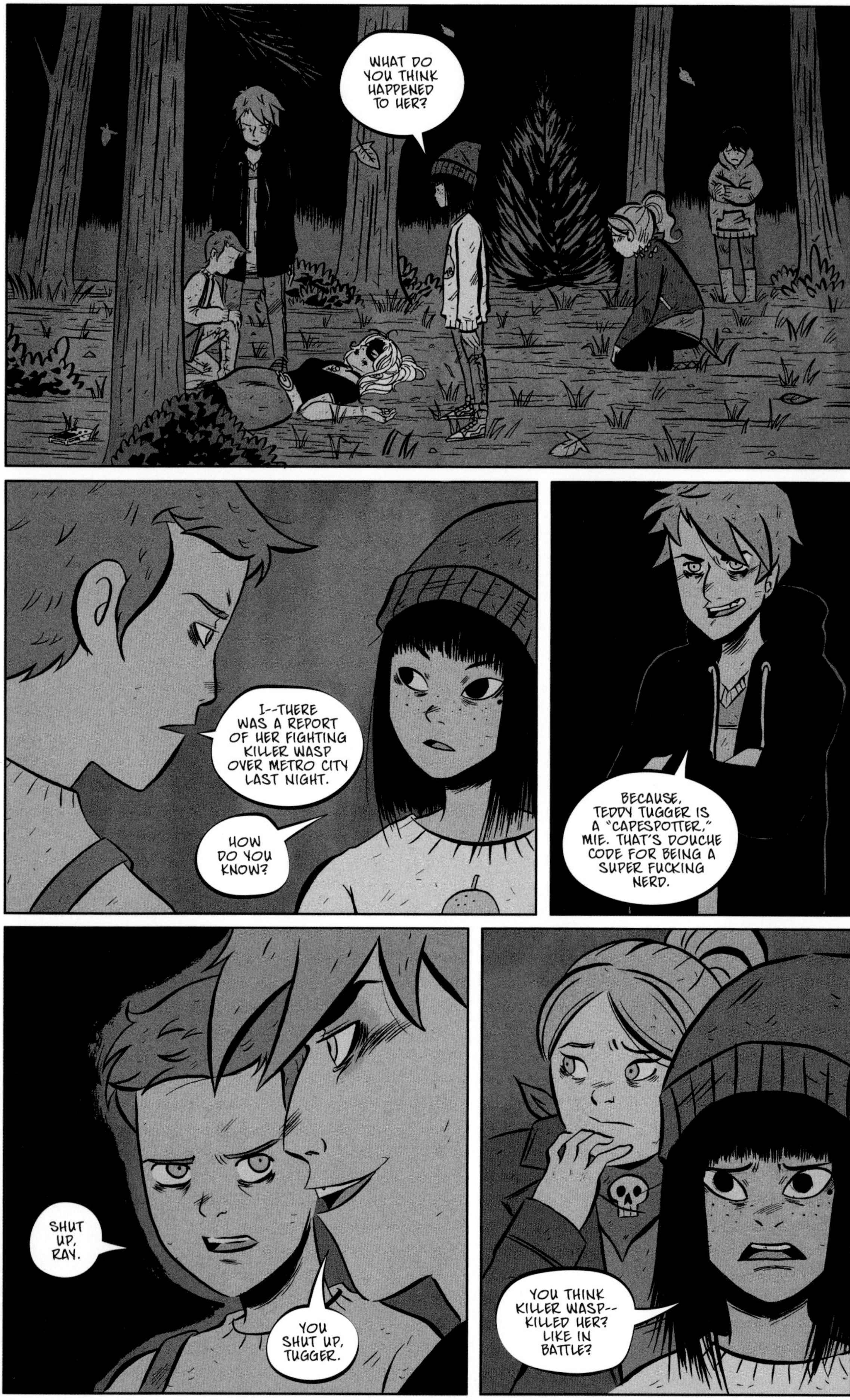
WHAT DO YOU THINK HAPPENED TO HER?
I--THERE WAS A REPORT OF HER FIGHTING KILLER WASP OVER METRO CITY LAST NIGHT.
HOW DO YOU KNOW?
BECAUSE, TEDDY TUGGER IS A "CAPESPOTTER," MIE. THAT'S DOUCHE CODE FOR BEING A SUPER FUCKING NERD.
SHUT UP, RAY.
YOU SHUT UP, TUGGER.
YOU THINK KILLER WASP--KILLED HER? LIKE IN BATTLE?

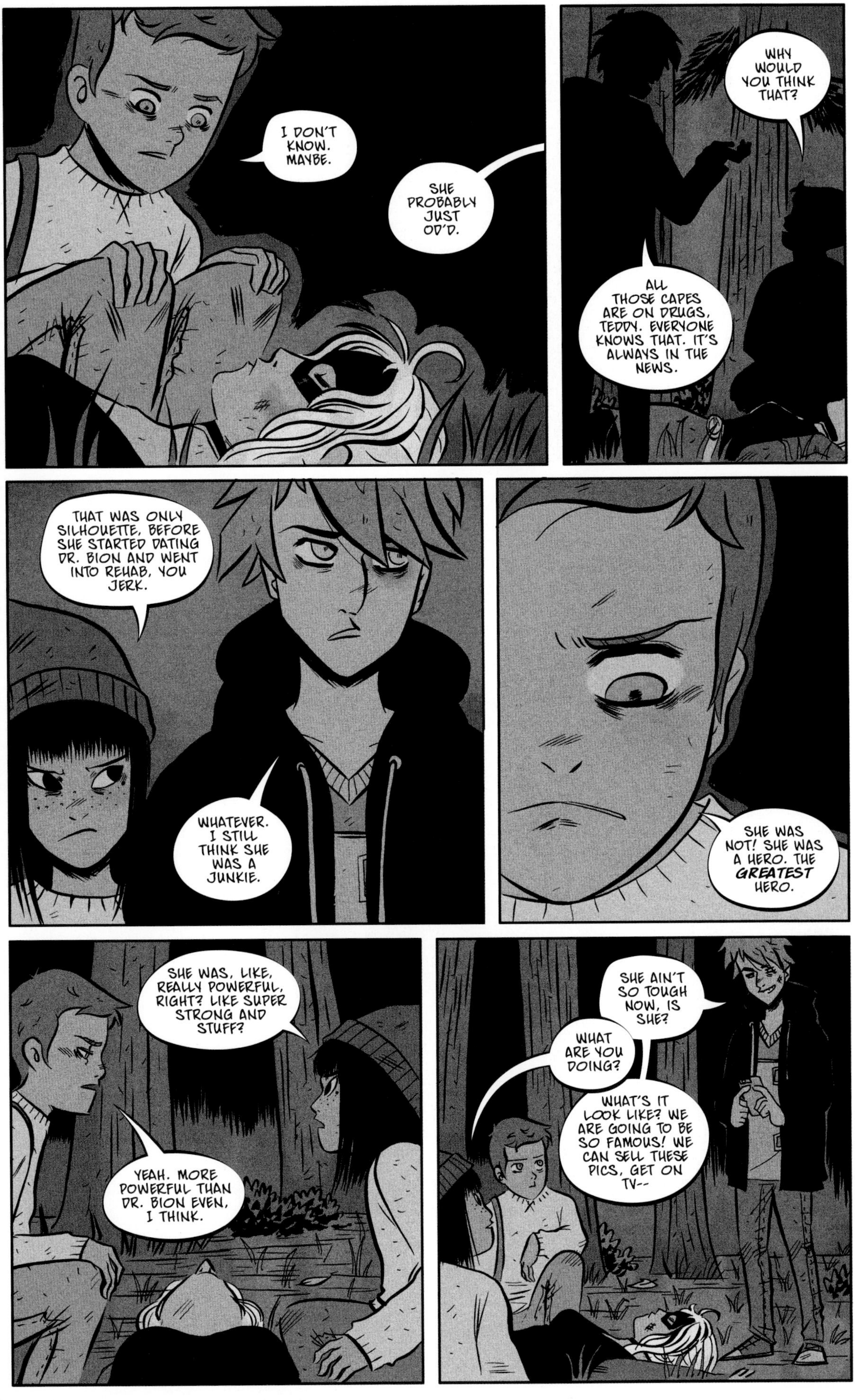
I DON'T KNOW. MAYBE.
SHE PROBABLY JUST OD'D.
WHY WOULD YOU THINK THAT?
ALL THOSE CAPES ARE ON DRUGS, TEDDY. EVERYONE KNOWS THAT. IT'S ALWAYS IN THE NEWS.
THAT WAS ONLY SILHOUETTE, BEFORE SHE STARTED DATING DR. BION AND WENT INTO REHAB, YOU JERK.
WHATEVER. I STILL THINK SHE WAS A JUNKIE.
SHE WAS NOT! SHE WAS A HERO. THE ***GREATEST*** HERO.
SHE WAS, LIKE, REALLY POWERFUL, RIGHT? LIKE SUPER STRONG AND STUFF?
YEAH. MORE POWERFUL THAN DR. BION EVEN, I THINK.
SHE AIN'T SO TOUGH NOW, IS SHE?
WHAT ARE YOU DOING?
WHAT'S IT LOOK LIKE? WE ARE GOING TO BE SO FAMOUS! WE CAN SELL THESE PICS, GET ON TV--

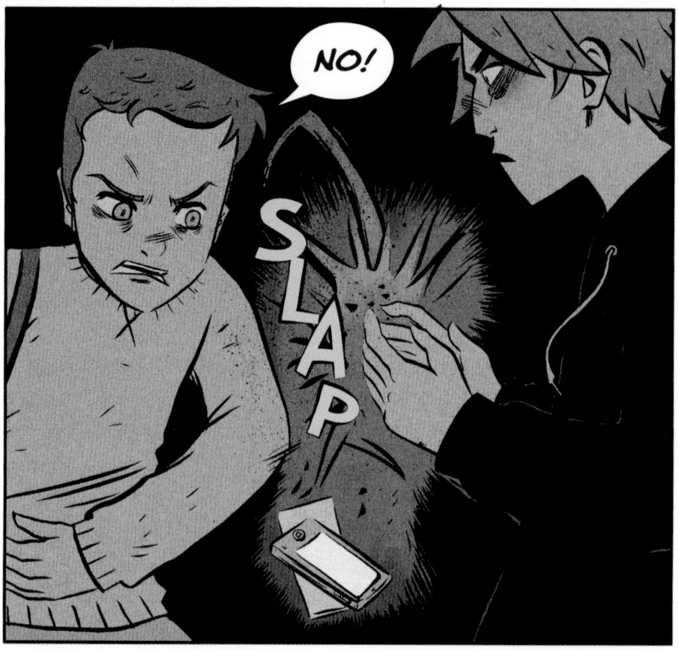
NO!
SLAP
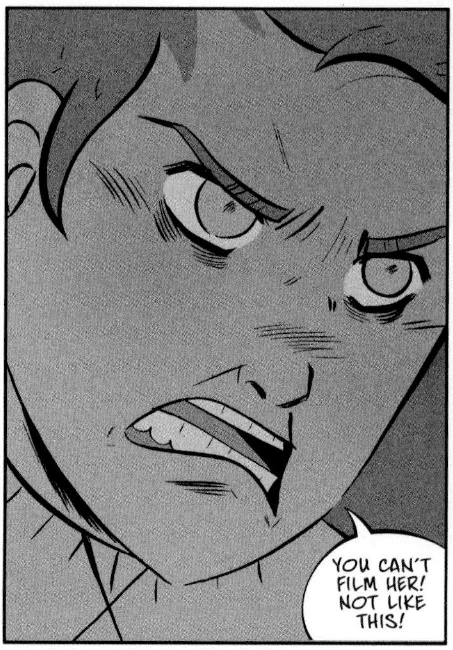
YOU CAN'T FILM HER! NOT LIKE THIS!
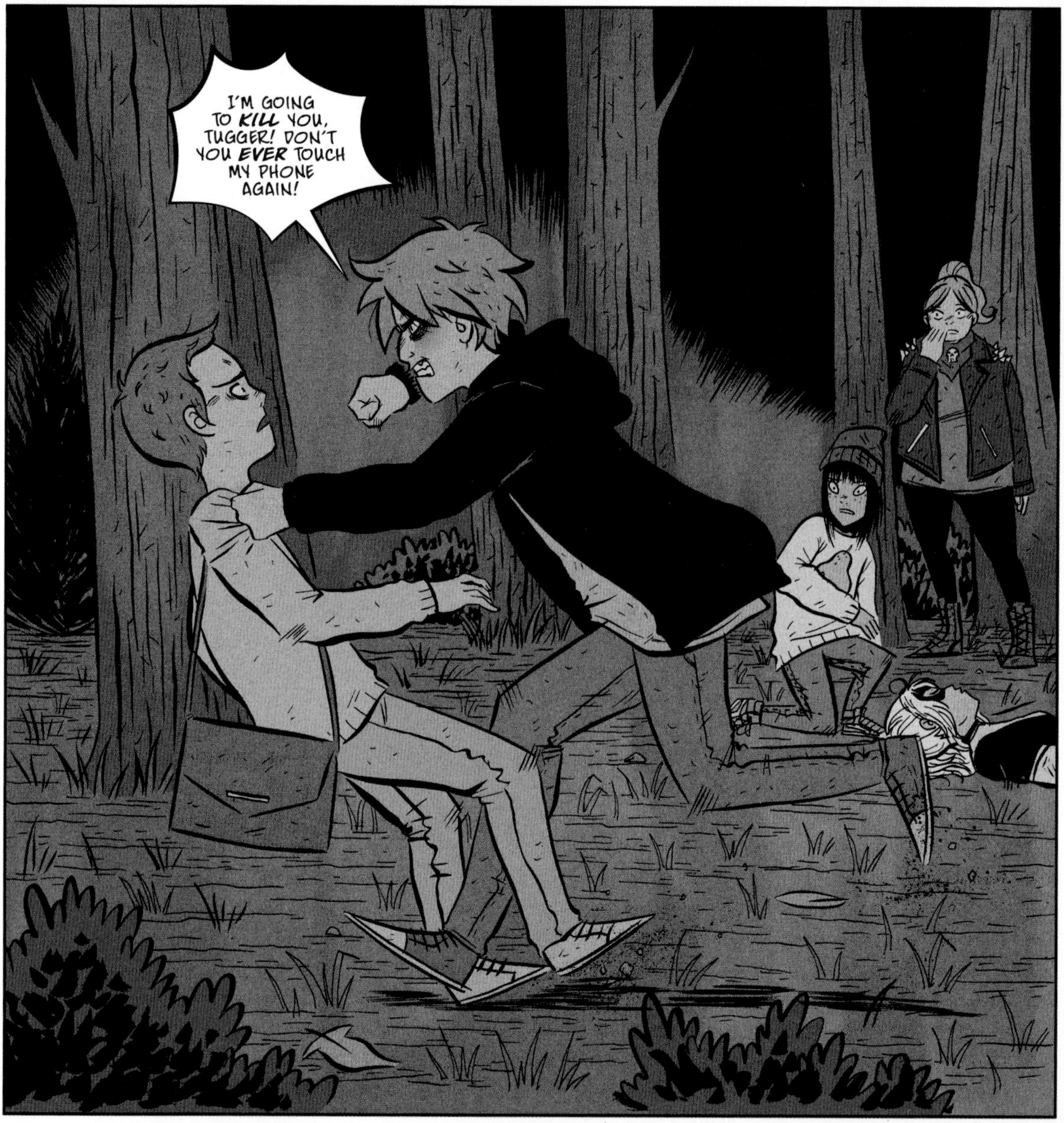
I'M GOING TO KILL YOU, TUGGER! DON'T YOU EVER TOUCH MY PHONE AGAIN!

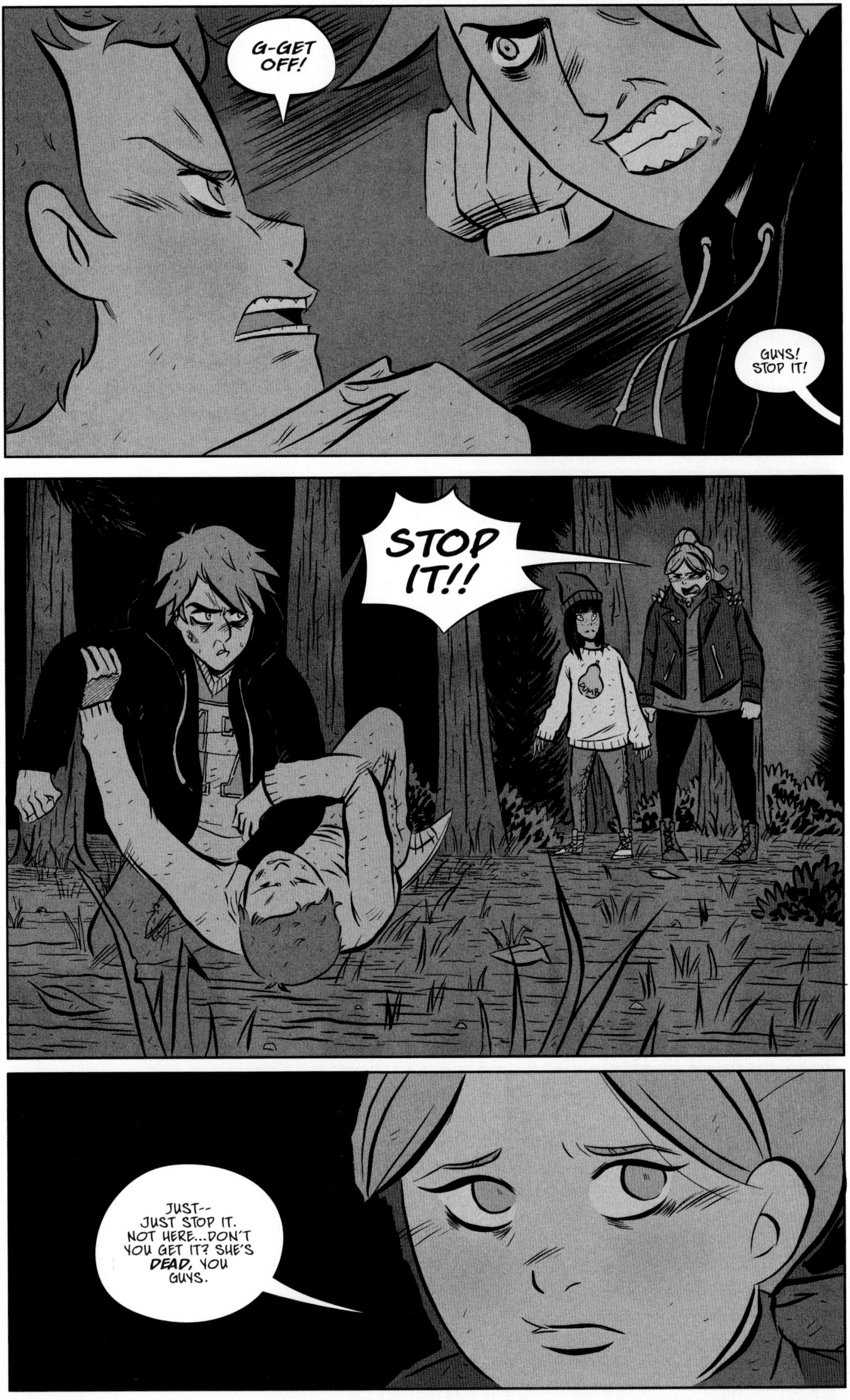
G-GET OFF!
GUYS! STOP IT!
STOP IT!!
DUMB
JUST-- JUST STOP IT. NOT HERE...DON'T YOU GET IT? SHE'S **DEAD**, YOU GUYS.

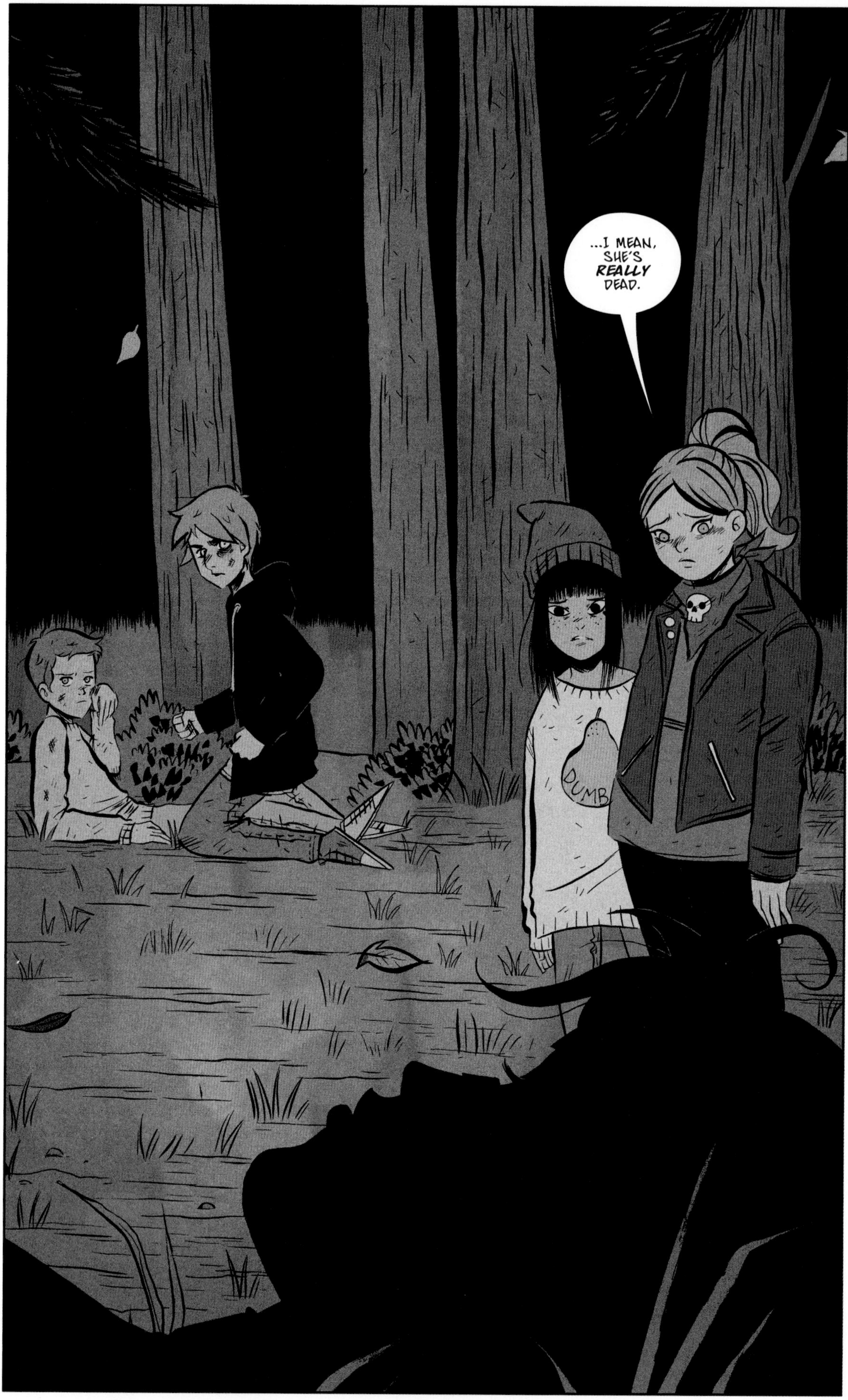
...I MEAN, SHE'S REALLY DEAD.
DUMB

MIE...I WANT TO GO HOME.

NOT YET.

BETTER NOT HAVE BROKE MY PHONE, TUGGER.

SO, WHAT *DO* WE DO?

LIKE *I SAID*, WE FILM HER, THEN SELL THE PICTURES.

MIE, LET'S GO.

I *SAID* NOT YET, MIKE! *STOP IT!*

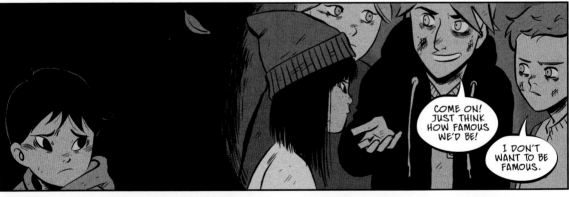

COME ON! JUST THINK HOW FAMOUS WE'D BE!

I DON'T WANT TO BE FAMOUS.

EVERYONE WANTS TO BE FAMOUS.

I DON'T. AND WE CAN'T PUT PICTURES ONLINE OR TELL *ANYONE.*

WHY NOT?

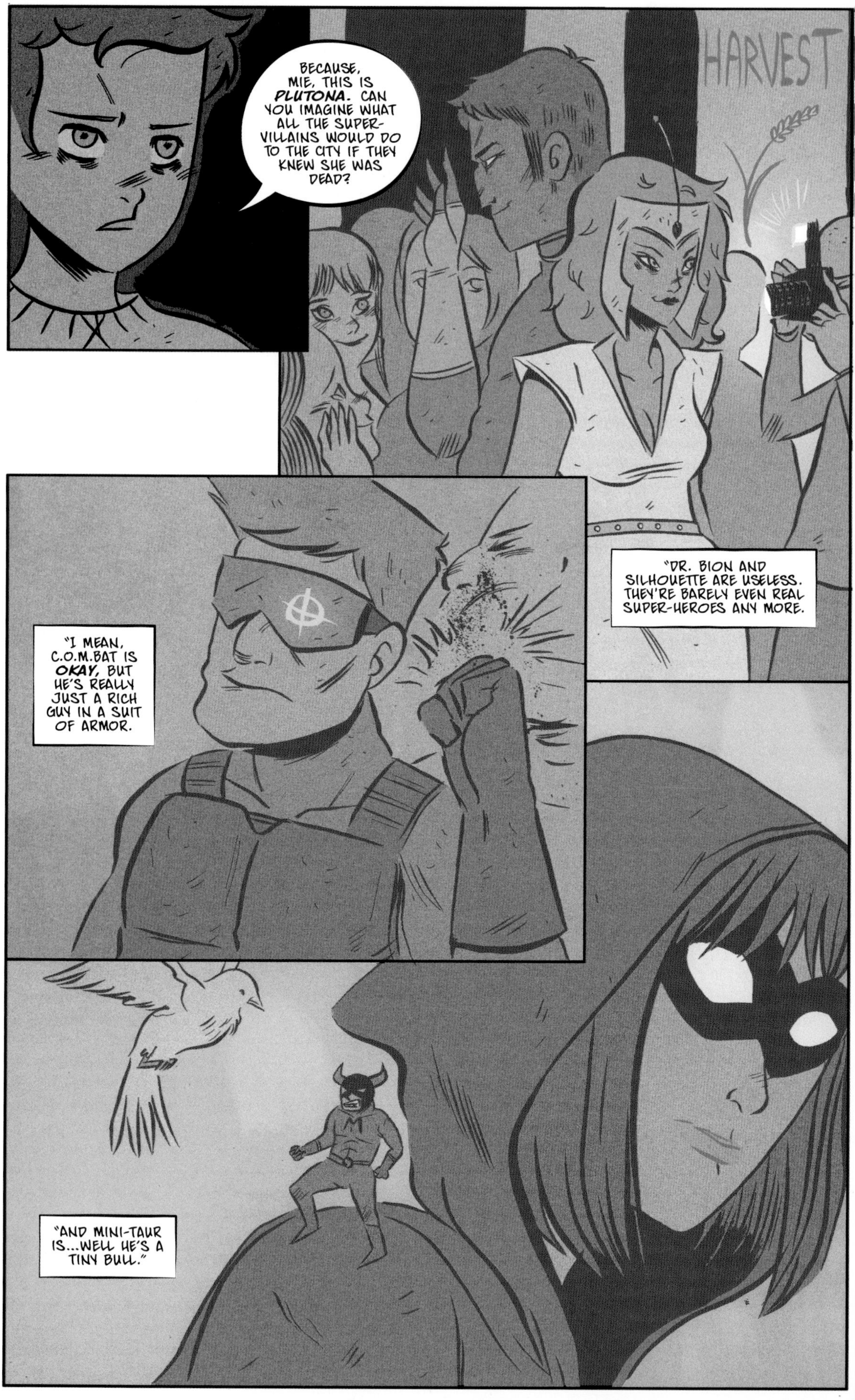
BECAUSE, MIE, THIS IS **PLUTONA.** CAN YOU IMAGINE WHAT ALL THE SUPER-VILLAINS WOULD DO TO THE CITY IF THEY KNEW SHE WAS DEAD?
HARVEST
"DR. BION AND SILHOUETTE ARE USELESS. THEY'RE BARELY EVEN REAL SUPER-HEROES ANY MORE.
"I MEAN, C.O.M.BAT IS **OKAY,** BUT HE'S REALLY JUST A RICH GUY IN A SUIT OF ARMOR.
"AND MINI-TAUR IS...WELL HE'S A TINY BULL."

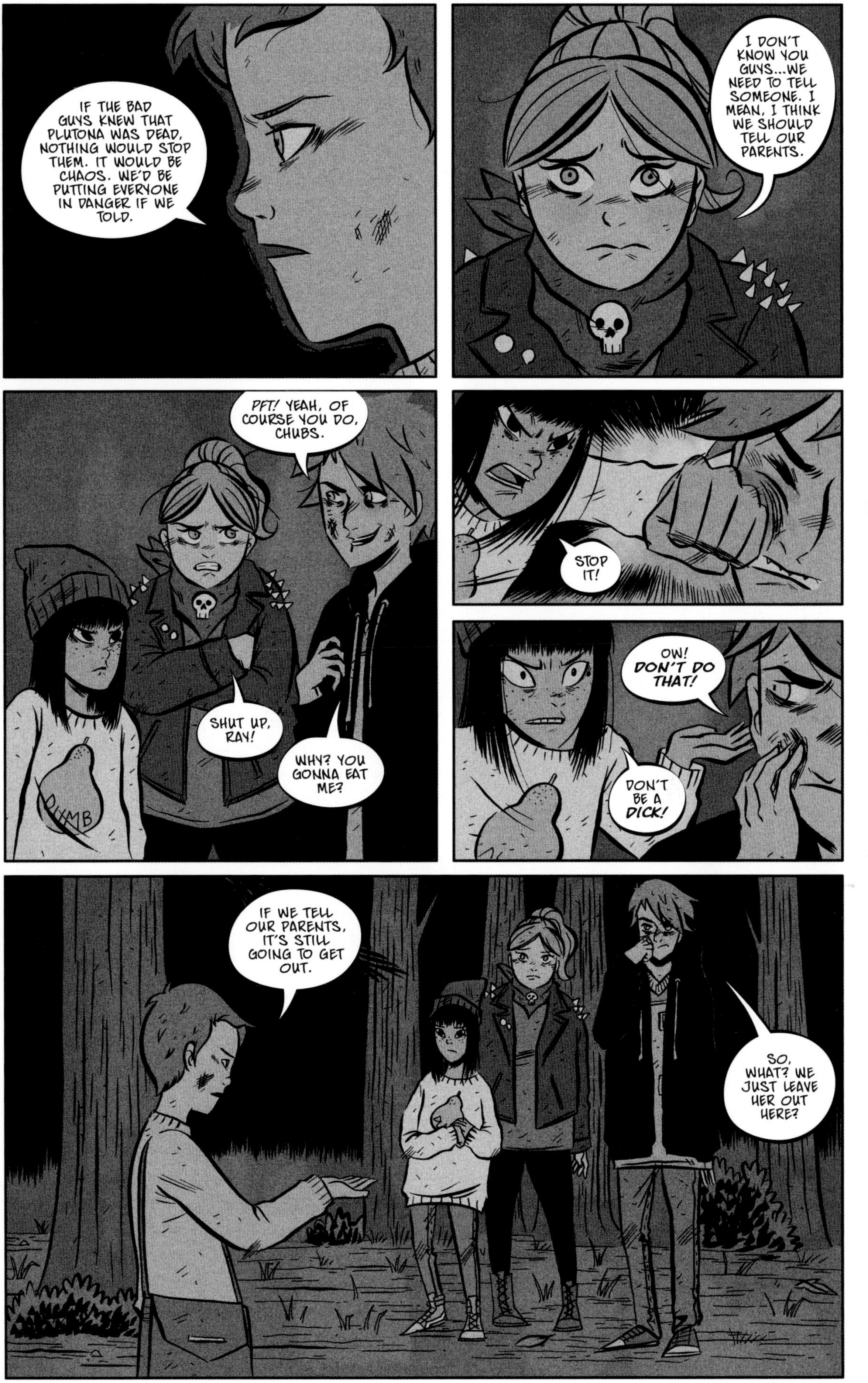
IF THE BAD GUYS KNEW THAT PLUTONA WAS DEAD, NOTHING WOULD STOP THEM. IT WOULD BE CHAOS. WE'D BE PUTTING EVERYONE IN DANGER IF WE TOLD.
I DON'T KNOW YOU GUYS...WE NEED TO TELL SOMEONE. I MEAN, I THINK WE SHOULD TELL OUR PARENTS.
PFT! YEAH, OF COURSE YOU DO, CHUBS.
SHUT UP, RAY!
WHY? YOU GONNA EAT ME?
DUMB
STOP IT!
OW! DON'T DO THAT!
DON'T BE A DICK!
IF WE TELL OUR PARENTS, IT'S STILL GOING TO GET OUT.
SO, WHAT? WE JUST LEAVE HER OUT HERE?

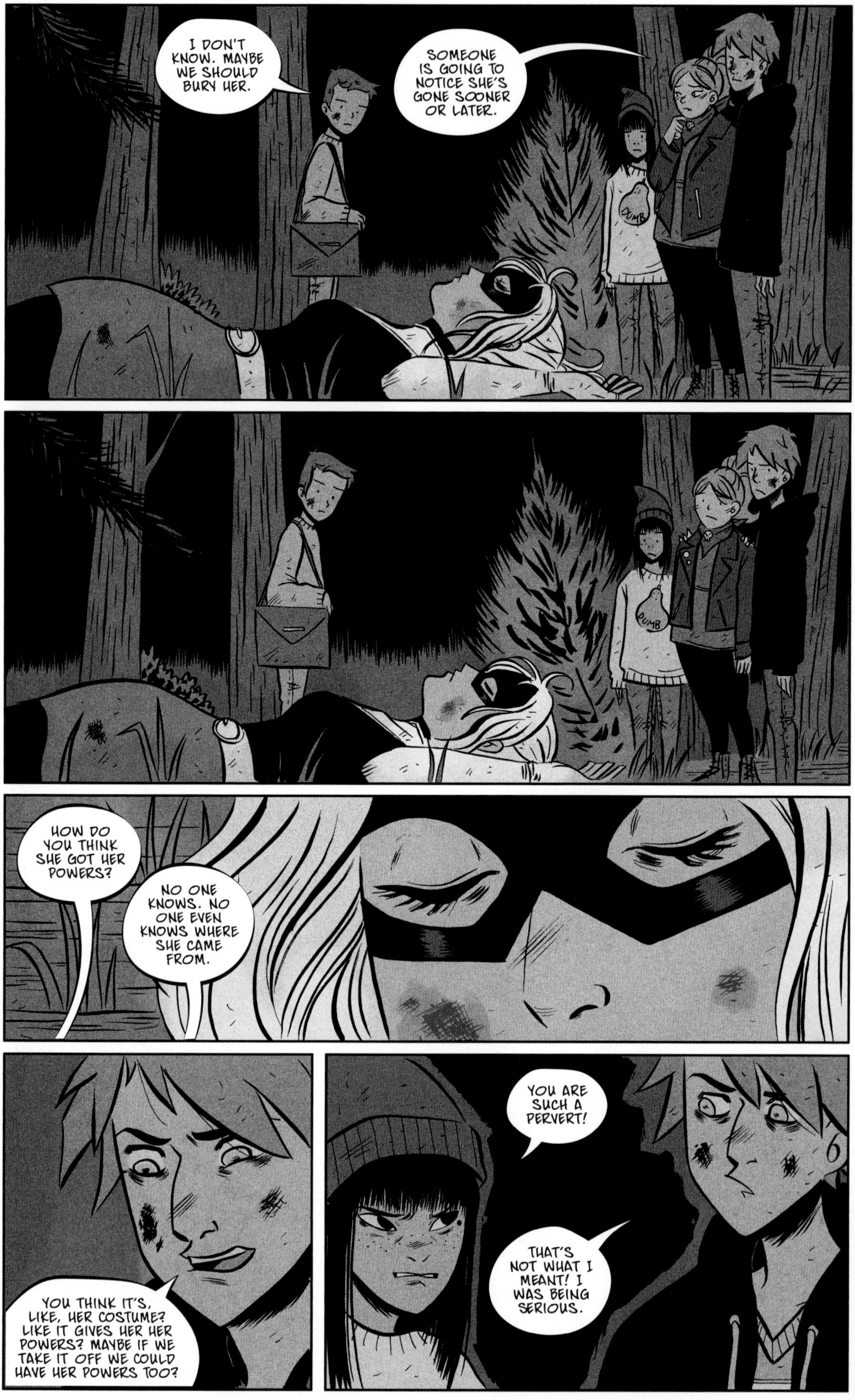
I DON'T KNOW. MAYBE WE SHOULD BURY HER.
SOMEONE IS GOING TO NOTICE SHE'S GONE SOONER OR LATER.
DUMB
DUMB
HOW DO YOU THINK SHE GOT HER POWERS?
NO ONE KNOWS. NO ONE EVEN KNOWS WHERE SHE CAME FROM.
YOU THINK IT'S, LIKE, HER COSTUME? LIKE IT GIVES HER HER POWERS? MAYBE IF WE TAKE IT OFF WE COULD HAVE HER POWERS TOO?
YOU ARE SUCH A PERVERT!
THAT'S NOT WHAT I MEANT! I WAS BEING SERIOUS.

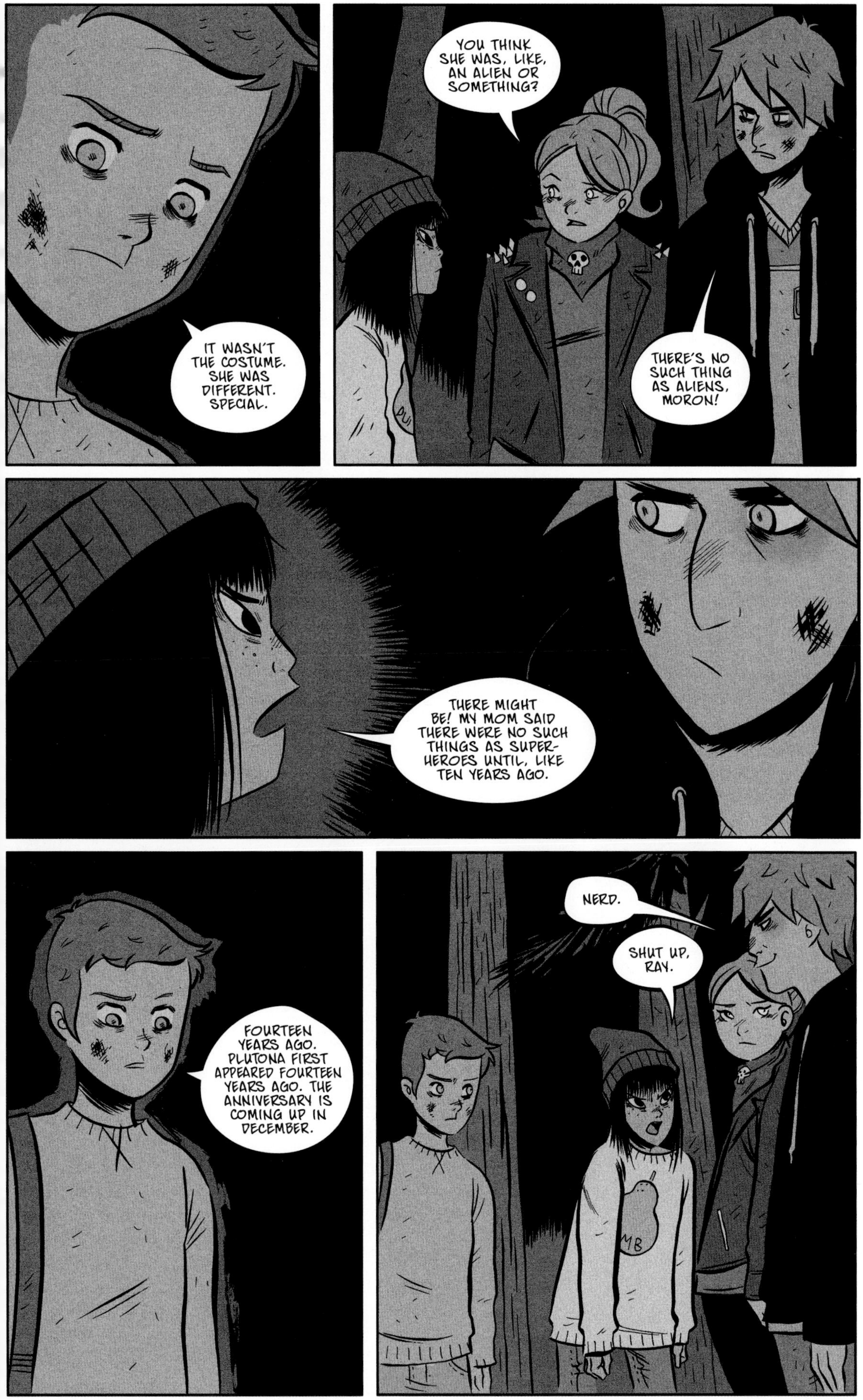
IT WASN'T THE COSTUME. SHE WAS DIFFERENT. SPECIAL.
YOU THINK SHE WAS, LIKE, AN ALIEN OR SOMETHING?
THERE'S NO SUCH THING AS ALIENS, MORON!
THERE MIGHT BE! MY MOM SAID THERE WERE NO SUCH THINGS AS SUPER-HEROES UNTIL, LIKE TEN YEARS AGO.
FOURTEEN YEARS AGO. PLUTONA FIRST APPEARED FOURTEEN YEARS AGO. THE ANNIVERSARY IS COMING UP IN DECEMBER.
NERD.
SHUT UP, RAY.

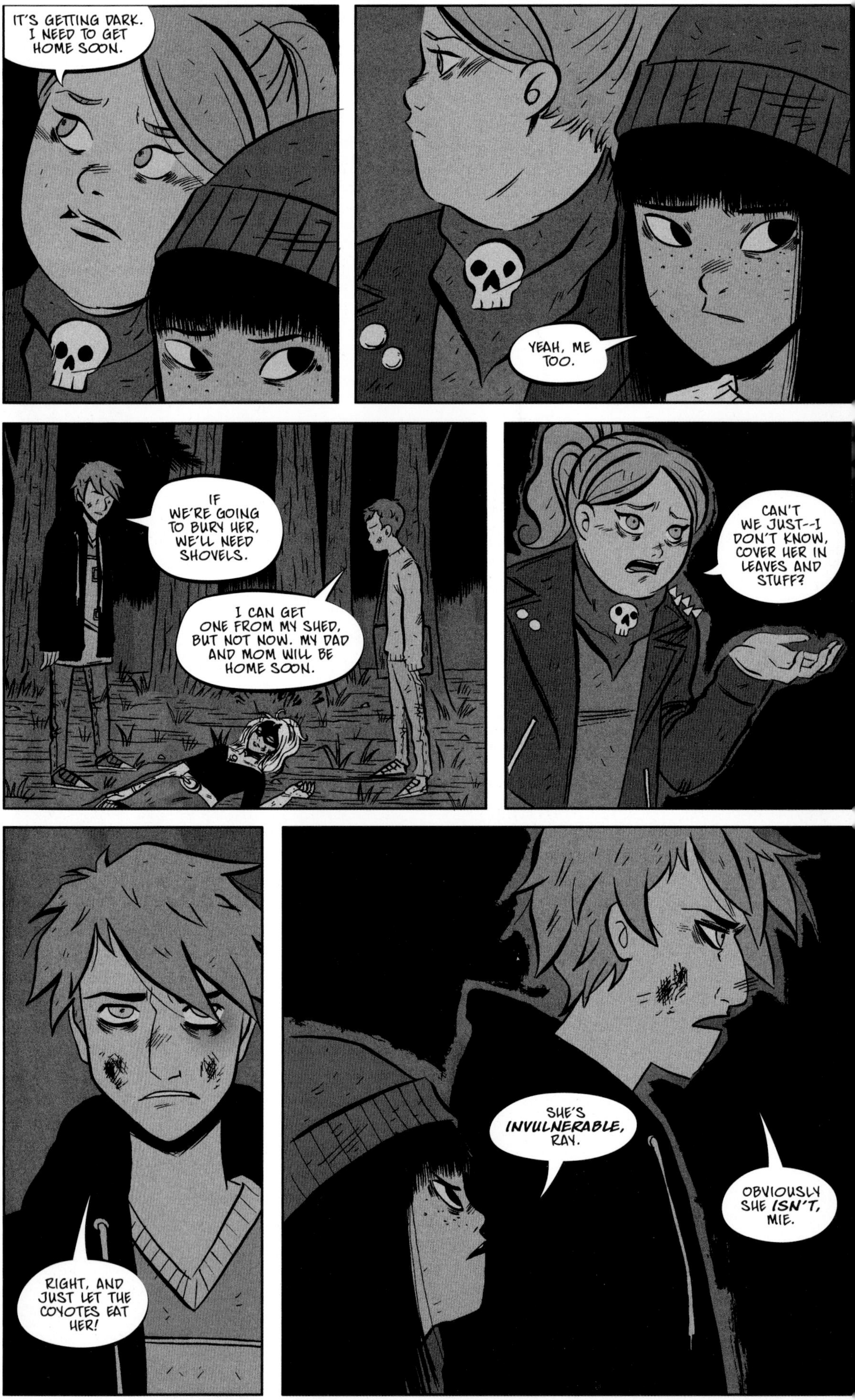
IT'S GETTING DARK. I NEED TO GET HOME SOON.
YEAH, ME TOO.
IF WE'RE GOING TO BURY HER, WE'LL NEED SHOVELS.
I CAN GET ONE FROM MY SHED, BUT NOT NOW. MY DAD AND MOM WILL BE HOME SOON.
CAN'T WE JUST--I DON'T KNOW, COVER HER IN LEAVES AND STUFF?
RIGHT, AND JUST LET THE COYOTES EAT HER!
SHE'S *INVULNERABLE*, RAY.
OBVIOUSLY SHE *ISN'T*, MIE.

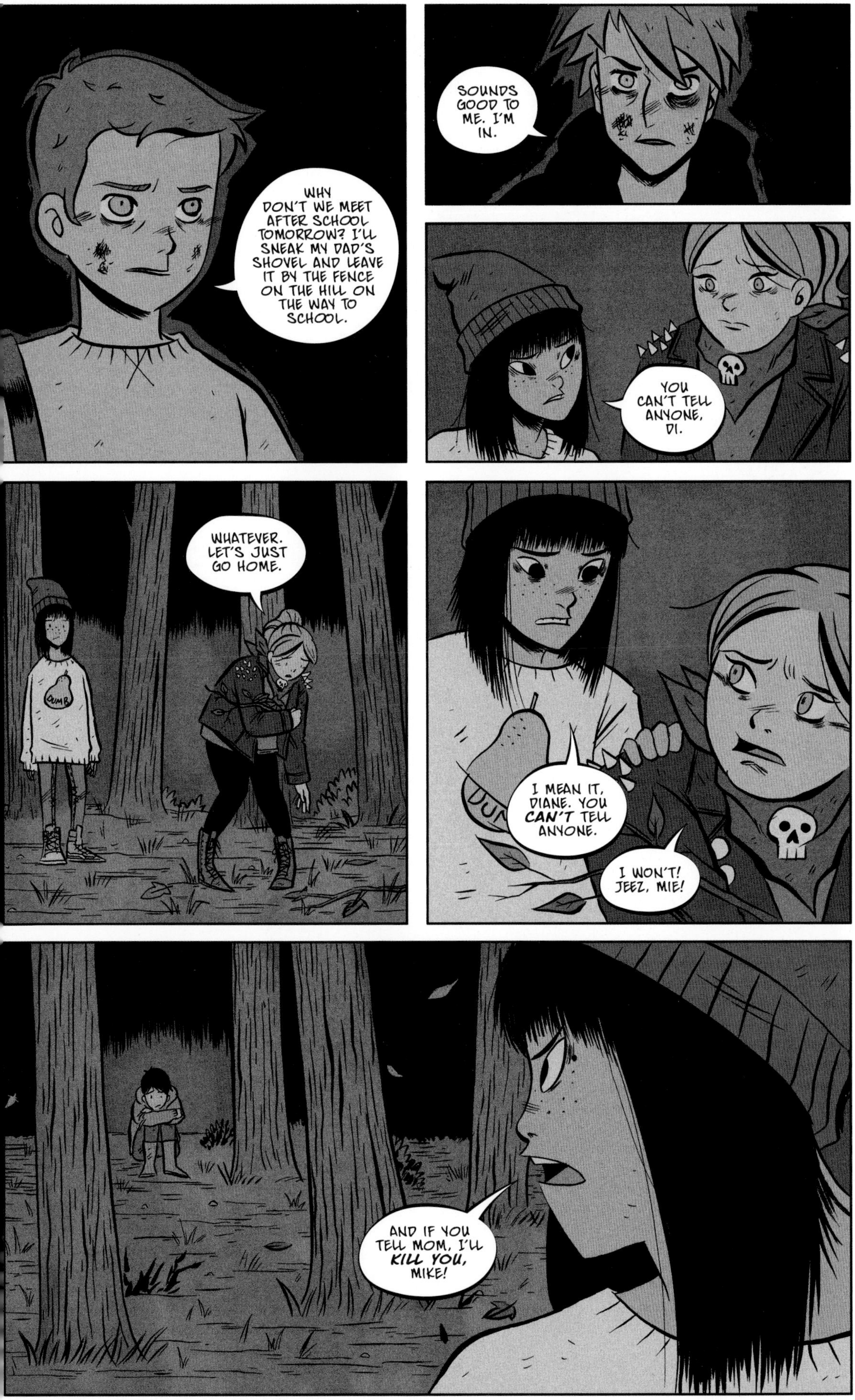
WHY DON'T WE MEET AFTER SCHOOL TOMORROW? I'LL SNEAK MY DAD'S SHOVEL AND LEAVE IT BY THE FENCE ON THE HILL ON THE WAY TO SCHOOL.
SOUNDS GOOD TO ME. I'M IN.
YOU CAN'T TELL ANYONE, DI.
WHATEVER. LET'S JUST GO HOME.
I MEAN IT, DIANE. YOU **CAN'T** TELL ANYONE.
I WON'T! JEEZ, MIE!
DUMB
AND IF YOU TELL MOM, I'LL **KILL YOU,** MIKE!

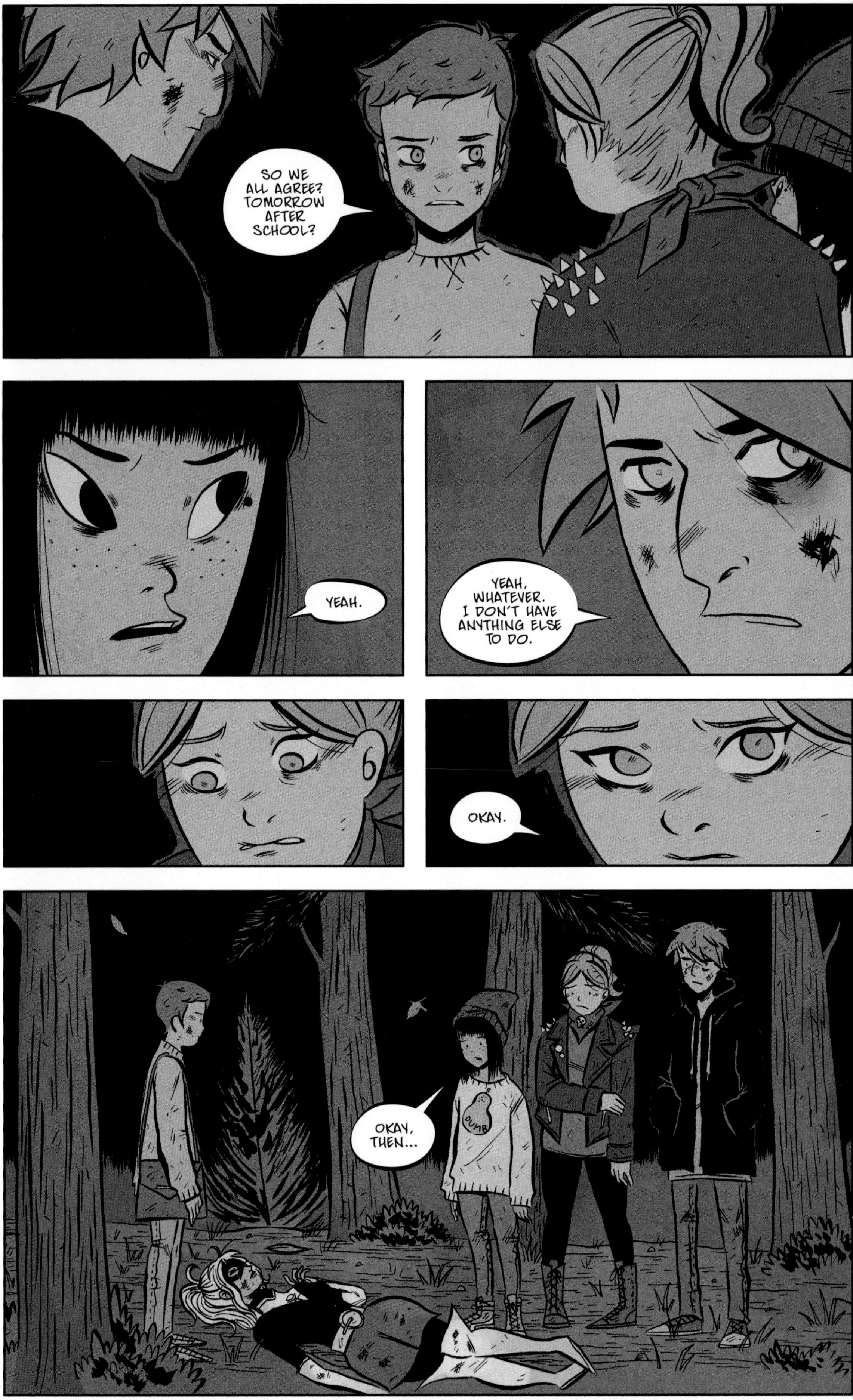
SO WE ALL AGREE? TOMORROW AFTER SCHOOL?
YEAH.
YEAH, WHATEVER. I DON'T HAVE ANYTHING ELSE TO DO.
OKAY.
DUMB
OKAY, THEN...

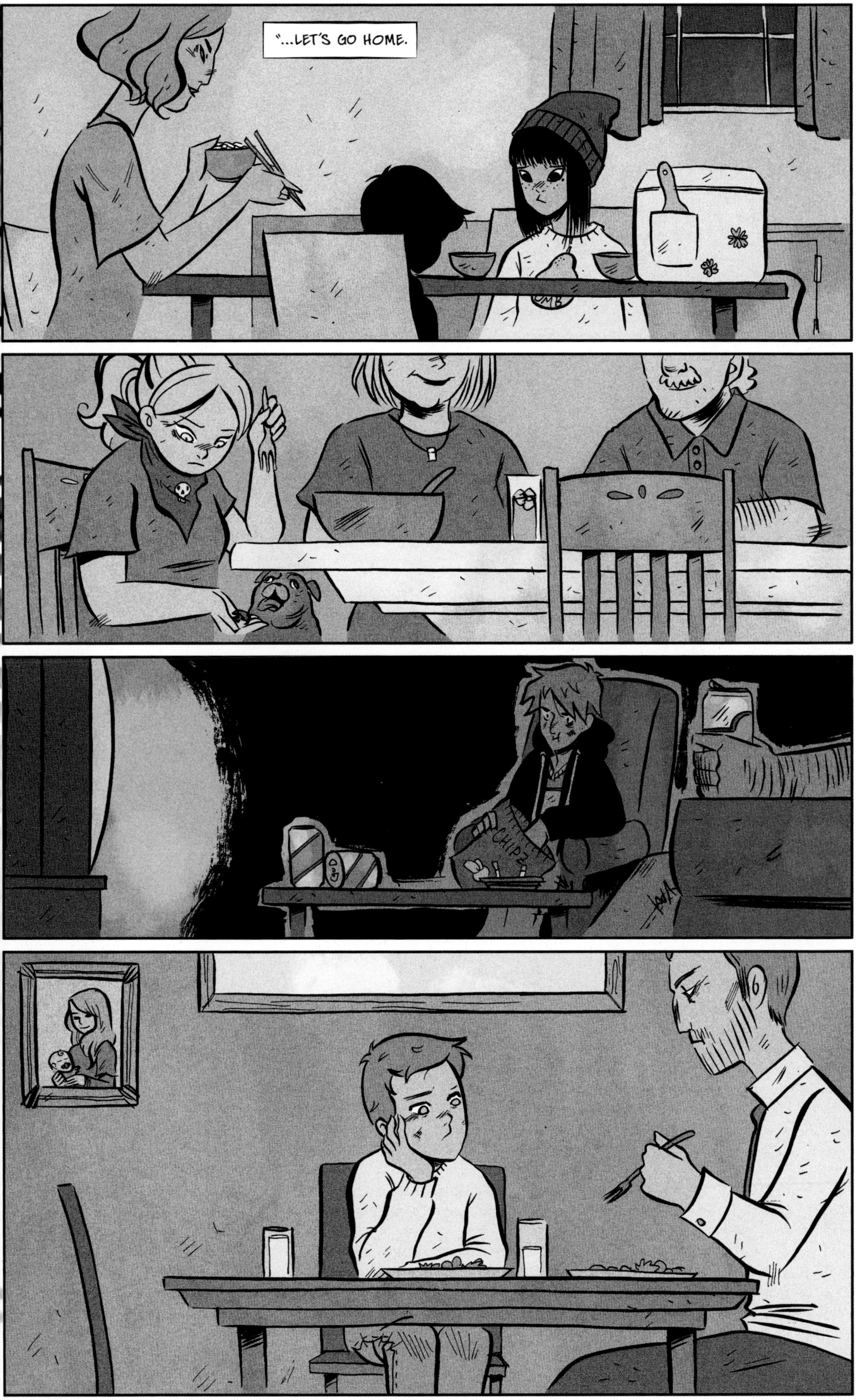
"...LET'S GO HOME.
CHIPZ

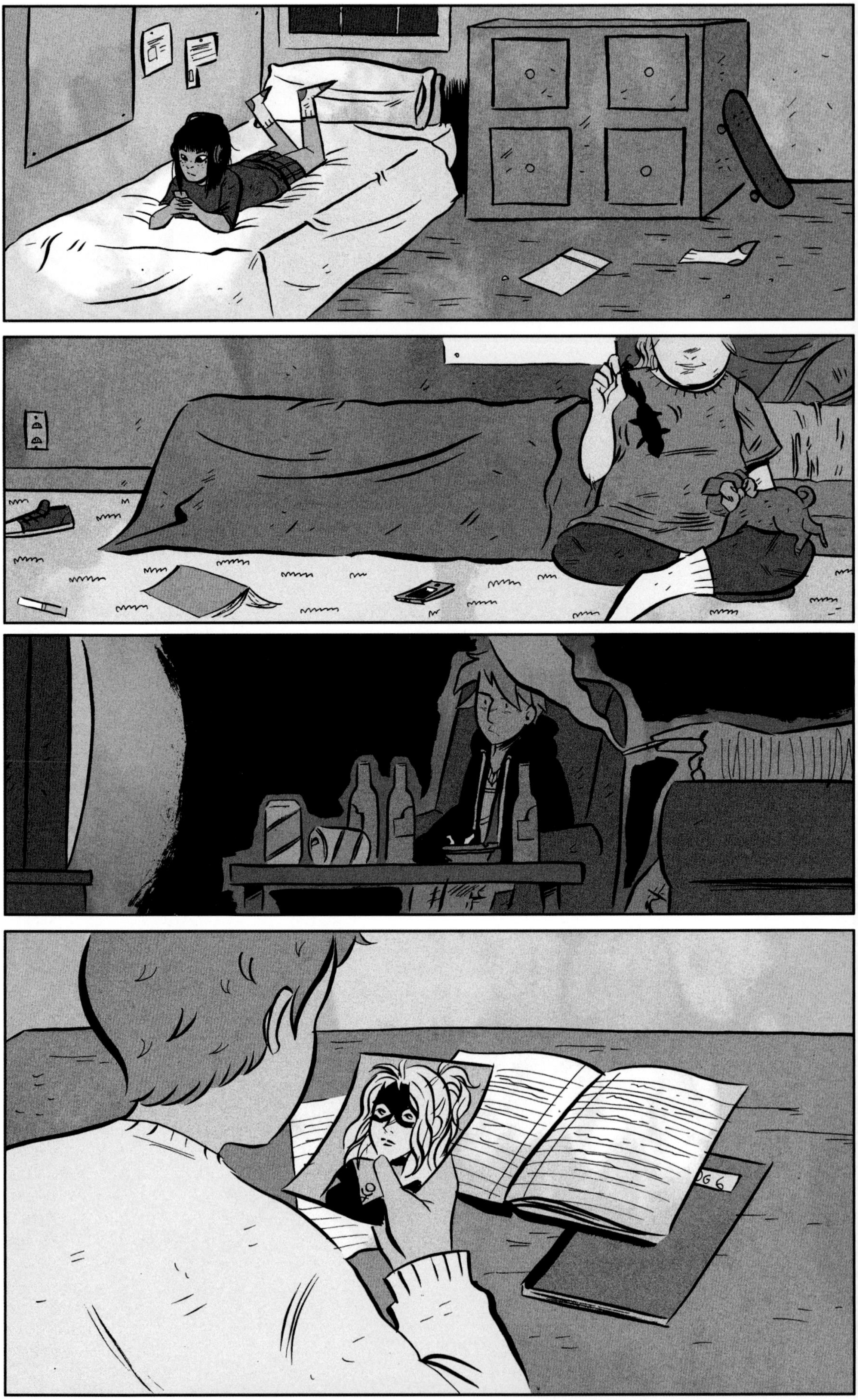

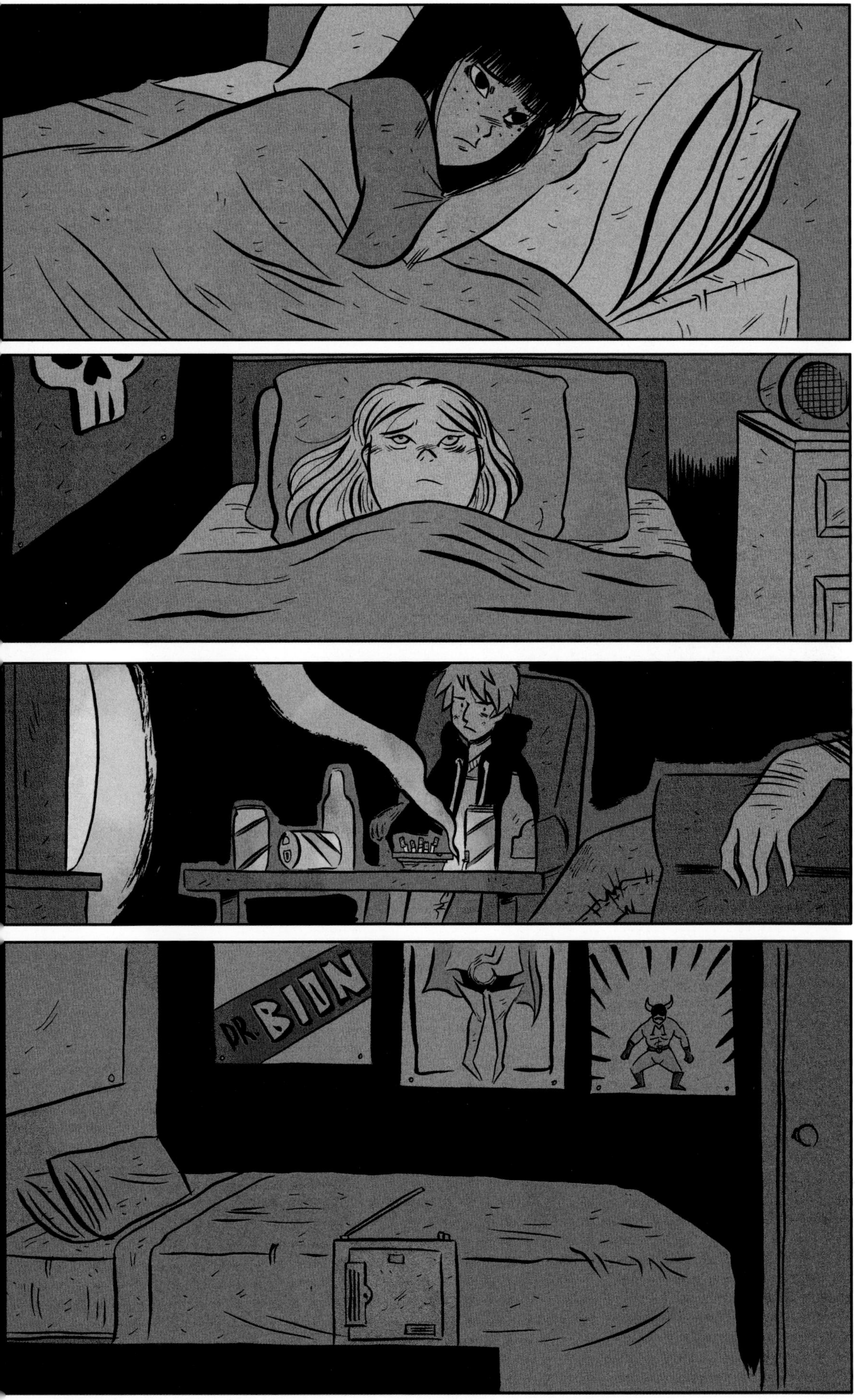
DR. BION

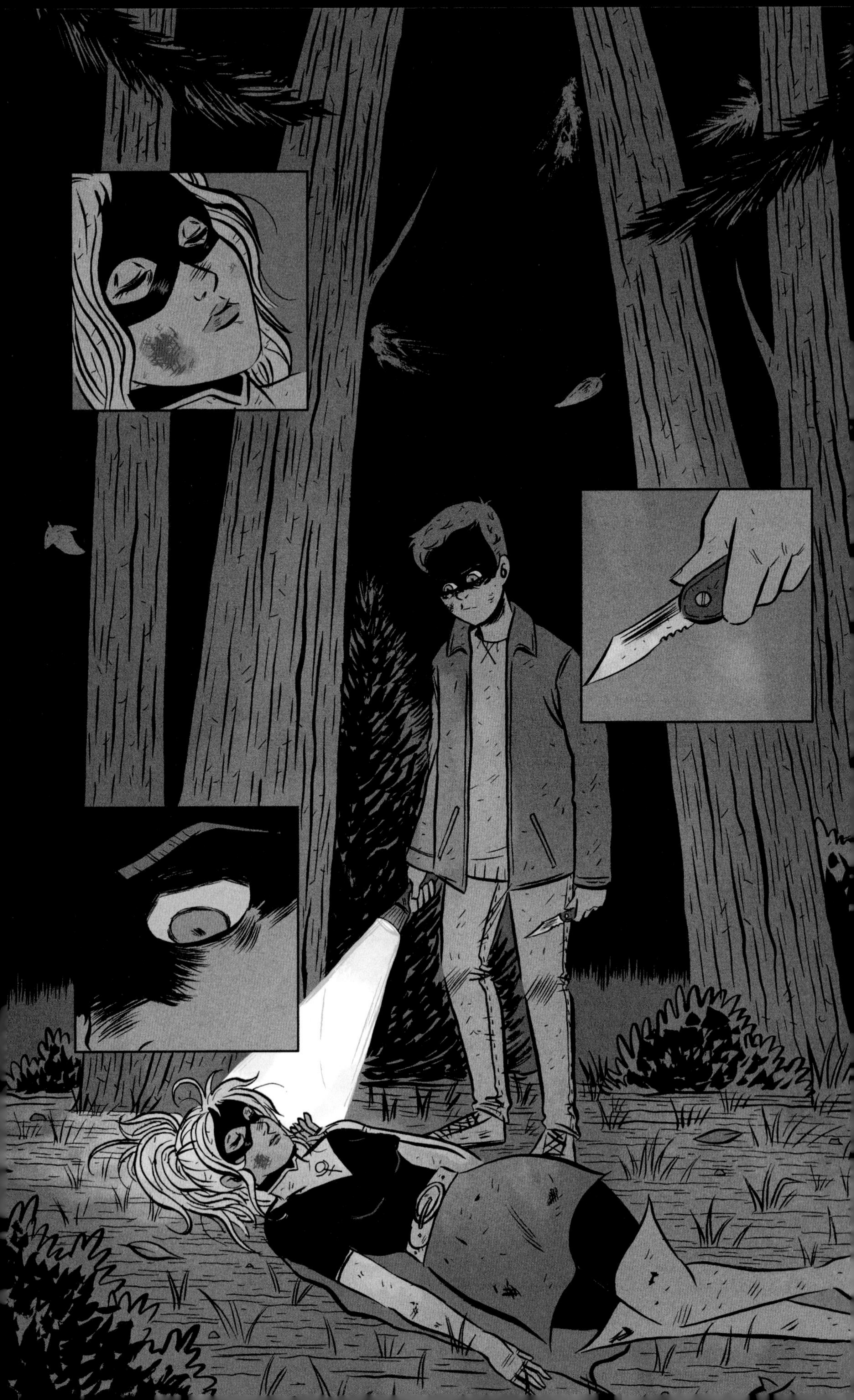

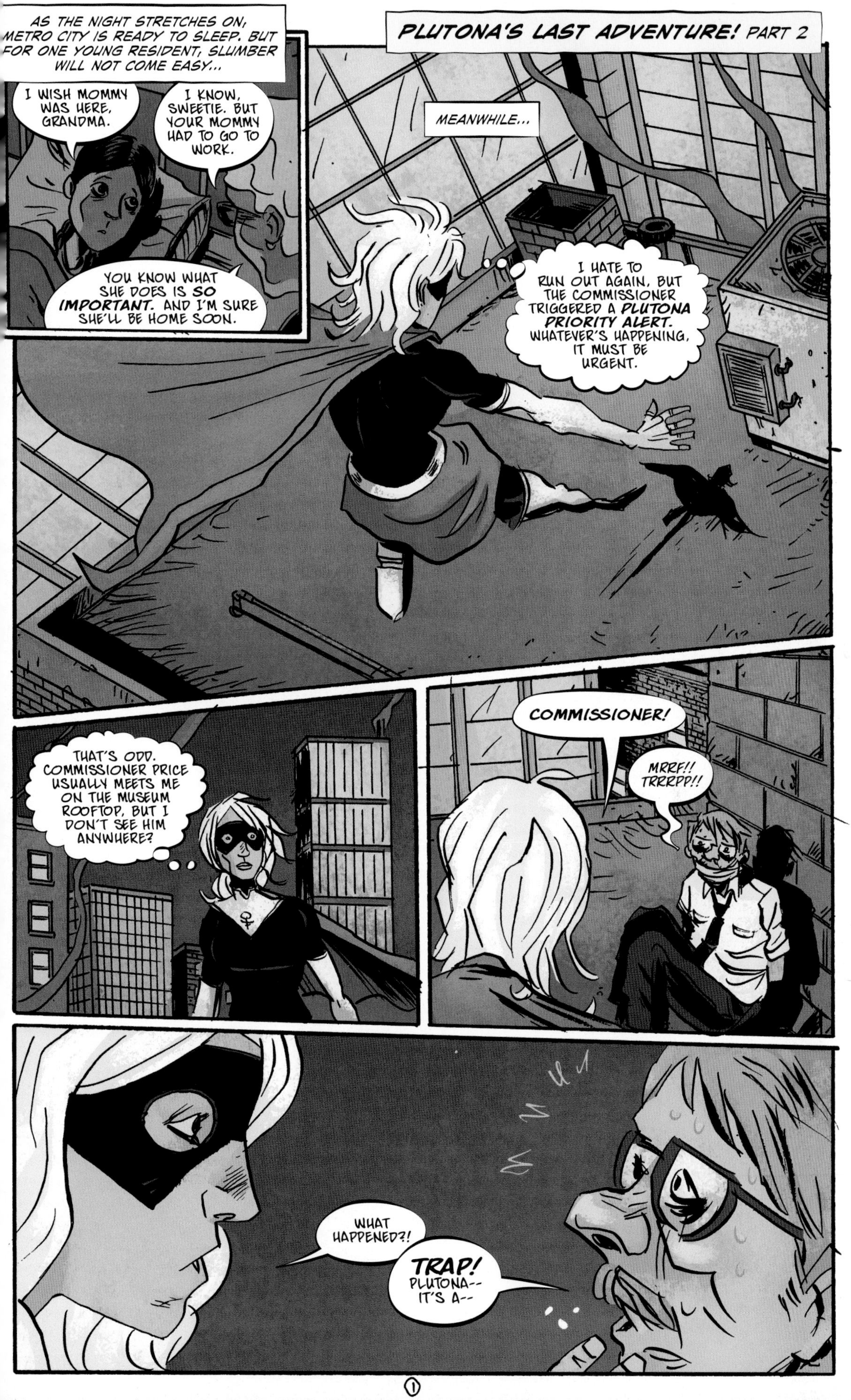
AS THE NIGHT STRETCHES ON, METRO CITY IS READY TO SLEEP. BUT FOR ONE YOUNG RESIDENT, SLUMBER WILL NOT COME EASY...
PLUTONA'S LAST ADVENTURE! PART 2
I WISH MOMMY WAS HERE, GRANDMA.
I KNOW, SWEETIE. BUT YOUR MOMMY HAD TO GO TO WORK.
YOU KNOW WHAT SHE DOES IS SO IMPORTANT. AND I'M SURE SHE'LL BE HOME SOON.
MEANWHILE...
I HATE TO RUN OUT AGAIN, BUT THE COMMISSIONER TRIGGERED A PLUTONA PRIORITY ALERT. WHATEVER'S HAPPENING, IT MUST BE URGENT.
THAT'S ODD. COMMISSIONER PRICE USUALLY MEETS ME ON THE MUSEUM ROOFTOP, BUT I DON'T SEE HIM ANYWHERE?
COMMISSIONER!
MRRF!! TRRRPP!!
WHAT HAPPENED?!
TRAP! PLUTONA-- IT'S A--

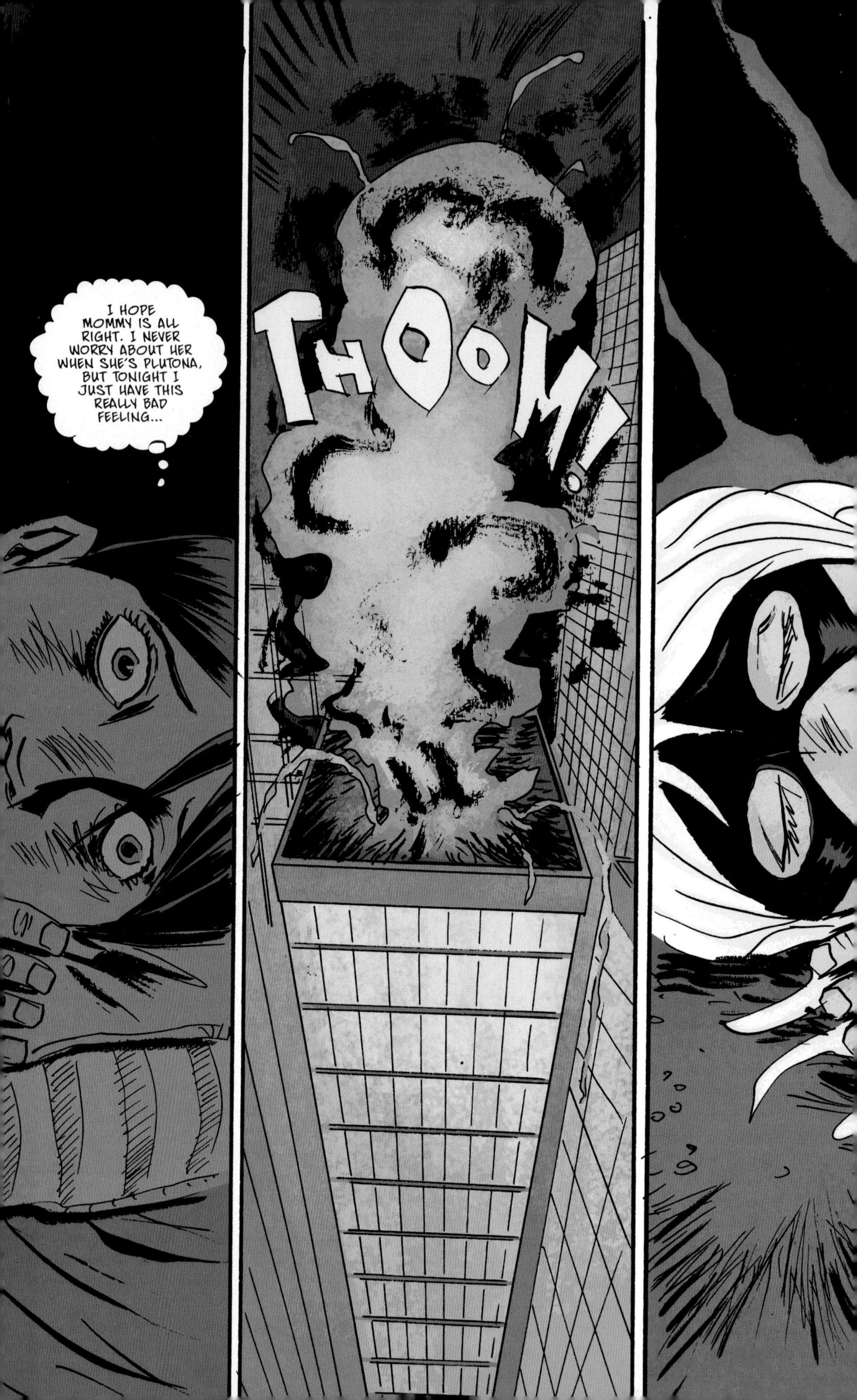
I HOPE MOMMY IS ALL RIGHT. I NEVER WORRY ABOUT HER WHEN SHE'S PLUTONA, BUT TONIGHT I JUST HAVE THIS REALLY BAD FEELING...
THOOM!!

CHAPTER

3

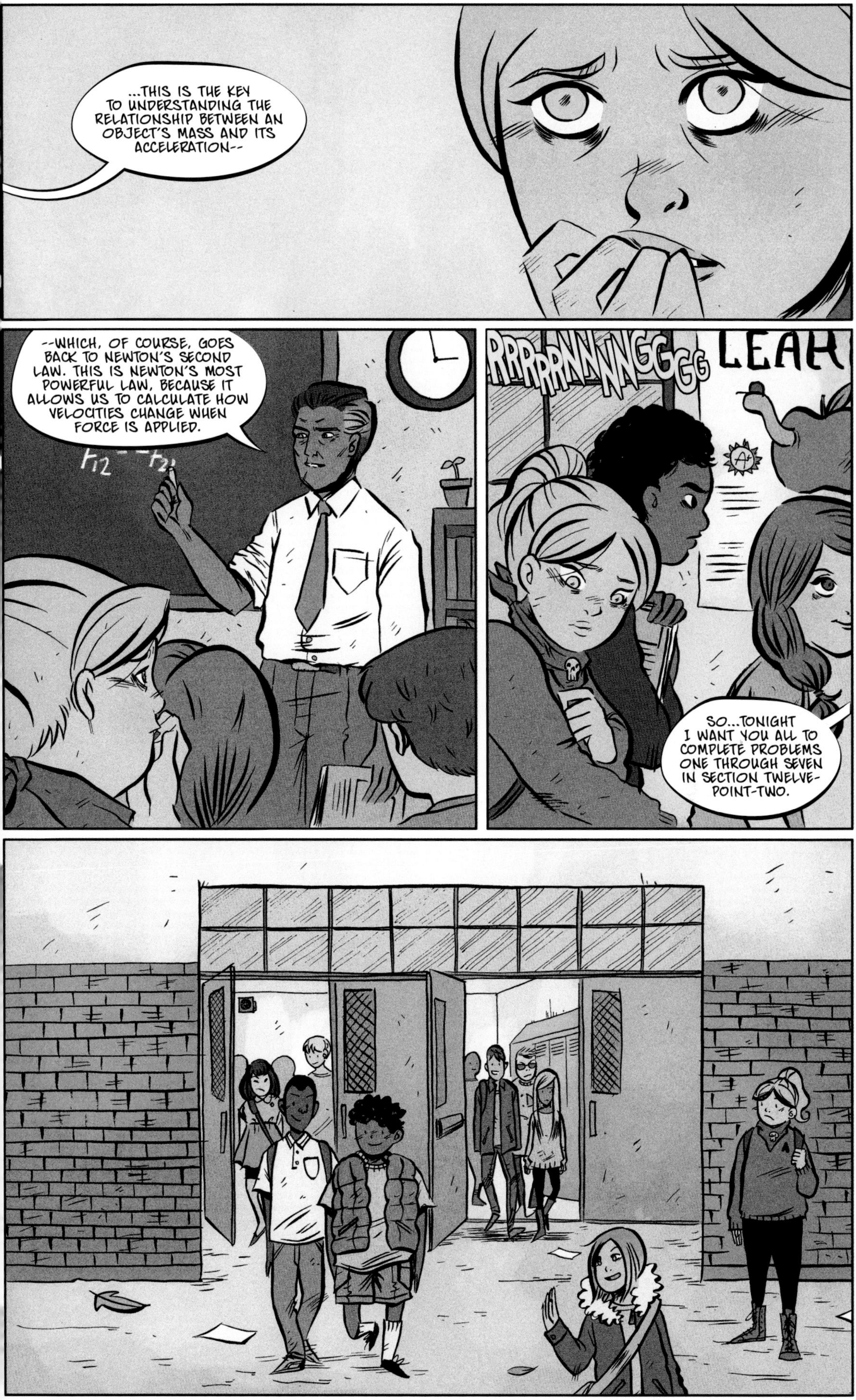
...THIS IS THE KEY TO UNDERSTANDING THE RELATIONSHIP BETWEEN AN OBJECT'S MASS AND ITS ACCELERATION--
--WHICH, OF COURSE, GOES BACK TO NEWTON'S SECOND LAW. THIS IS NEWTON'S MOST POWERFUL LAW, BECAUSE IT ALLOWS US TO CALCULATE HOW VELOCITIES CHANGE WHEN FORCE IS APPLIED.
RRRRRNNNNGGGG
LEAR
SO...TONIGHT I WANT YOU ALL TO COMPLETE PROBLEMS ONE THROUGH SEVEN IN SECTION TWELVE-POINT-TWO.

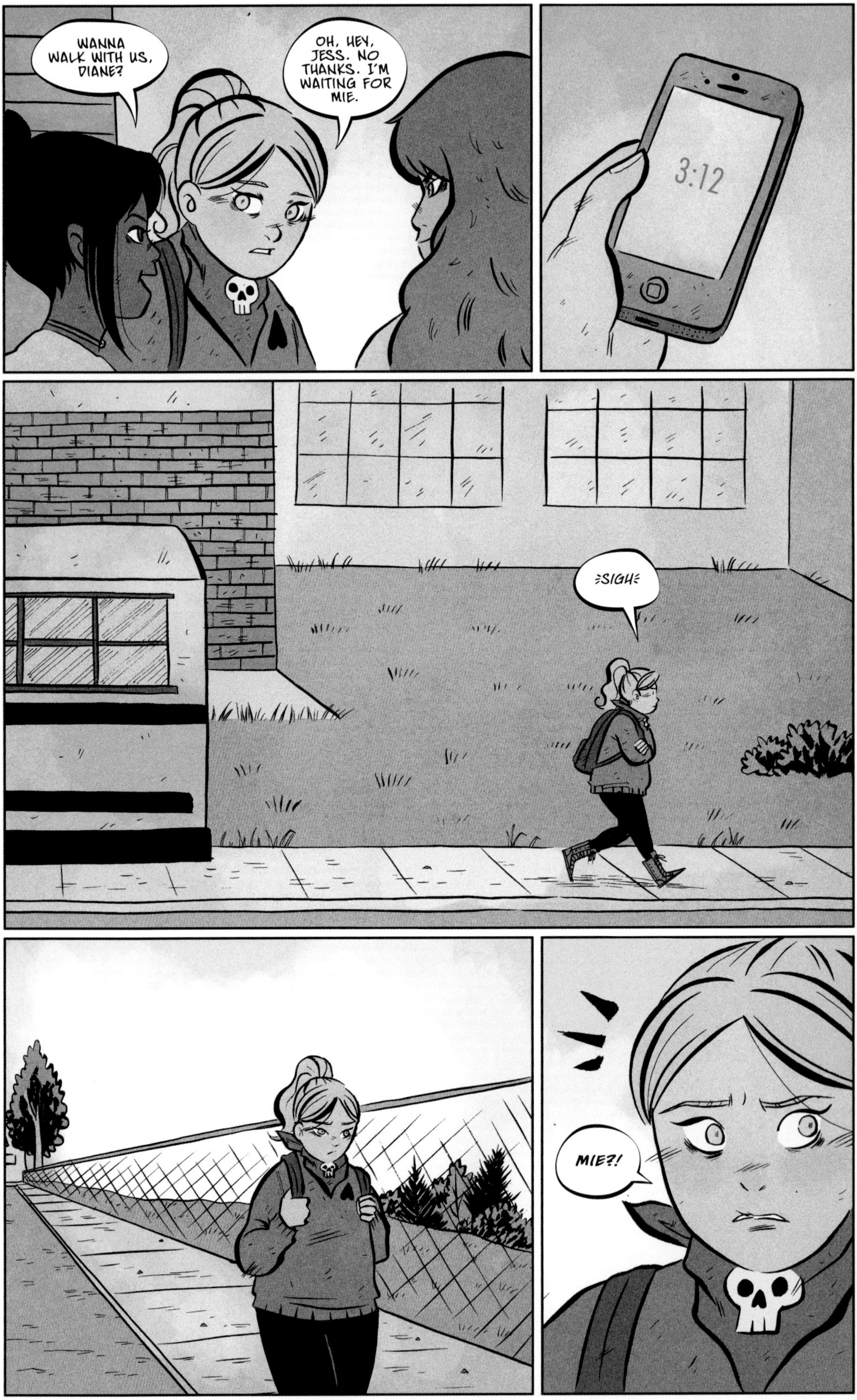
WANNA WALK WITH US, DIANE?
OH, HEY, JESS. NO THANKS. I'M WAITING FOR MIE.
3:12
SIGH
MIE?!

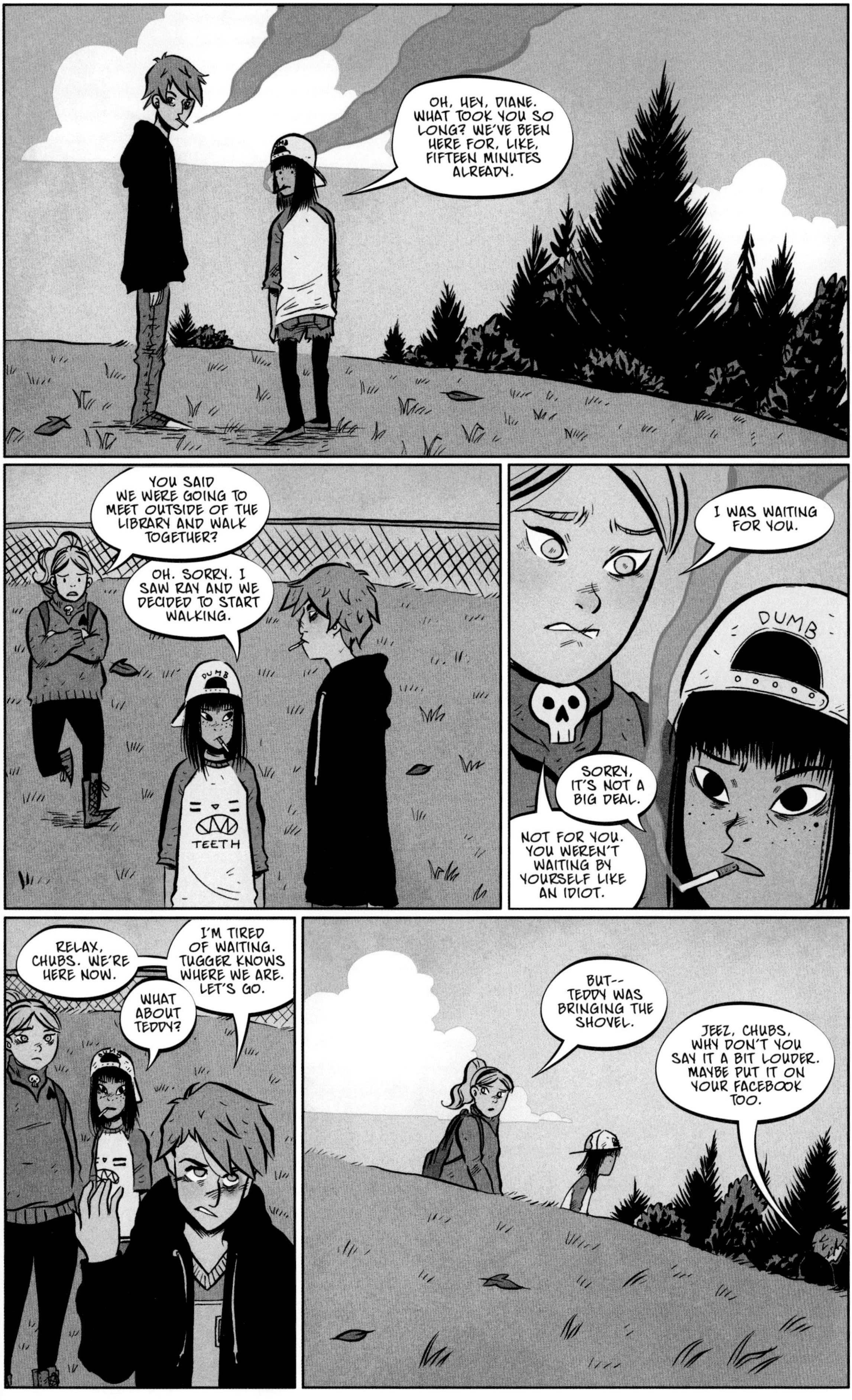
OH, HEY, DIANE. WHAT TOOK YOU SO LONG? WE'VE BEEN HERE FOR, LIKE, FIFTEEN MINUTES ALREADY.
YOU SAID WE WERE GOING TO MEET OUTSIDE OF THE LIBRARY AND WALK TOGETHER?
OH. SORRY. I SAW RAY AND WE DECIDED TO START WALKING.
DUMB
TEETH
I WAS WAITING FOR YOU.
DUMB
SORRY, IT'S NOT A BIG DEAL.
NOT FOR YOU. YOU WEREN'T WAITING BY YOURSELF LIKE AN IDIOT.
RELAX, CHUBS. WE'RE HERE NOW.
I'M TIRED OF WAITING. TUGGER KNOWS WHERE WE ARE. LET'S GO.
WHAT ABOUT TEDDY?
BUT-- TEDDY WAS BRINGING THE SHOVEL.
JEEZ, CHUBS, WHY DON'T YOU SAY IT A BIT LOUDER. MAYBE PUT IT ON YOUR FACEBOOK TOO.

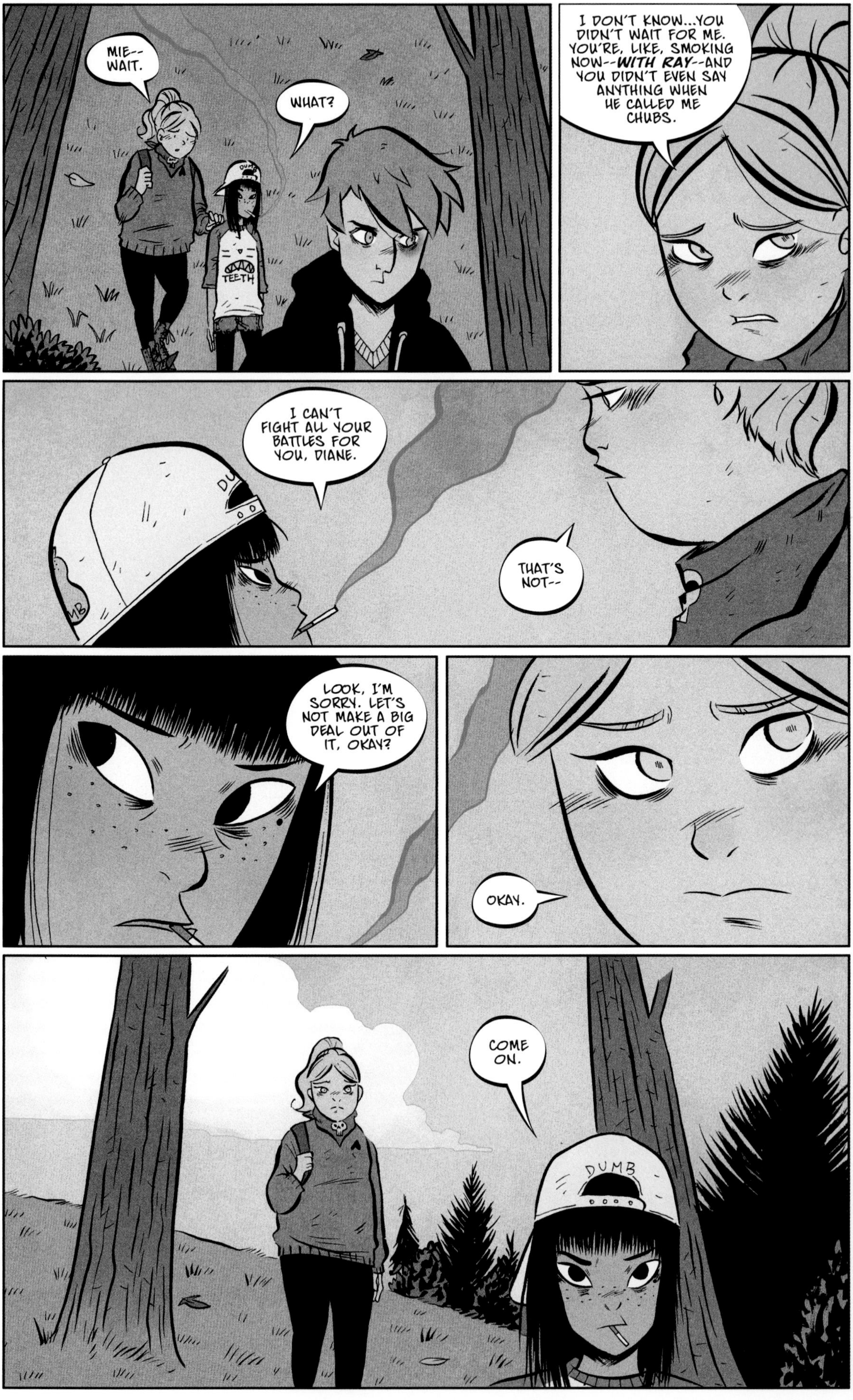
MIE--
WAIT.
WHAT?
I DON'T KNOW...YOU DIDN'T WAIT FOR ME. YOU'RE, LIKE, SMOKING NOW--WITH RAY--AND YOU DIDN'T EVEN SAY ANYTHING WHEN HE CALLED ME CHUBS.
DUMB
TEETH
I CAN'T FIGHT ALL YOUR BATTLES FOR YOU, DIANE.
THAT'S NOT--
LOOK, I'M SORRY. LET'S NOT MAKE A BIG DEAL OUT OF IT, OKAY?
OKAY.
COME ON.
DUMB

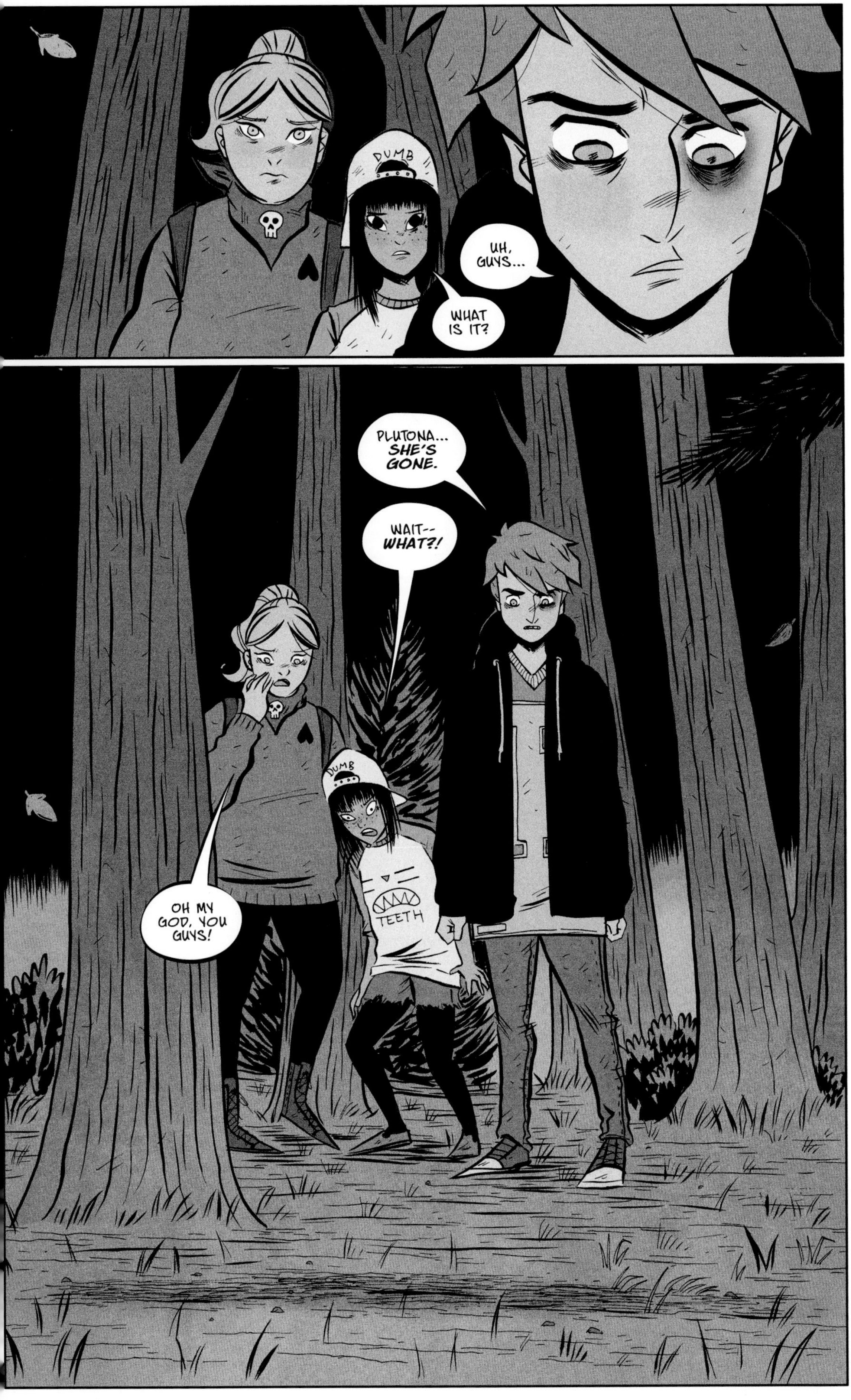
DUMB
UH, GUYS...
WHAT IS IT?
PLUTONA... SHE'S GONE.
WAIT-- WHAT?!
DUMB
OH MY GOD, YOU GUYS!
TEETH

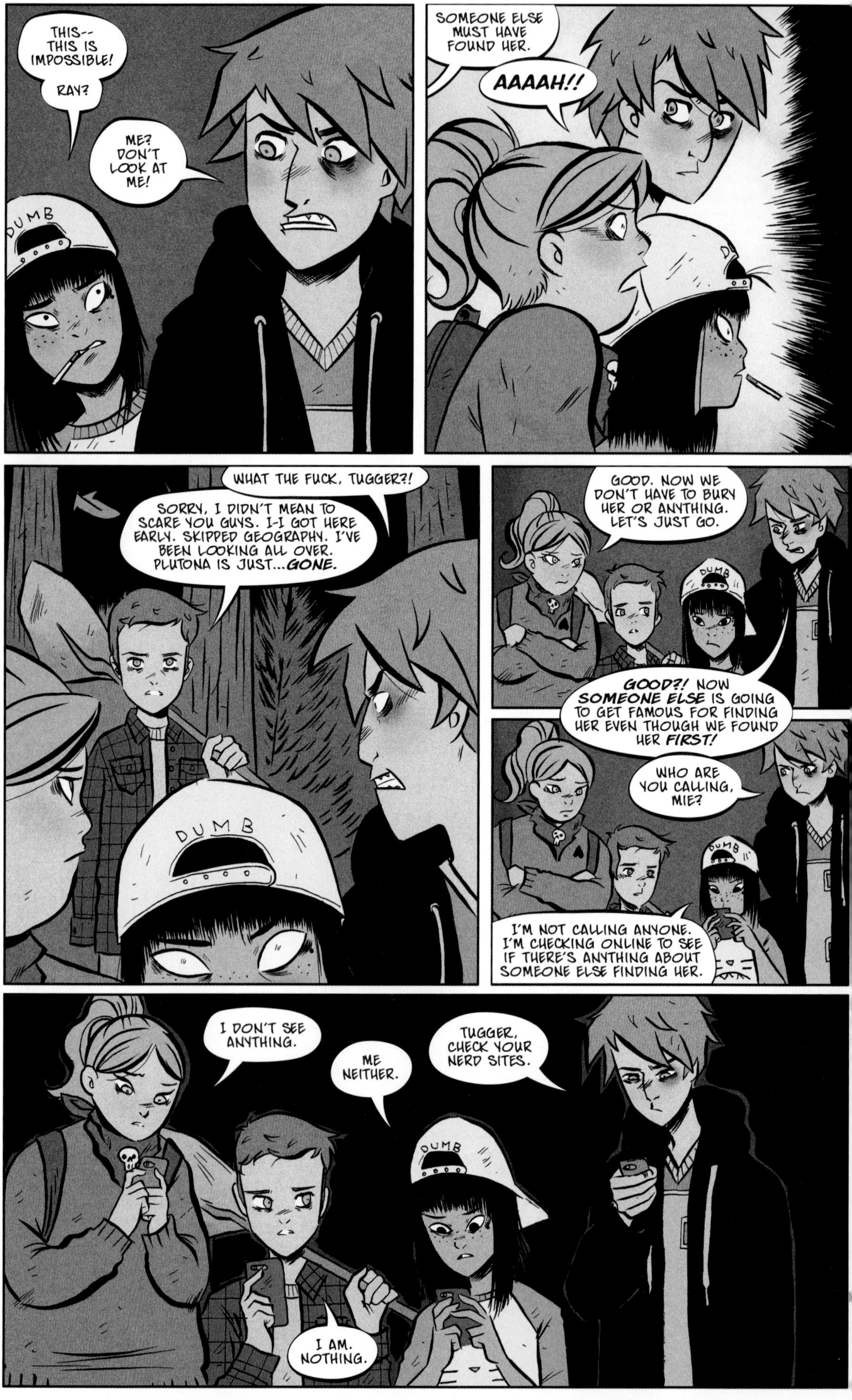
THIS-- THIS IS IMPOSSIBLE!
RAY?
ME? DON'T LOOK AT ME!
SOMEONE ELSE MUST HAVE FOUND HER.
AAAAH!!
WHAT THE FUCK, TUGGER?!
SORRY, I DIDN'T MEAN TO SCARE YOU GUYS. I-I GOT HERE EARLY. SKIPPED GEOGRAPHY. I'VE BEEN LOOKING ALL OVER. PLUTONA IS JUST...GONE.
DUMB
GOOD. NOW WE DON'T HAVE TO BURY HER OR ANYTHING. LET'S JUST GO.
GOOD?! NOW SOMEONE ELSE IS GOING TO GET FAMOUS FOR FINDING HER EVEN THOUGH WE FOUND HER FIRST!
WHO ARE YOU CALLING, MIE?
I'M NOT CALLING ANYONE. I'M CHECKING ONLINE TO SEE IF THERE'S ANYTHING ABOUT SOMEONE ELSE FINDING HER.
I DON'T SEE ANYTHING.
ME NEITHER.
TUGGER, CHECK YOUR NERD SITES.
I AM. NOTHING.

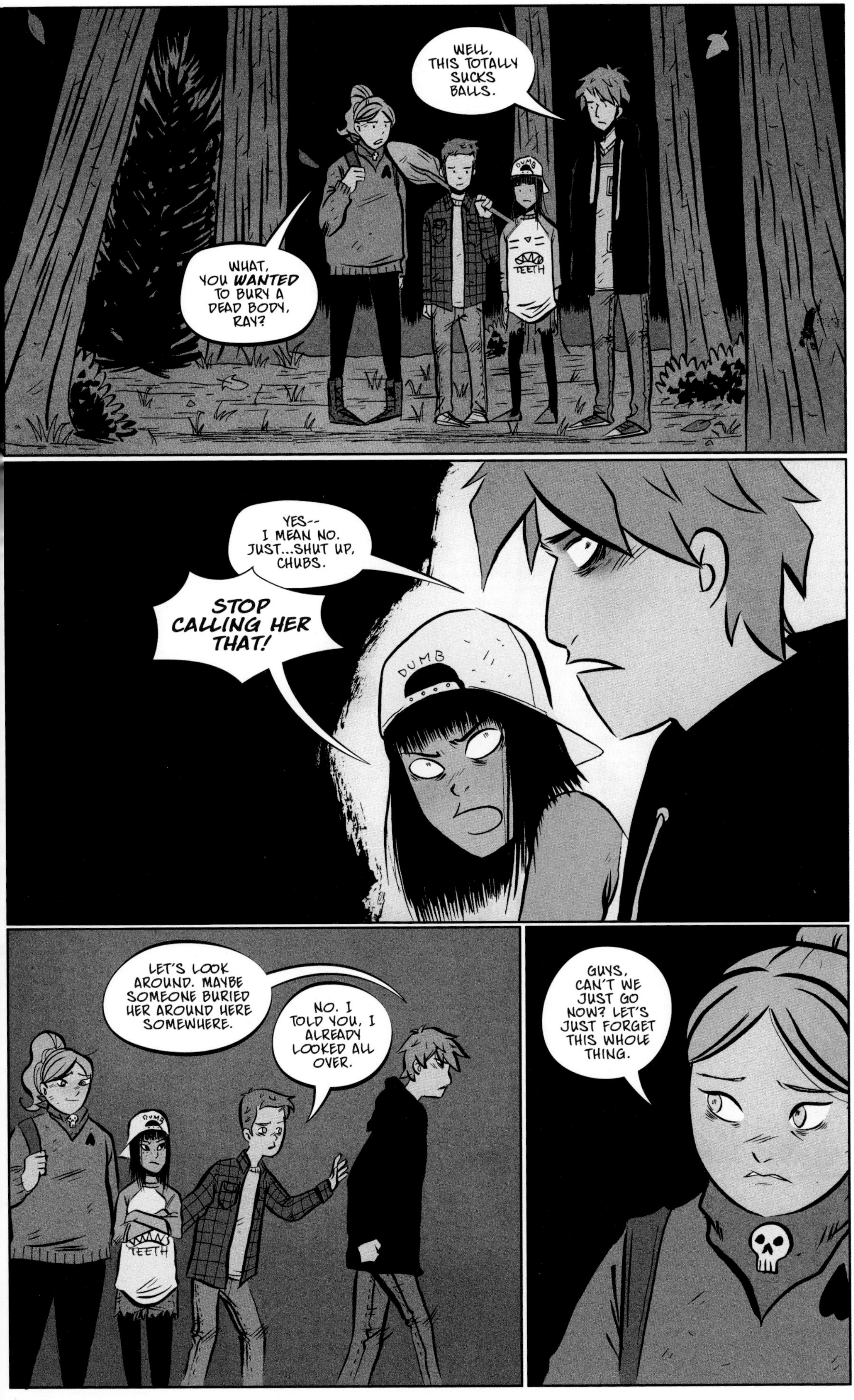
WELL, THIS TOTALLY SUCKS BALLS.
WHAT, YOU WANTED TO BURY A DEAD BODY, RAY?
DUMB
TEETH
YES-- I MEAN NO. JUST...SHUT UP, CHUBS.
STOP CALLING HER THAT!
DUMB
LET'S LOOK AROUND. MAYBE SOMEONE BURIED HER AROUND HERE SOMEWHERE.
NO. I TOLD YOU, I ALREADY LOOKED ALL OVER.
DUMB
TEETH
GUYS, CAN'T WE JUST GO NOW? LET'S JUST FORGET THIS WHOLE THING.

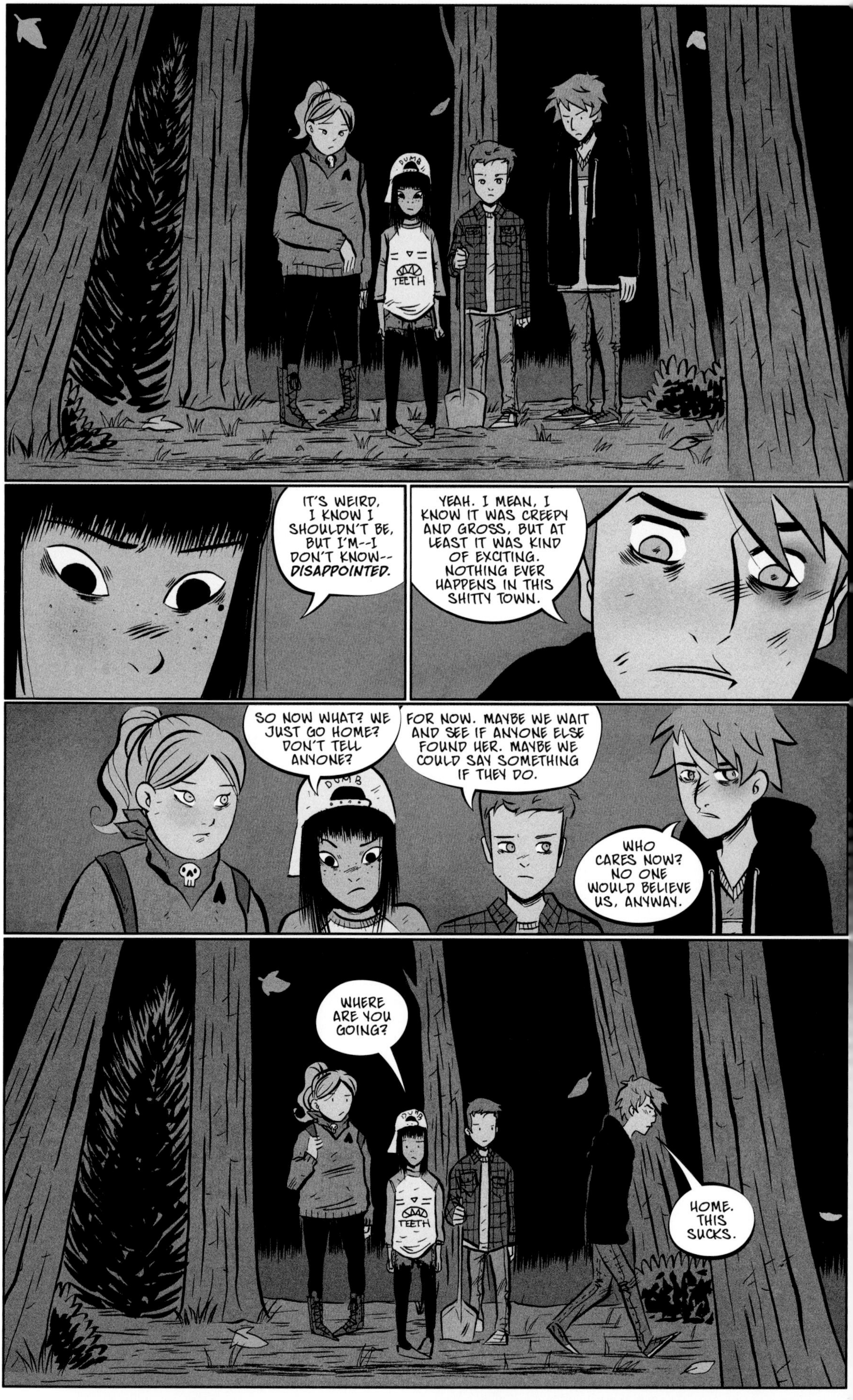
DUMB
TEETH
IT'S WEIRD, I KNOW I SHOULDN'T BE, BUT I'M--I DON'T KNOW-- *DISAPPOINTED.*
YEAH. I MEAN, I KNOW IT WAS CREEPY AND GROSS, BUT AT LEAST IT WAS KIND OF EXCITING. NOTHING EVER HAPPENS IN THIS SHITTY TOWN.
SO NOW WHAT? WE JUST GO HOME? DON'T TELL ANYONE?
DUMB
FOR NOW. MAYBE WE WAIT AND SEE IF ANYONE ELSE FOUND HER. MAYBE WE COULD SAY SOMETHING IF THEY DO.
WHO CARES NOW? NO ONE WOULD BELIEVE US, ANYWAY.
WHERE ARE YOU GOING?
DUMB
TEETH
HOME. THIS SUCKS.

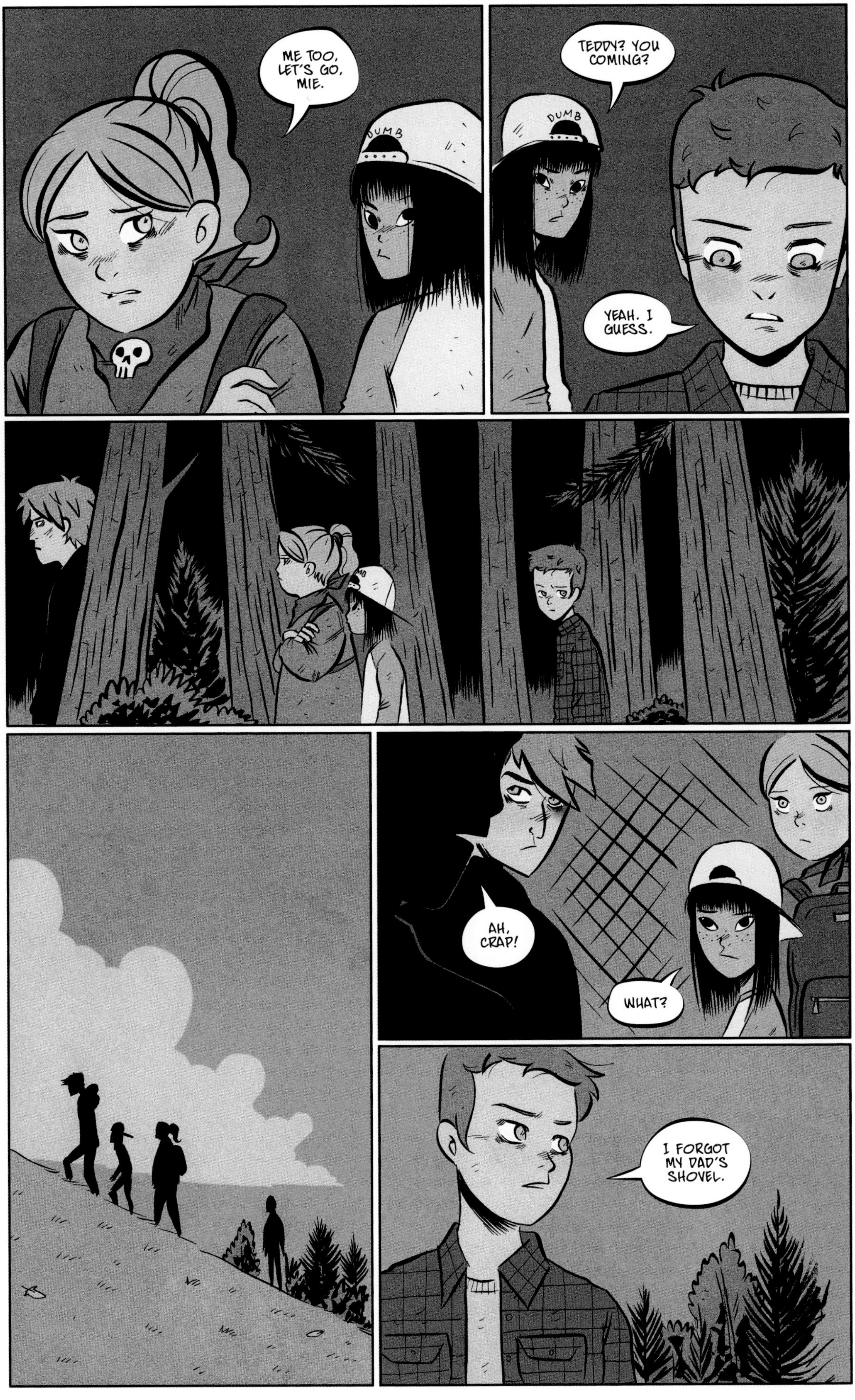
ME TOO, LET'S GO, MIE.
TEDDY? YOU COMING?
YEAH. I GUESS.
AH, CRAP!
WHAT?
I FORGOT MY DAD'S SHOVEL.

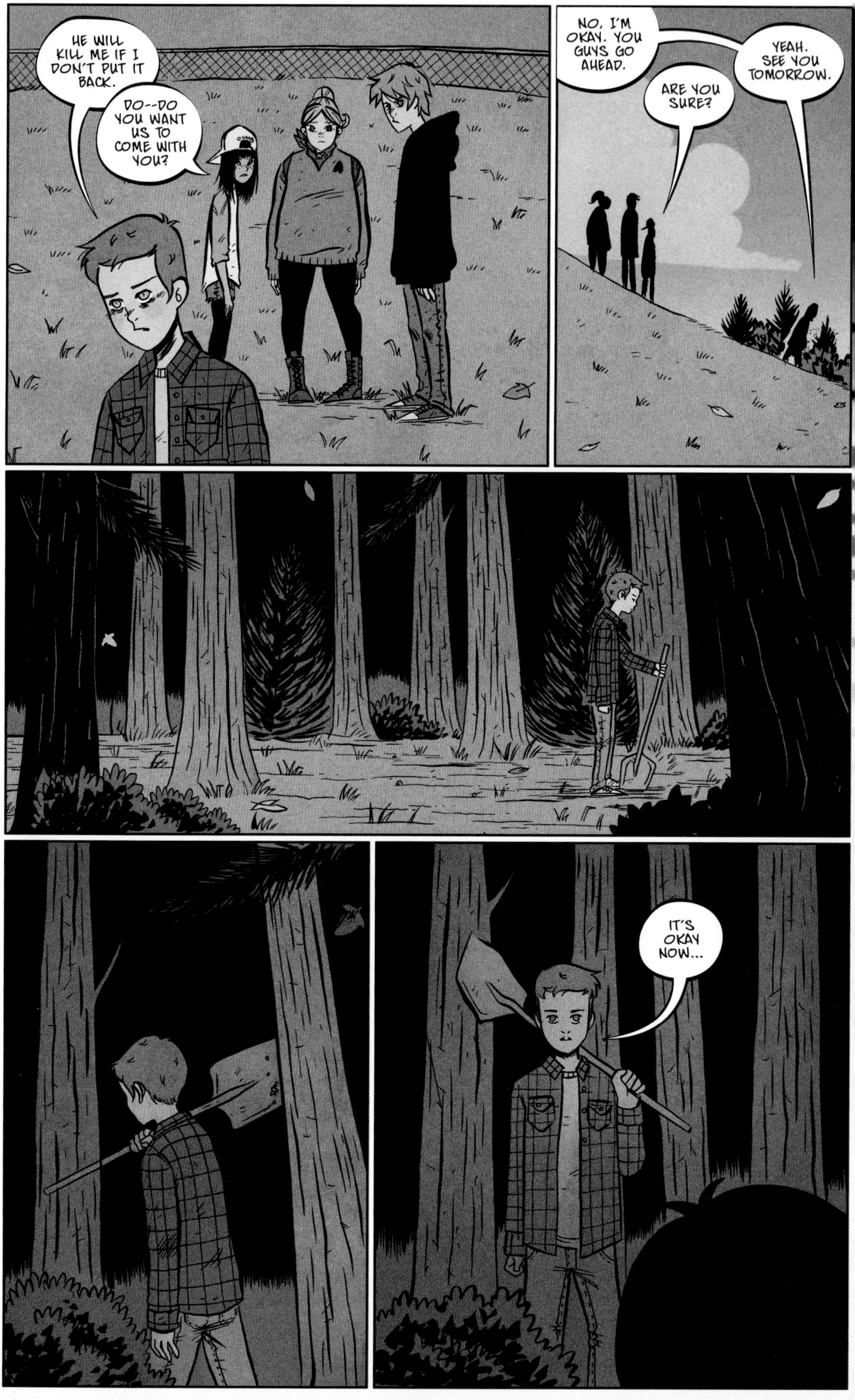
HE WILL KILL ME IF I DON'T PUT IT BACK.
DO--DO YOU WANT US TO COME WITH YOU?
NO, I'M OKAY. YOU GUYS GO AHEAD.
ARE YOU SURE?
YEAH. SEE YOU TOMORROW.
IT'S OKAY NOW...

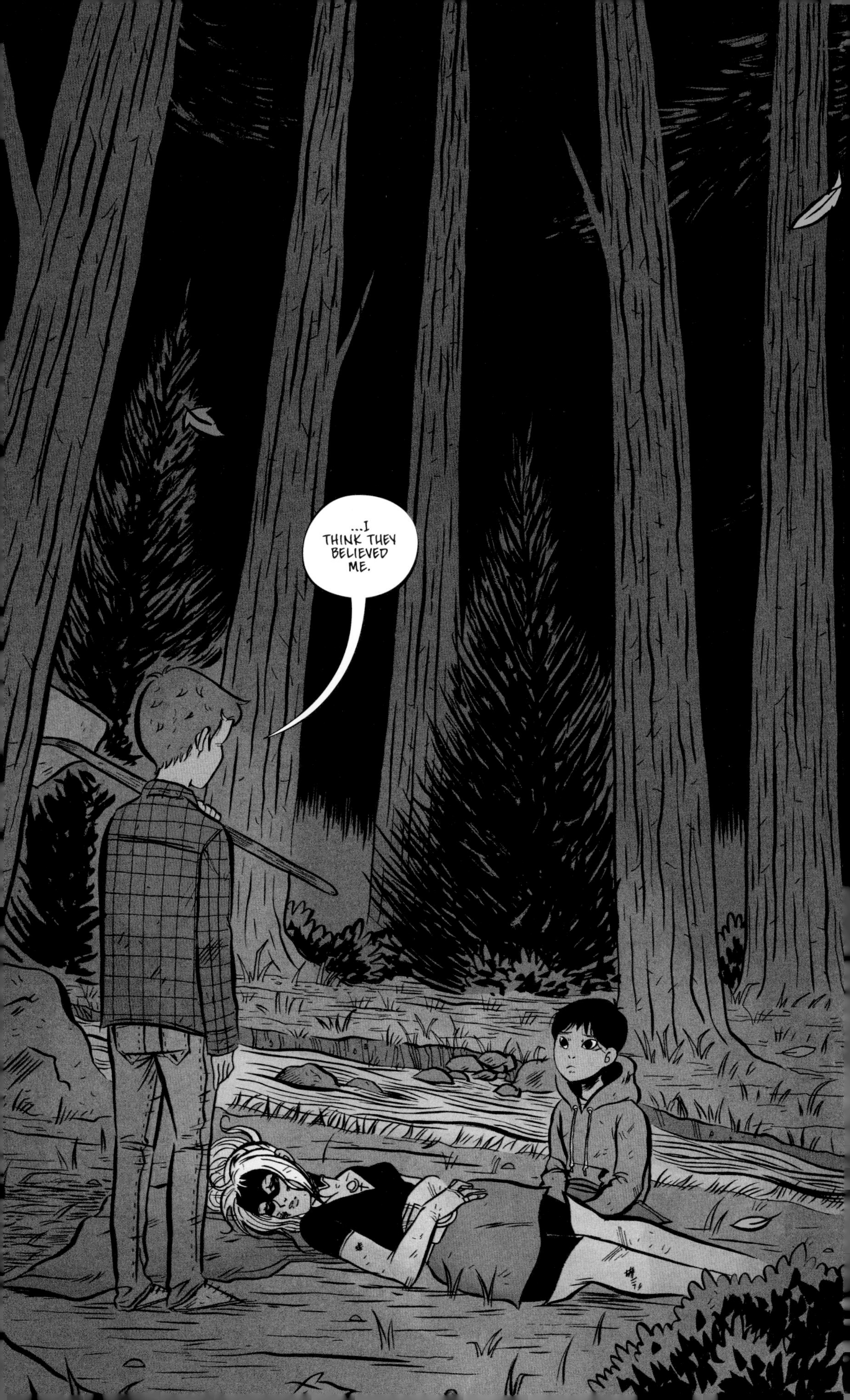
...I THINK THEY BELIEVED ME.

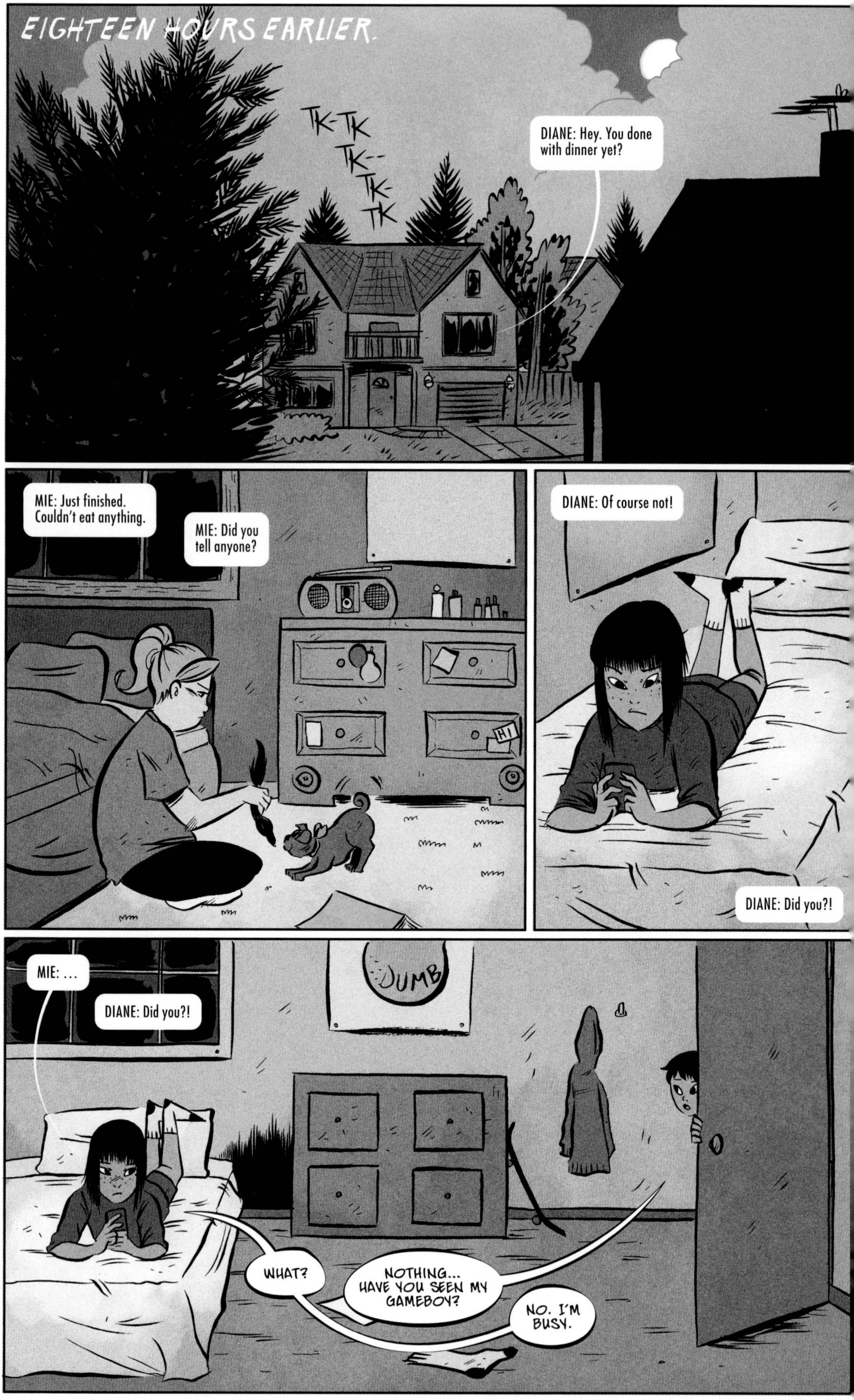
EIGHTEEN HOURS EARLIER.
TK-TK TK-- TK- TK
DIANE: Hey. You done with dinner yet?
MIE: Just finished. Couldn't eat anything.
MIE: Did you tell anyone?
HI
DIANE: Of course not!
DIANE: Did you?!
DUMB
MIE: ...
DIANE: Did you?!
WHAT?
NOTHING... HAVE YOU SEEN MY GAMEBOY?
NO. I'M BUSY.

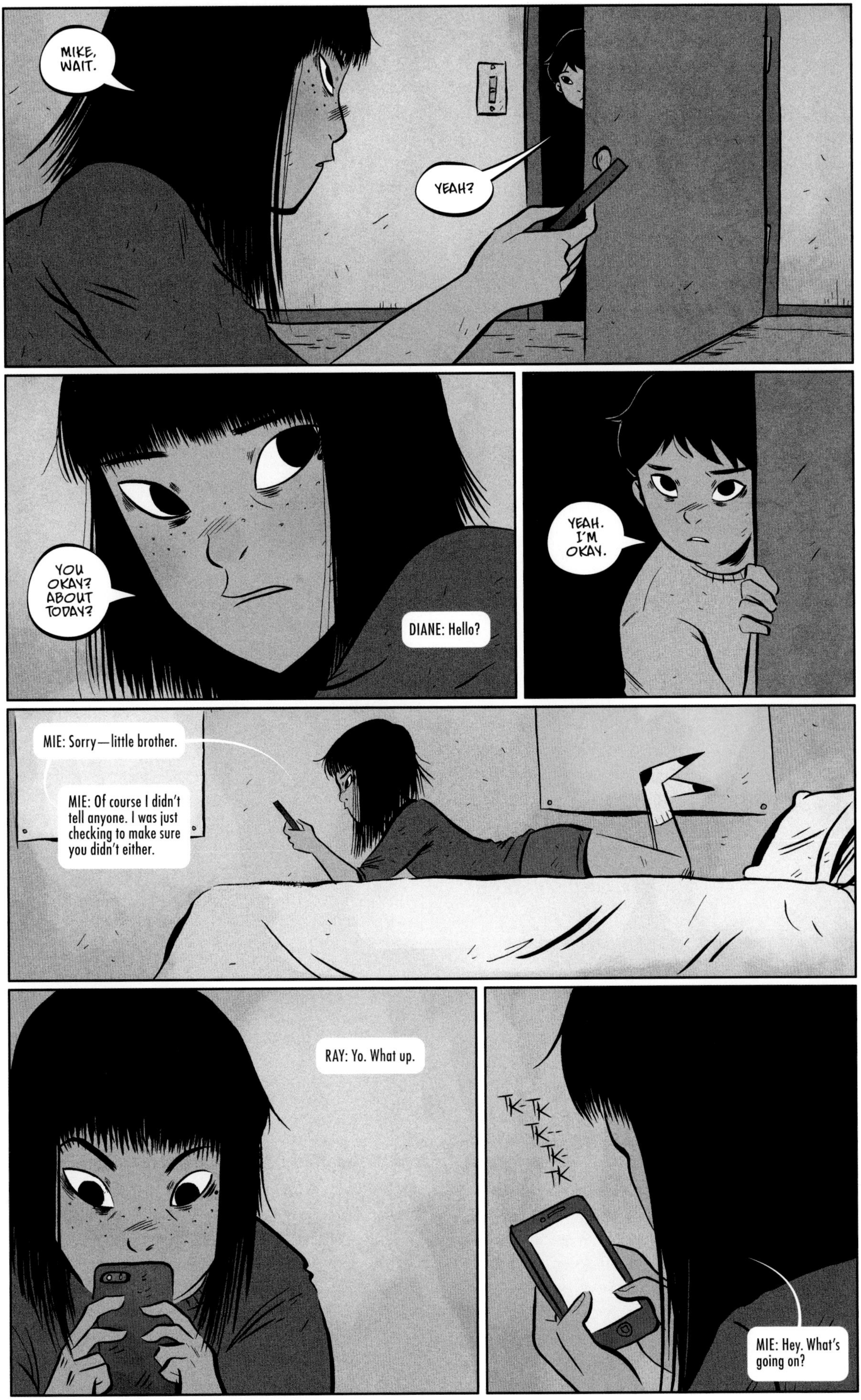
MIKE, WAIT.
YEAH?
YOU OKAY? ABOUT TODAY?
DIANE: Hello?
YEAH. I'M OKAY.
MIE: Sorry—little brother.
MIE: Of course I didn't tell anyone. I was just checking to make sure you didn't either.
RAY: Yo. What up.
TK-TK TK-- TK- TK
MIE: Hey. What's going on?

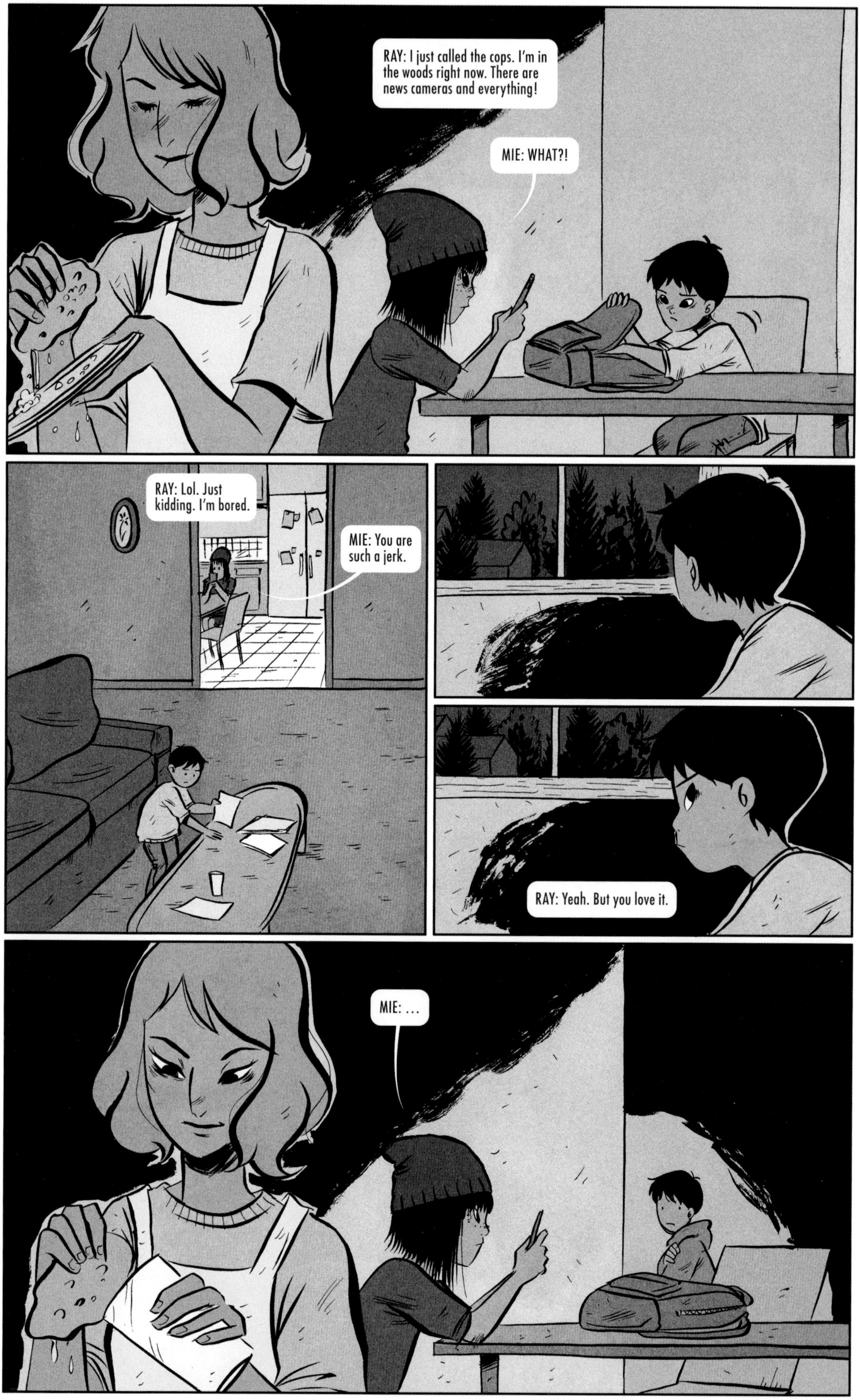
RAY: I just called the cops. I'm in the woods right now. There are news cameras and everything!
MIE: WHAT?!
RAY: Lol. Just kidding. I'm bored.
MIE: You are such a jerk.
RAY: Yeah. But you love it.
MIE: ...

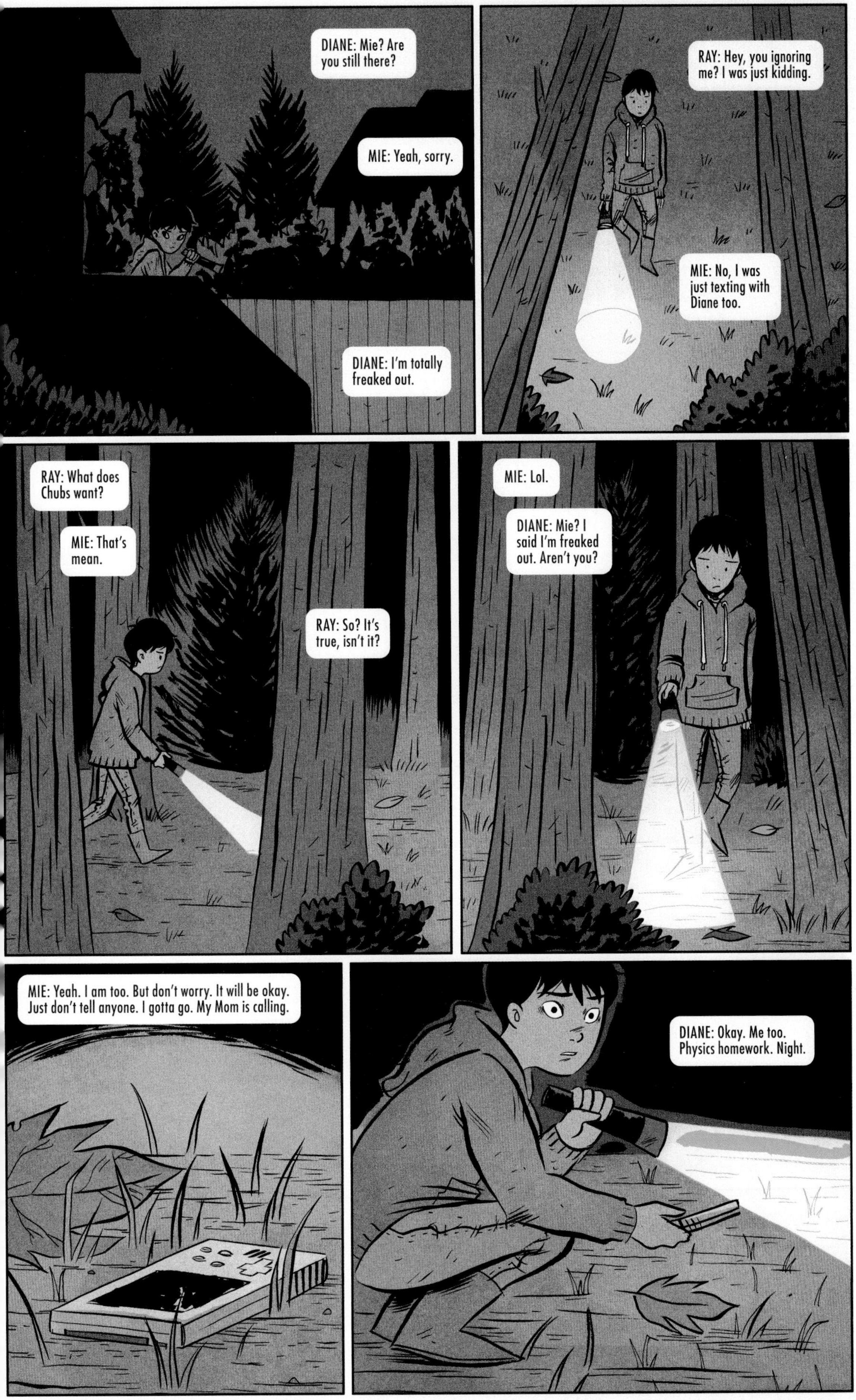
DIANE: Mie? Are you still there?
MIE: Yeah, sorry.
DIANE: I'm totally freaked out.
RAY: Hey, you ignoring me? I was just kidding.
MIE: No, I was just texting with Diane too.
RAY: What does Chubs want?
MIE: That's mean.
RAY: So? It's true, isn't it?
MIE: Lol.
DIANE: Mie? I said I'm freaked out. Aren't you?
MIE: Yeah. I am too. But don't worry. It will be okay. Just don't tell anyone. I gotta go. My Mom is calling.
DIANE: Okay. Me too. Physics homework. Night.

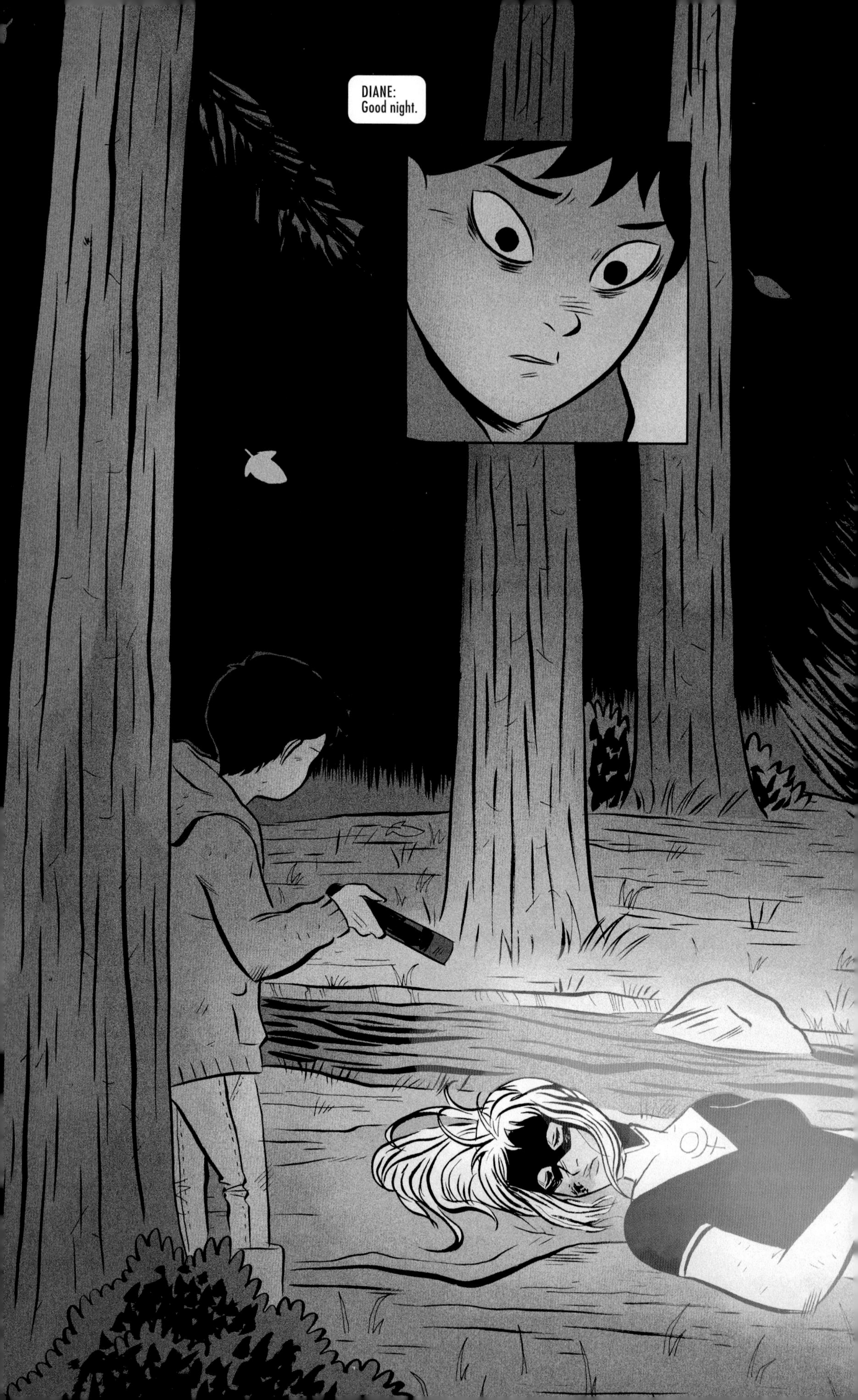
DIANE:
Good night.

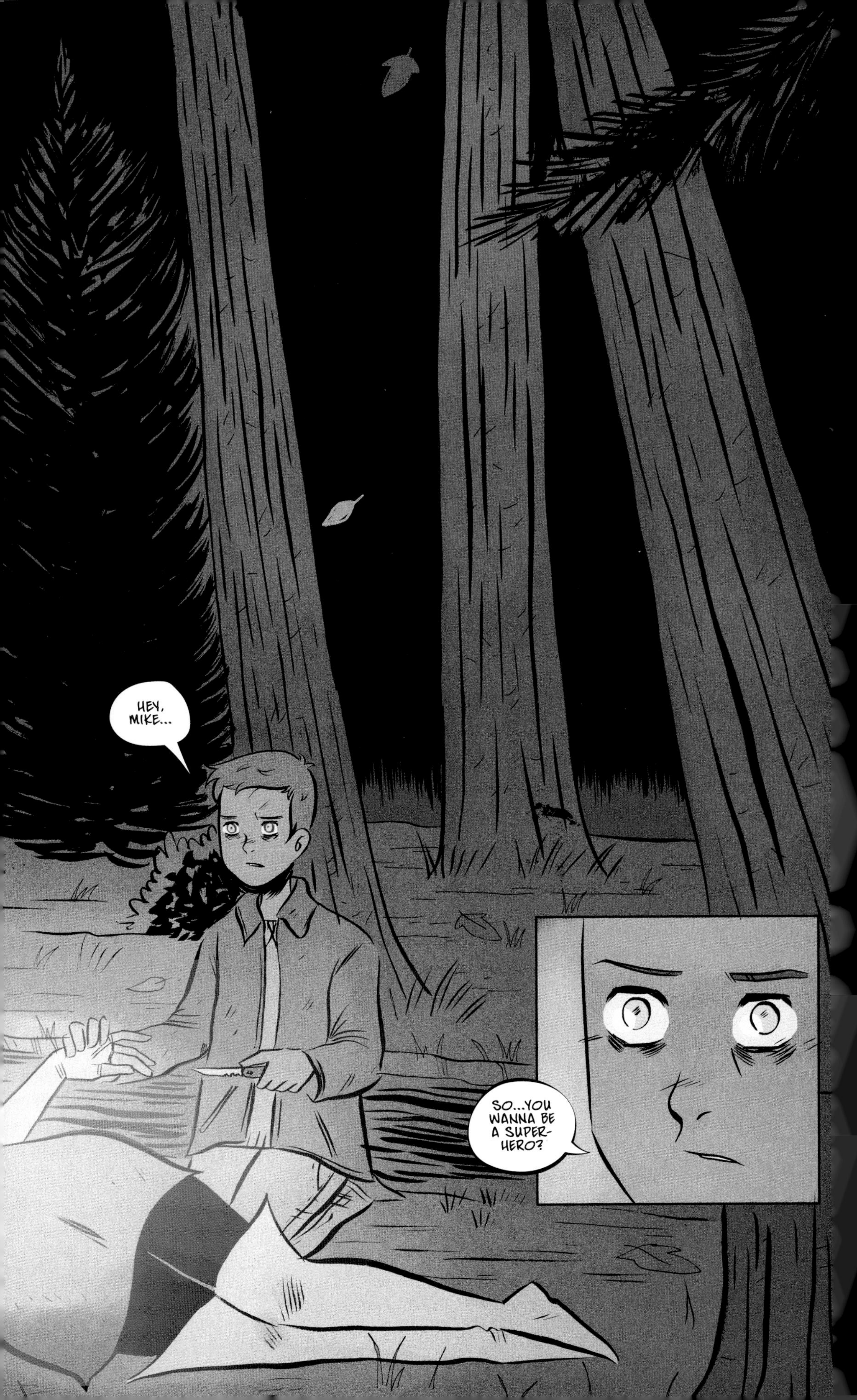
HEY, MIKE...
SO...YOU WANNA BE A SUPER-HERO?

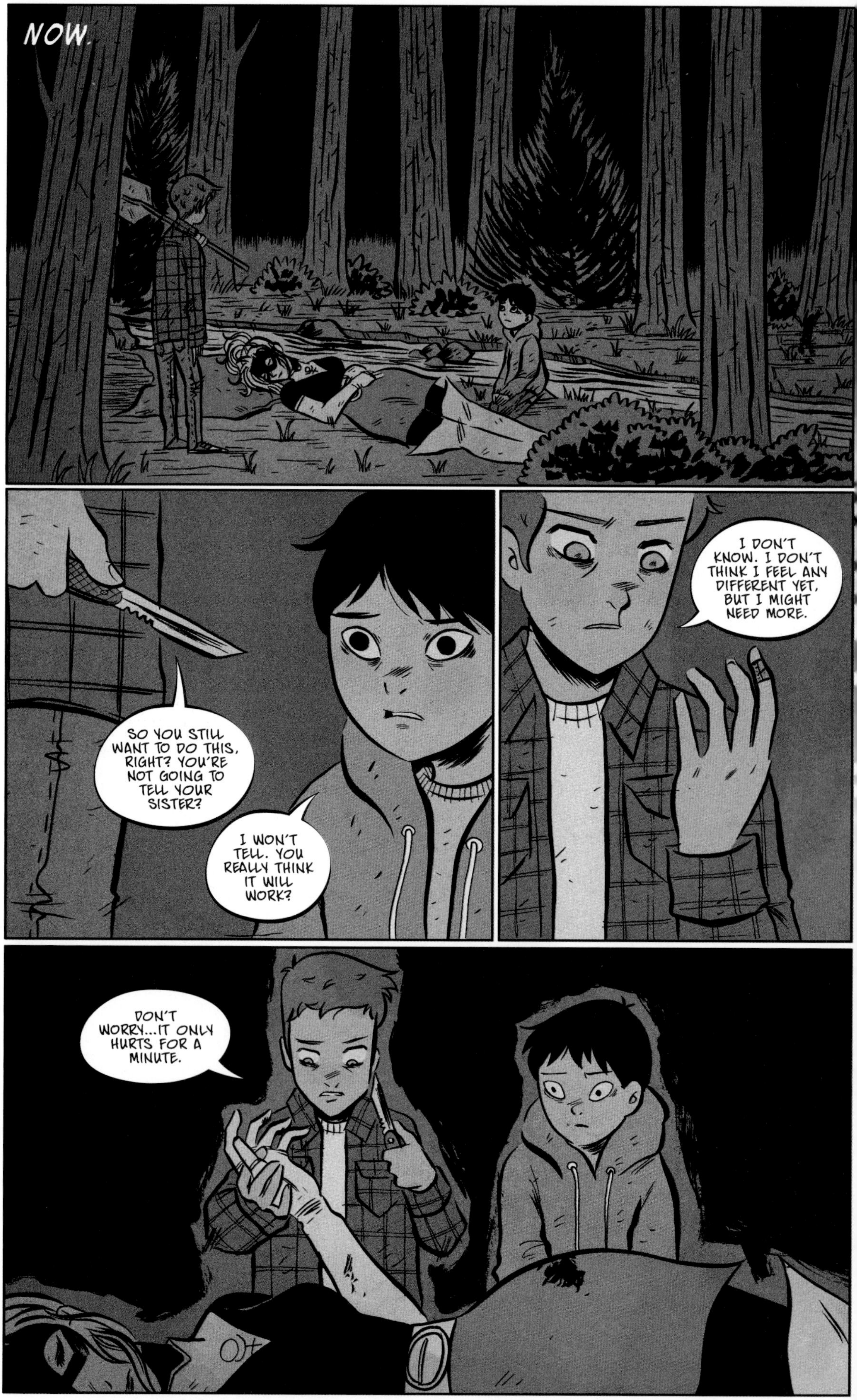
NOW.
SO YOU STILL WANT TO DO THIS, RIGHT? YOU'RE NOT GOING TO TELL YOUR SISTER?
I WON'T TELL. YOU REALLY THINK IT WILL WORK?
I DON'T KNOW. I DON'T THINK I FEEL ANY DIFFERENT YET, BUT I MIGHT NEED MORE.
DON'T WORRY...IT ONLY HURTS FOR A MINUTE.

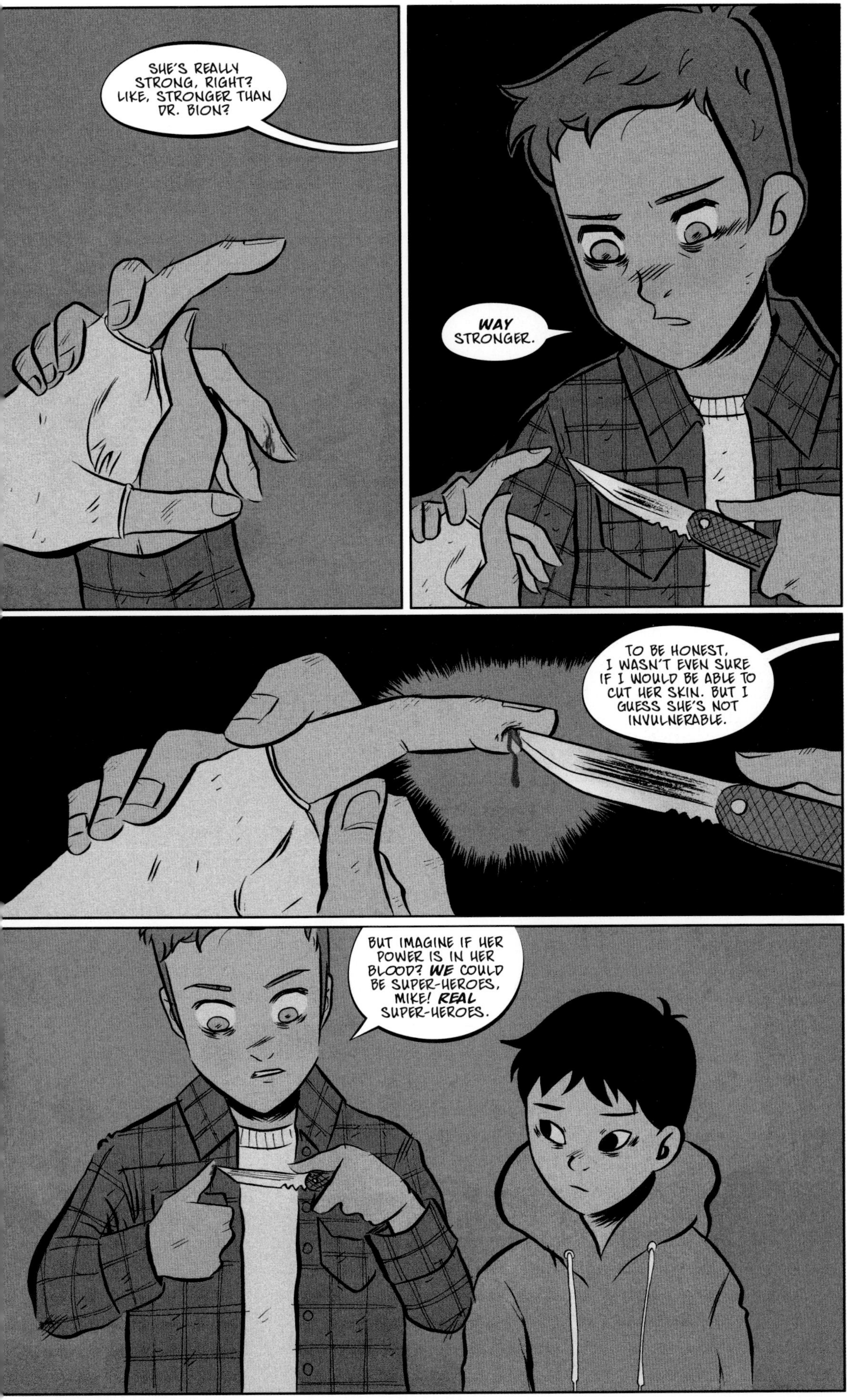

SHE'S REALLY STRONG, RIGHT? LIKE, STRONGER THAN DR. BION?
WAY STRONGER.
TO BE HONEST, I WASN'T EVEN SURE IF I WOULD BE ABLE TO CUT HER SKIN. BUT I GUESS SHE'S NOT INVULNERABLE.
BUT IMAGINE IF HER POWER IS IN HER BLOOD? WE COULD BE SUPER-HEROES, MIKE! REAL SUPER-HEROES.

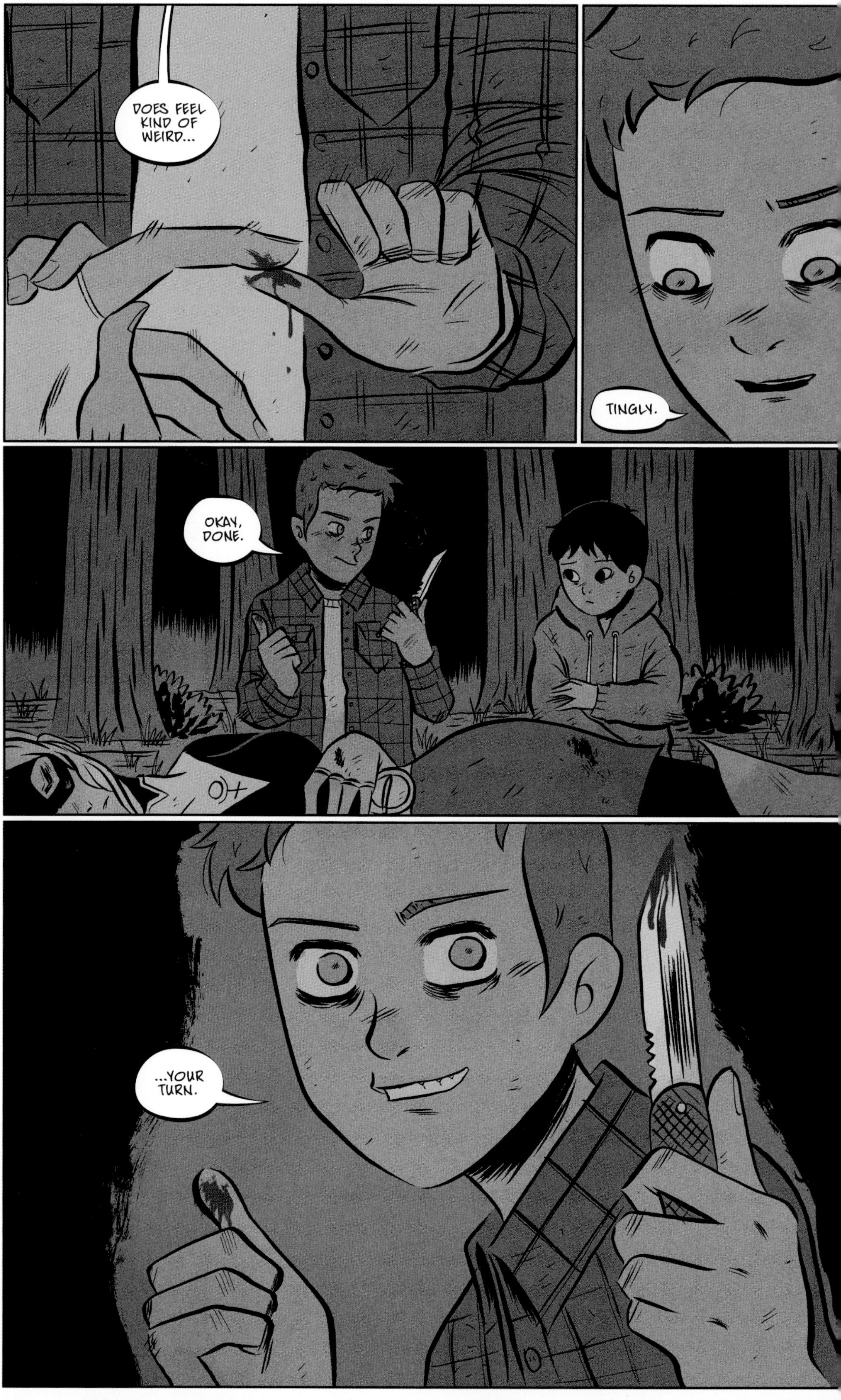
DOES FEEL KIND OF WEIRD...
TINGLY.
OKAY, DONE.
...YOUR TURN.

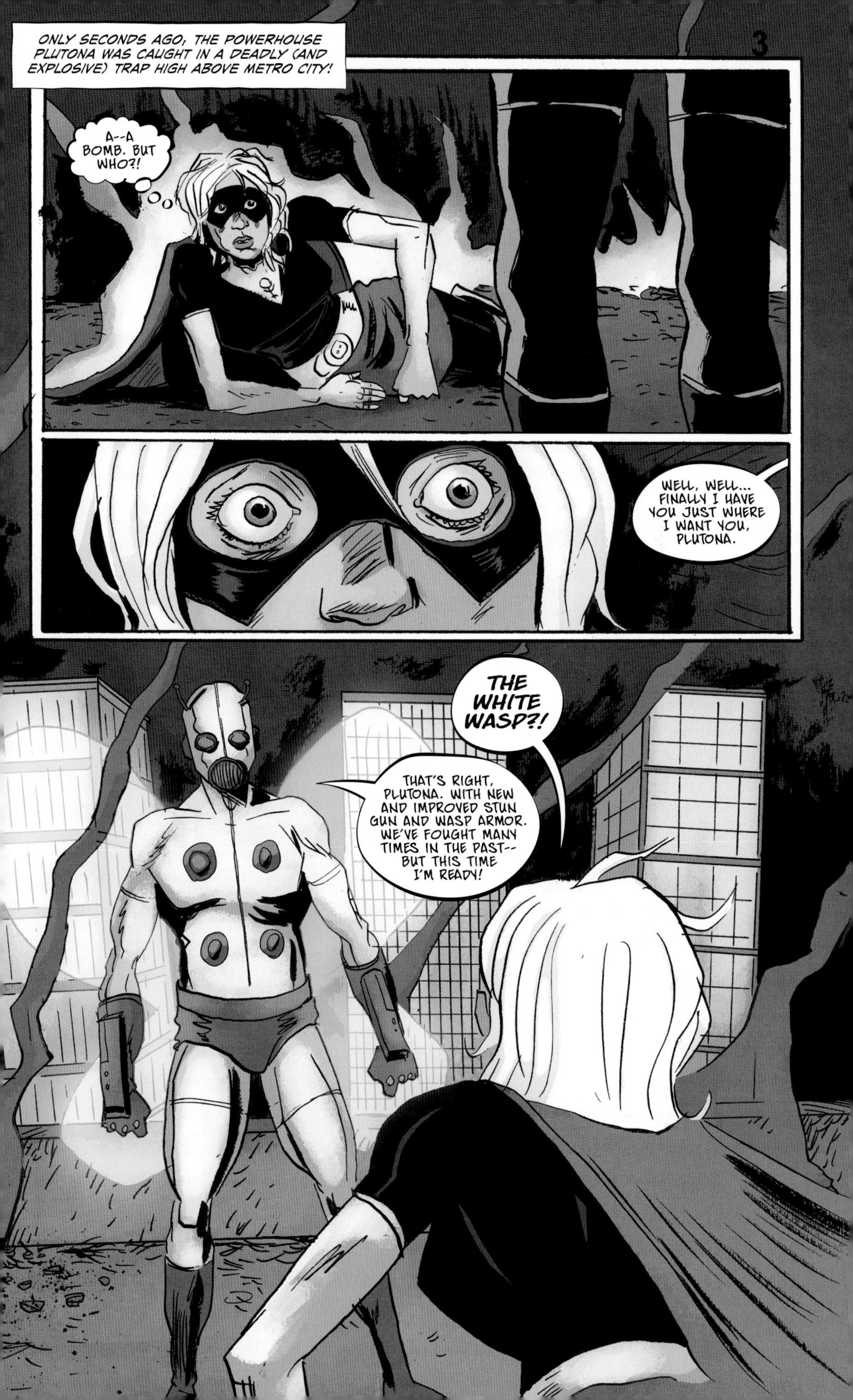
3
ONLY SECONDS AGO, THE POWERHOUSE PLUTONA WAS CAUGHT IN A DEADLY (AND EXPLOSIVE) TRAP HIGH ABOVE METRO CITY!
A--A BOMB. BUT WHO?!
WELL, WELL... FINALLY I HAVE YOU JUST WHERE I WANT YOU, PLUTONA.
THAT'S RIGHT, PLUTONA. WITH NEW AND IMPROVED STUN GUN AND WASP ARMOR. WE'VE FOUGHT MANY TIMES IN THE PAST-- BUT THIS TIME I'M READY!
THE WHITE WASP?!

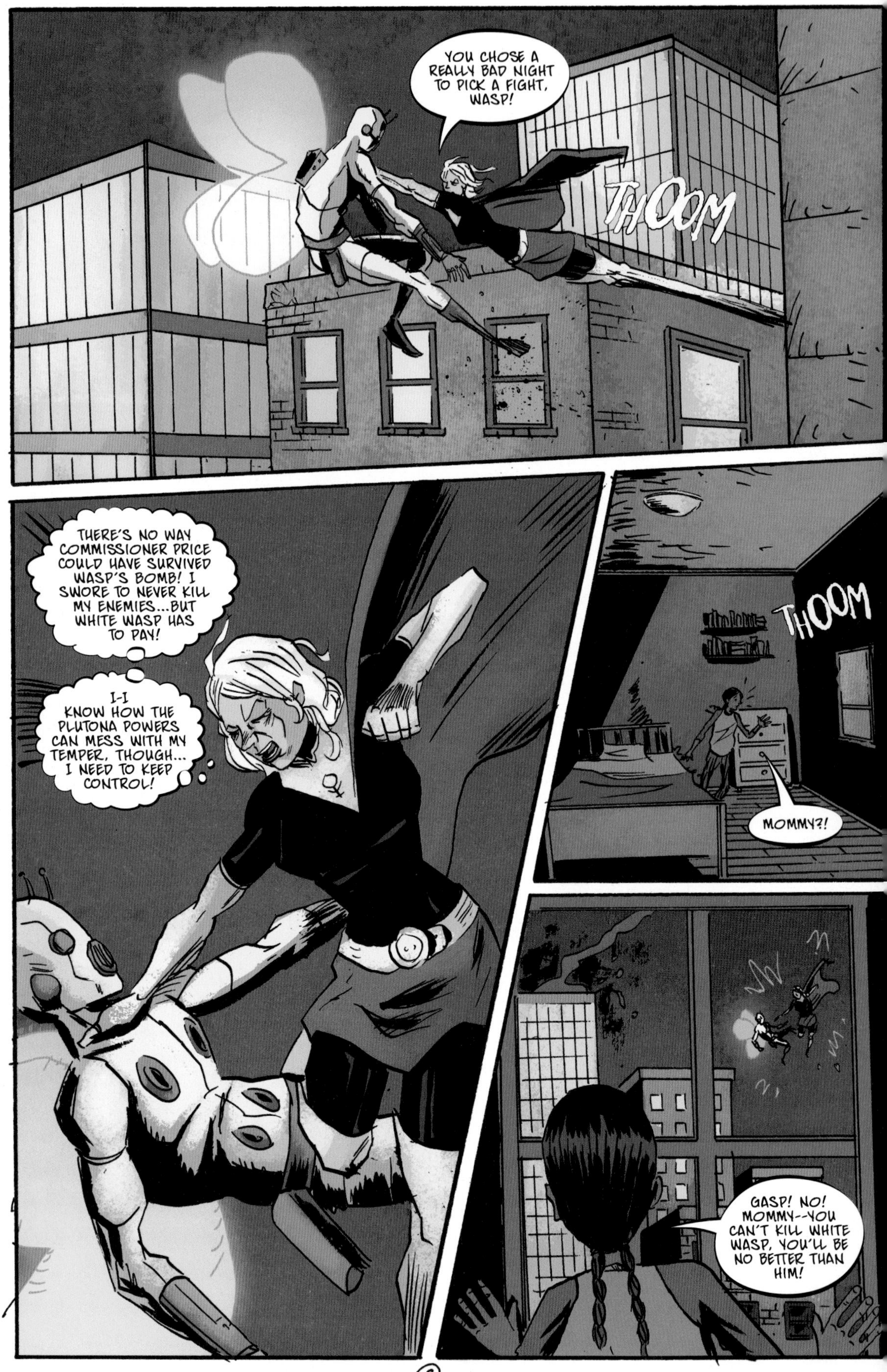
YOU CHOSE A REALLY BAD NIGHT TO PICK A FIGHT, WASP!
THOOM
THERE'S NO WAY COMMISSIONER PRICE COULD HAVE SURVIVED WASP'S BOMB! I SWORE TO NEVER KILL MY ENEMIES...BUT WHITE WASP HAS TO PAY!
I-I KNOW HOW THE PLUTONA POWERS CAN MESS WITH MY TEMPER, THOUGH... I NEED TO KEEP CONTROL!
THOOM
MOMMY?!
GASP! NO! MOMMY--YOU CAN'T KILL WHITE WASP, YOU'LL BE NO BETTER THAN HIM!

CHAPTER

4

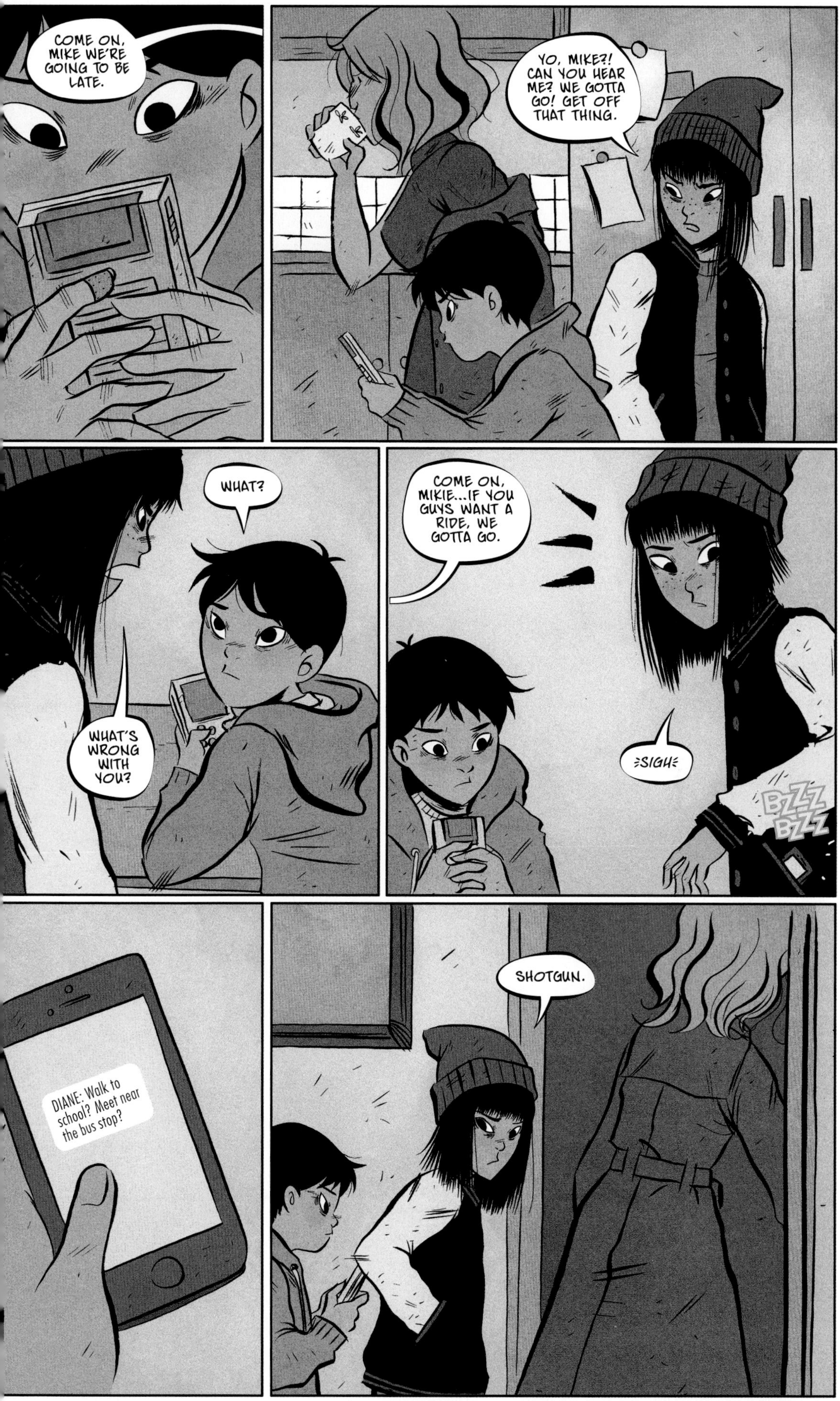
COME ON, MIKE WE'RE GOING TO BE LATE.
YO, MIKE?! CAN YOU HEAR ME? WE GOTTA GO! GET OFF THAT THING.
WHAT?
WHAT'S WRONG WITH YOU?
COME ON, MIKIE...IF YOU GUYS WANT A RIDE, WE GOTTA GO.
SIGH
BZZZ BZZZ
DIANE: Walk to school? Meet near the bus stop?
SHOTGUN.

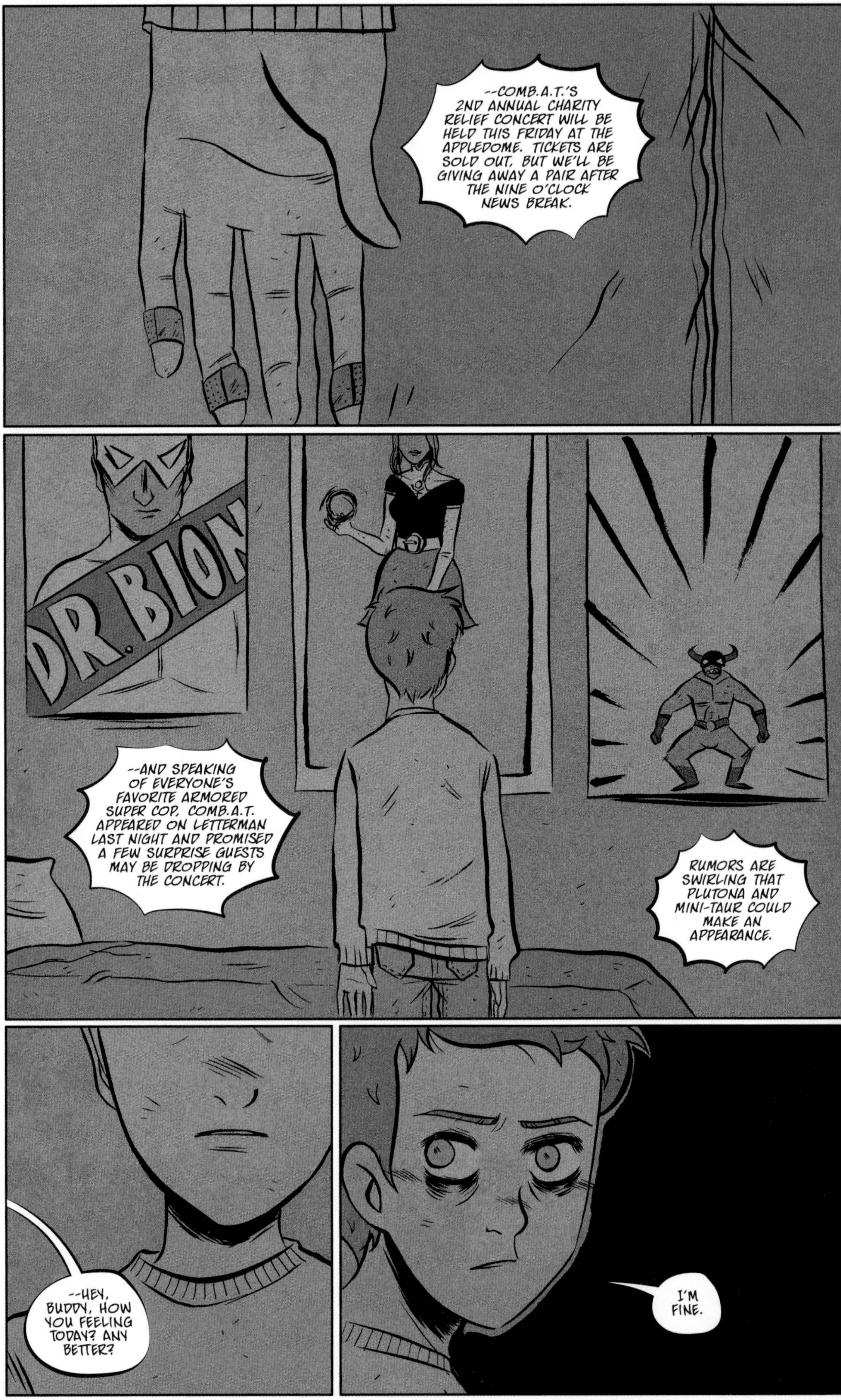
--COMB.A.T.'S 2ND ANNUAL CHARITY RELIEF CONCERT WILL BE HELD THIS FRIDAY AT THE APPLEDOME. TICKETS ARE SOLD OUT, BUT WE'LL BE GIVING AWAY A PAIR AFTER THE NINE O'CLOCK NEWS BREAK.
DR. BION
--AND SPEAKING OF EVERYONE'S FAVORITE ARMORED SUPER COP, COMB.A.T. APPEARED ON LETTERMAN LAST NIGHT AND PROMISED A FEW SURPRISE GUESTS MAY BE DROPPING BY THE CONCERT.
RUMORS ARE SWIRLING THAT PLUTONA AND MINI-TAUR COULD MAKE AN APPEARANCE.
--HEY, BUDDY, HOW YOU FEELING TODAY? ANY BETTER?
I'M FINE.

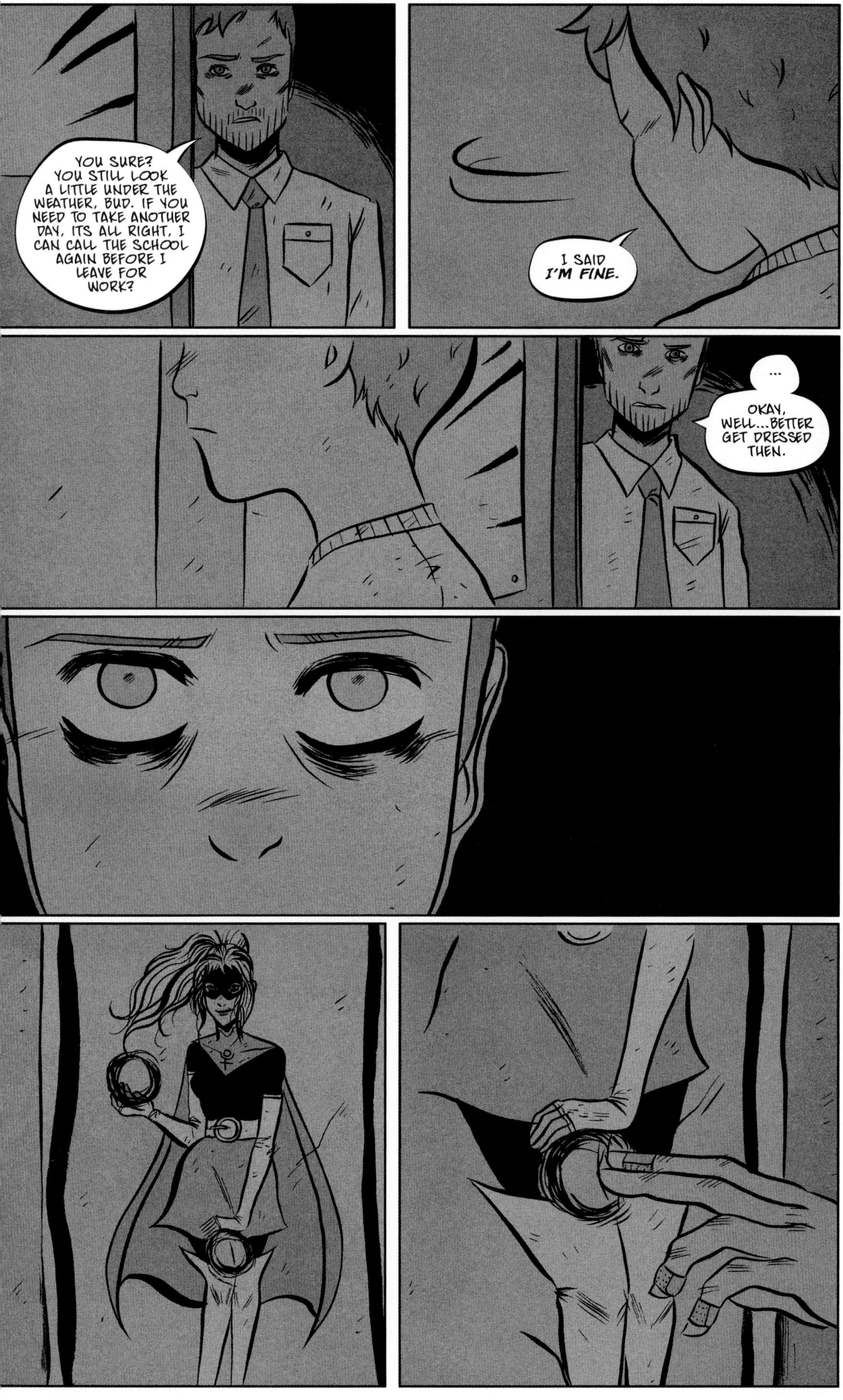
YOU SURE? YOU STILL LOOK A LITTLE UNDER THE WEATHER, BUD. IF YOU NEED TO TAKE ANOTHER DAY, ITS ALL RIGHT, I CAN CALL THE SCHOOL AGAIN BEFORE I LEAVE FOR WORK?
I SAID *I'M FINE.*
...
OKAY, WELL...BETTER GET DRESSED THEN.

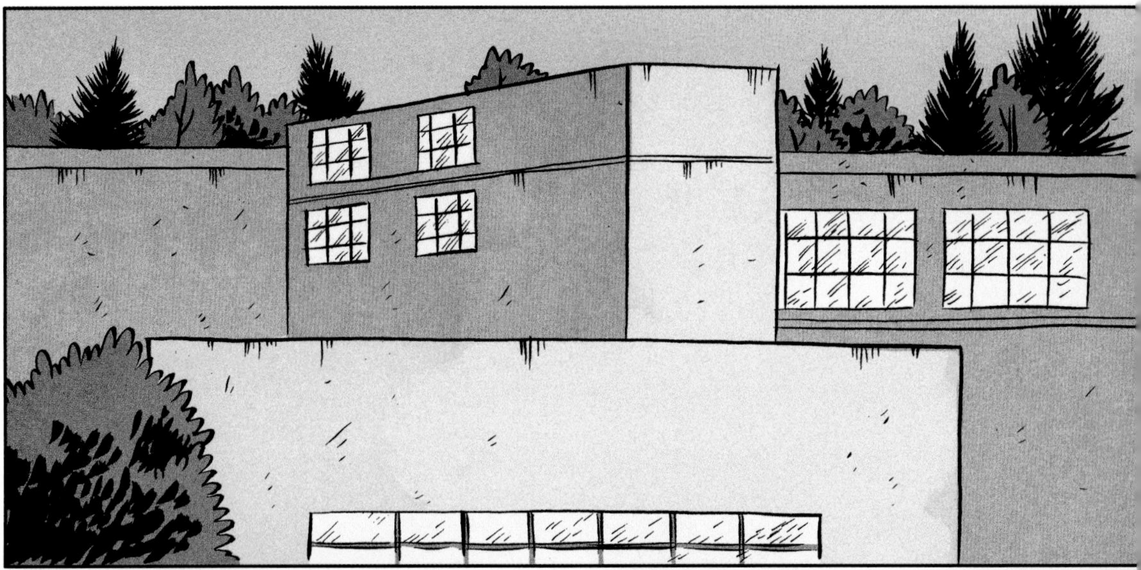
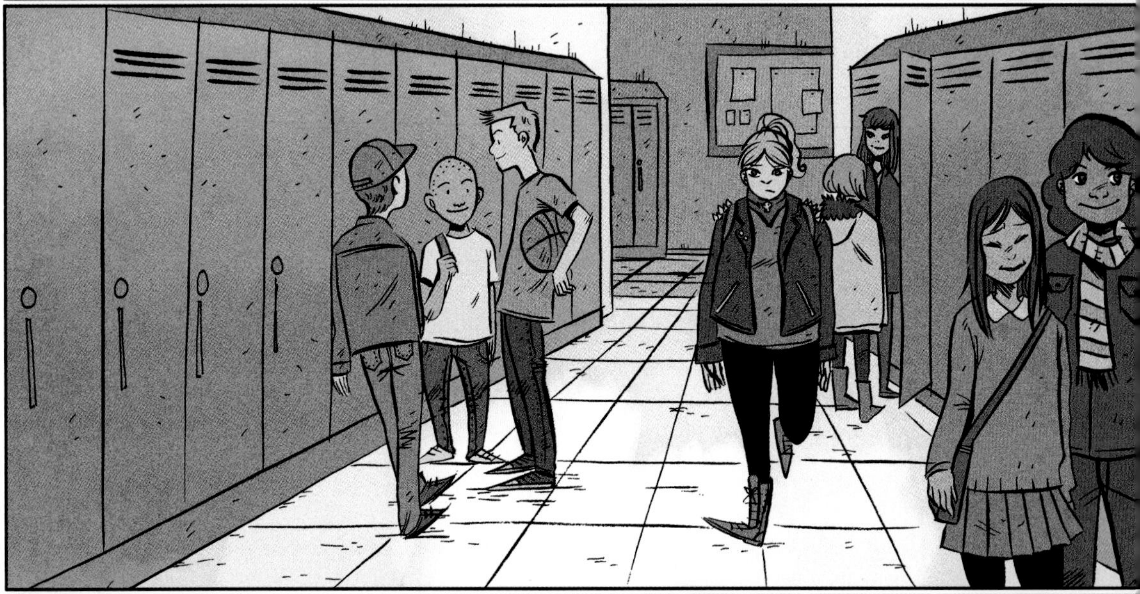
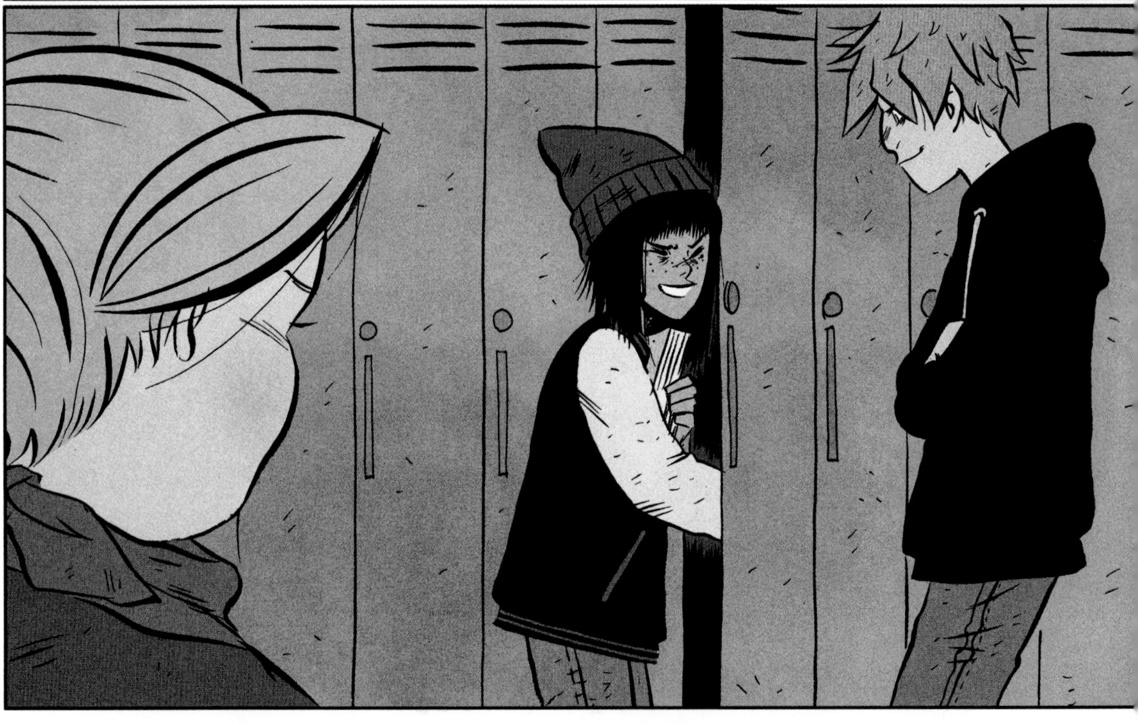

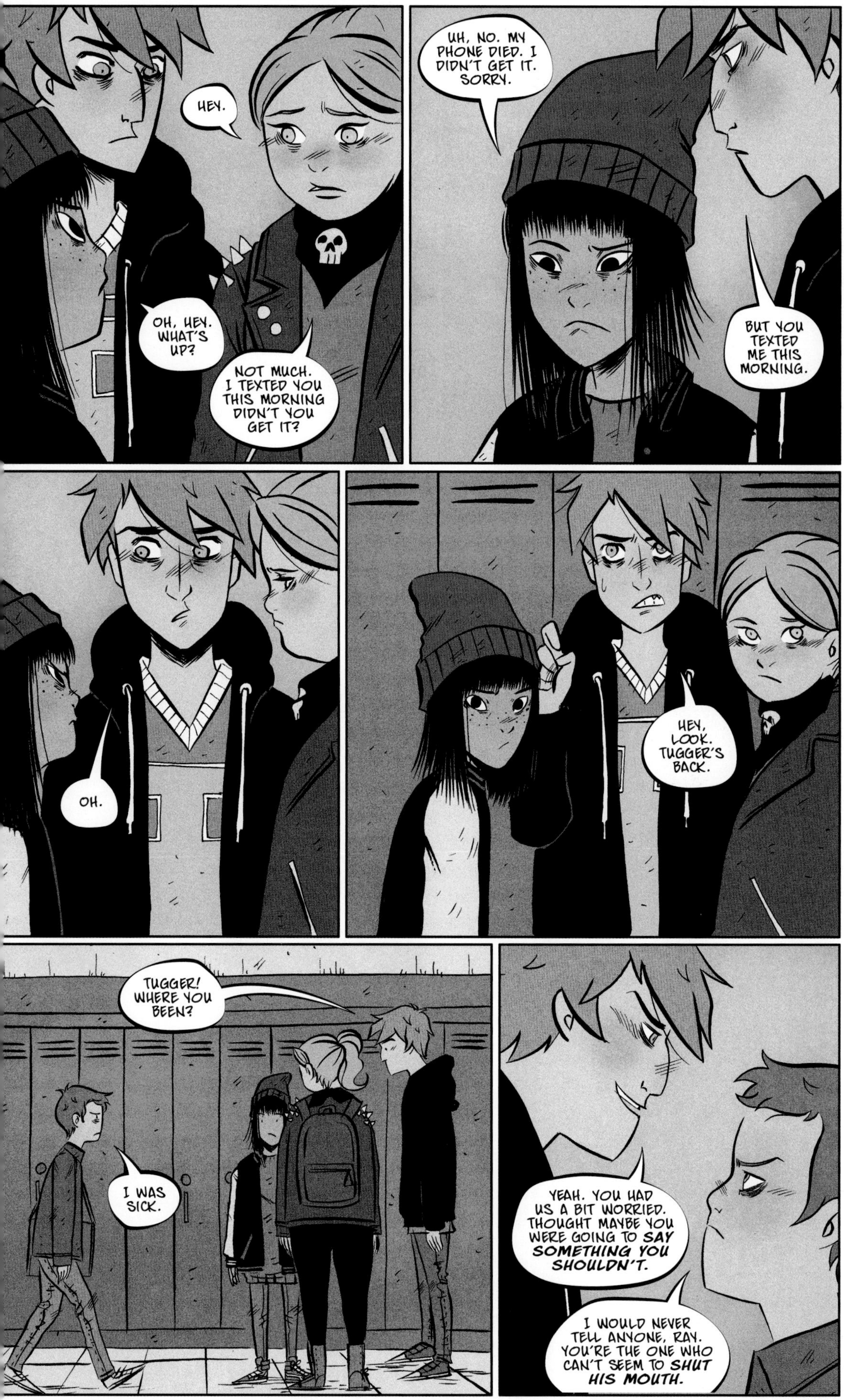
HEY.
OH, HEY. WHAT'S UP?
NOT MUCH. I TEXTED YOU THIS MORNING DIDN'T YOU GET IT?
UH, NO. MY PHONE DIED. I DIDN'T GET IT. SORRY.
BUT YOU TEXTED ME THIS MORNING.
OH.
HEY, LOOK. TUGGER'S BACK.
TUGGER! WHERE YOU BEEN?
I WAS SICK.
YEAH. YOU HAD US A BIT WORRIED. THOUGHT MAYBE YOU WERE GOING TO SAY SOMETHING YOU SHOULDN'T.
I WOULD NEVER TELL ANYONE, RAY. YOU'RE THE ONE WHO CAN'T SEEM TO SHUT HIS MOUTH.

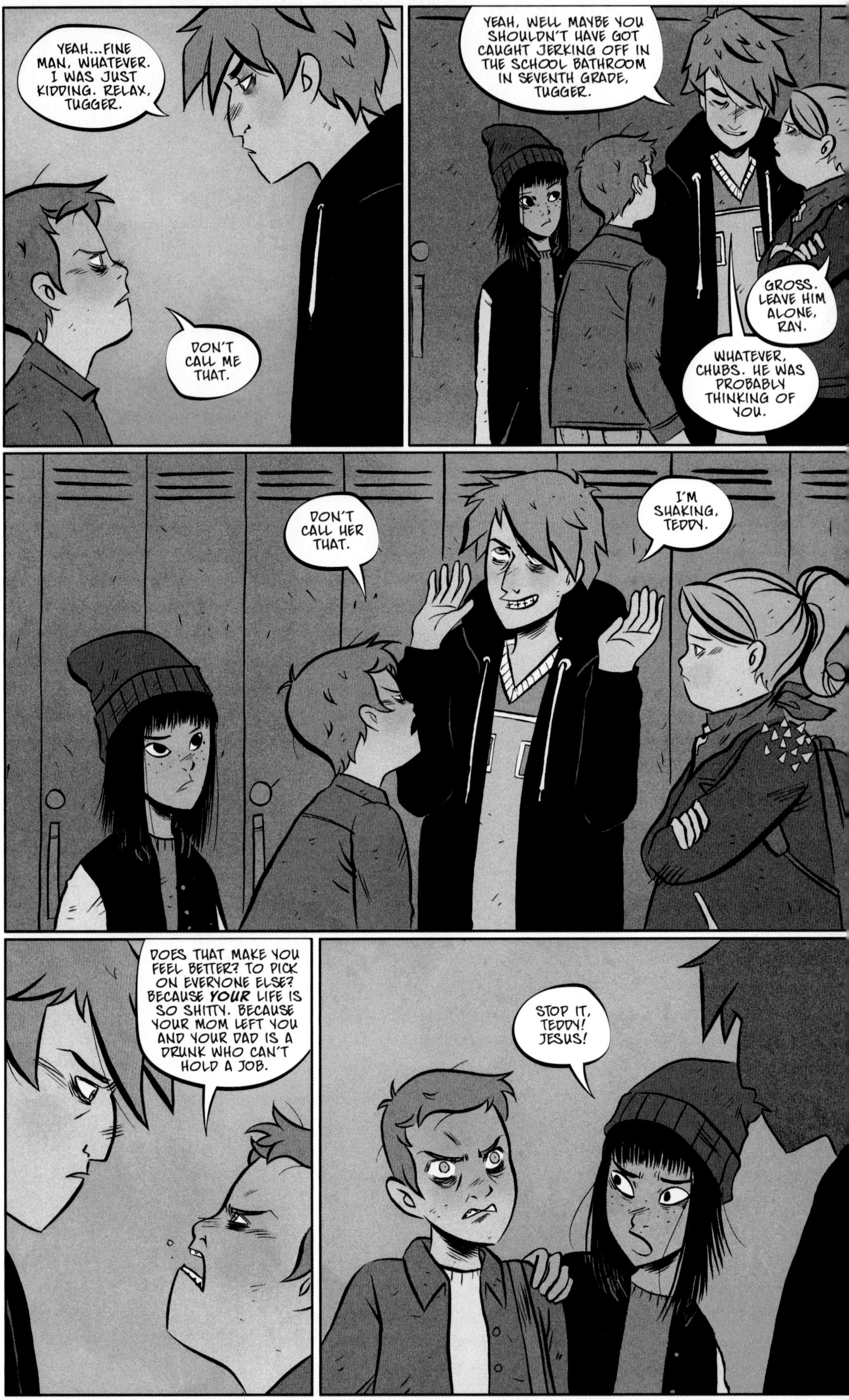
YEAH...FINE MAN, WHATEVER. I WAS JUST KIDDING. RELAX, TUGGER.
DON'T CALL ME THAT.
YEAH, WELL MAYBE YOU SHOULDN'T HAVE GOT CAUGHT JERKING OFF IN THE SCHOOL BATHROOM IN SEVENTH GRADE, TUGGER.
GROSS. LEAVE HIM ALONE, RAY.
WHATEVER, CHUBS. HE WAS PROBABLY THINKING OF YOU.
DON'T CALL HER THAT.
I'M SHAKING, TEDDY.
DOES THAT MAKE YOU FEEL BETTER? TO PICK ON EVERYONE ELSE? BECAUSE *YOUR* LIFE IS SO SHITTY. BECAUSE YOUR MOM LEFT YOU AND YOUR DAD IS A DRUNK WHO CAN'T HOLD A JOB.
STOP IT, TEDDY! JESUS!

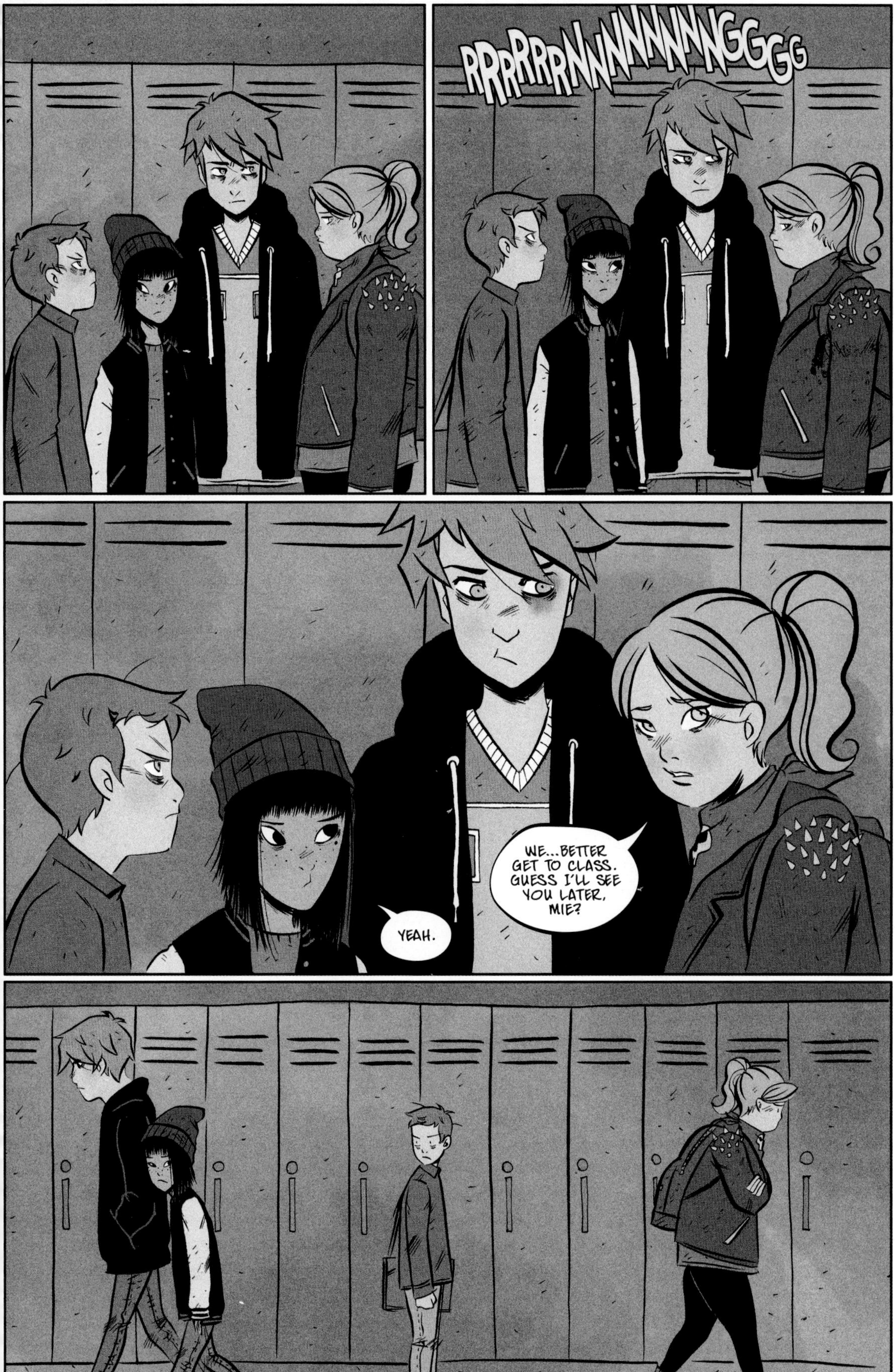
RRRRRNNNNNNNGGGG
WE...BETTER GET TO CLASS. GUESS I'LL SEE YOU LATER, MIE?
YEAH.

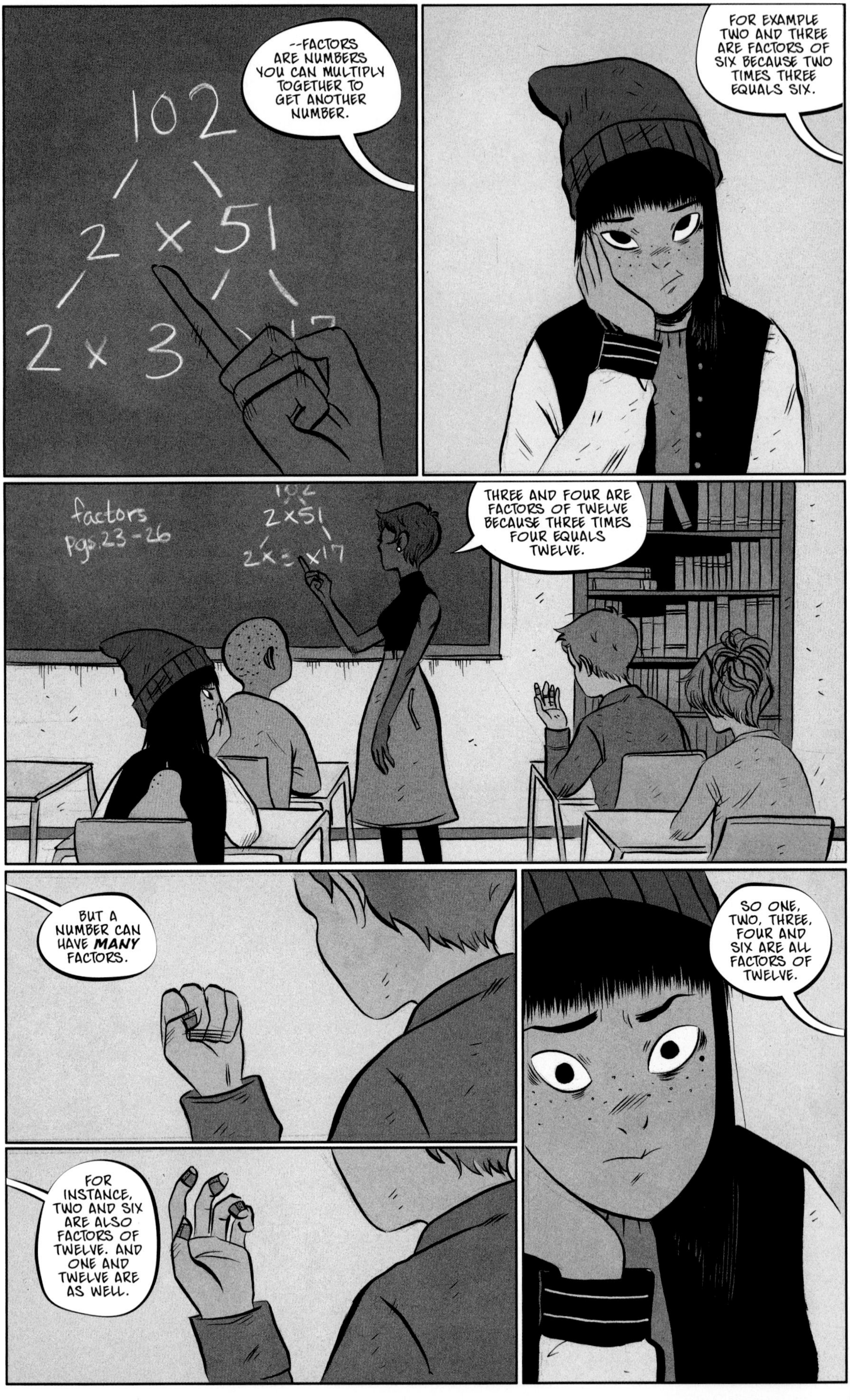
--FACTORS ARE NUMBERS YOU CAN MULTIPLY TOGETHER TO GET ANOTHER NUMBER.
102
2 x 51
2 x 3
FOR EXAMPLE TWO AND THREE ARE FACTORS OF SIX BECAUSE TWO TIMES THREE EQUALS SIX.
factors
pgs. 23 - 26
2x51
THREE AND FOUR ARE FACTORS OF TWELVE BECAUSE THREE TIMES FOUR EQUALS TWELVE.
BUT A NUMBER CAN HAVE **MANY** FACTORS.
FOR INSTANCE, TWO AND SIX ARE ALSO FACTORS OF TWELVE. AND ONE AND TWELVE ARE AS WELL.
SO ONE, TWO, THREE, FOUR AND SIX ARE ALL FACTORS OF TWELVE.

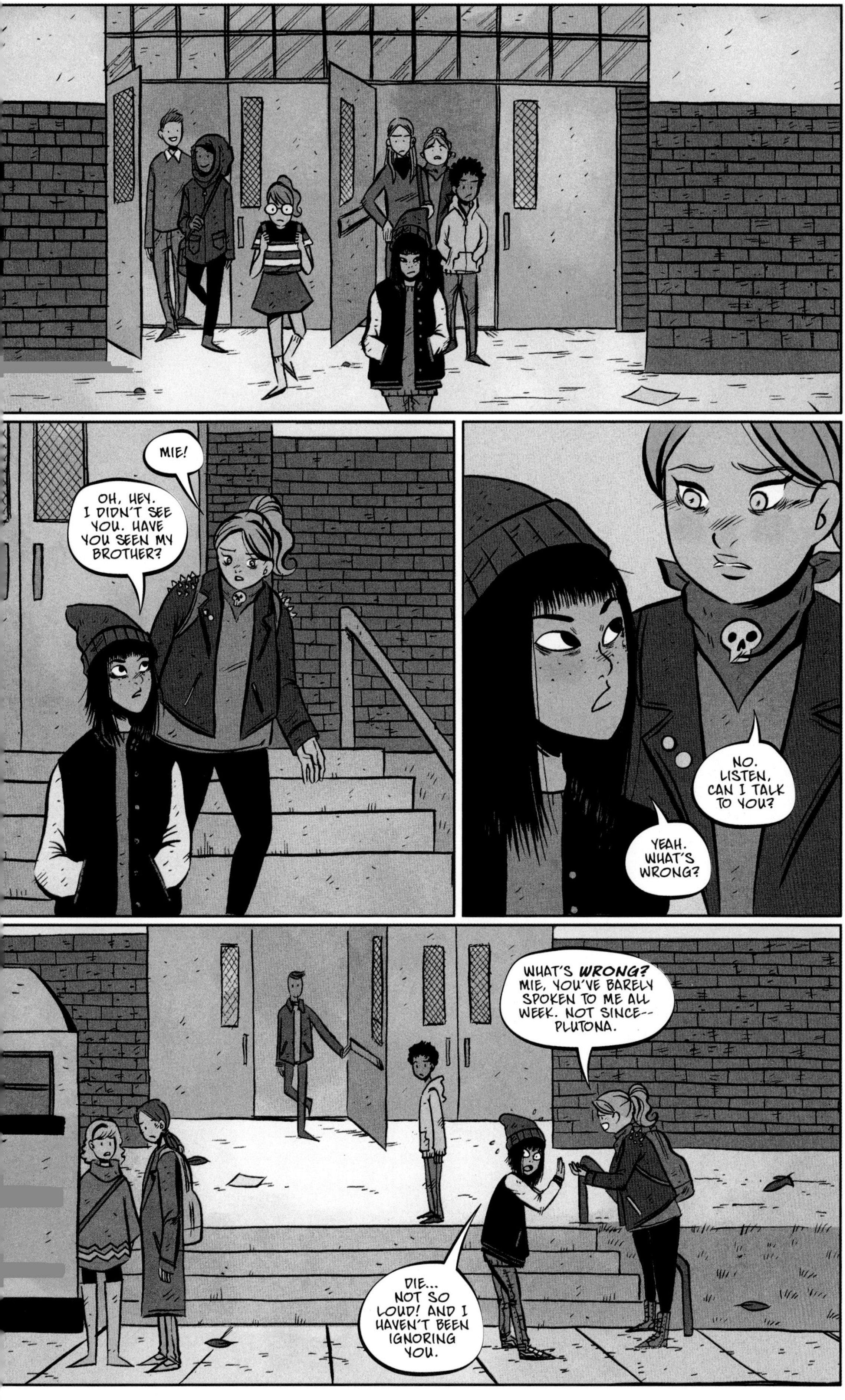
MIE!
OH, HEY. I DIDN'T SEE YOU. HAVE YOU SEEN MY BROTHER?
NO. LISTEN, CAN I TALK TO YOU?
YEAH. WHAT'S WRONG?
WHAT'S ***WRONG?*** MIE, YOU'VE BARELY SPOKEN TO ME ALL WEEK. NOT SINCE-- PLUTONA.
DIE... NOT SO LOUD! AND I HAVEN'T BEEN IGNORING YOU.

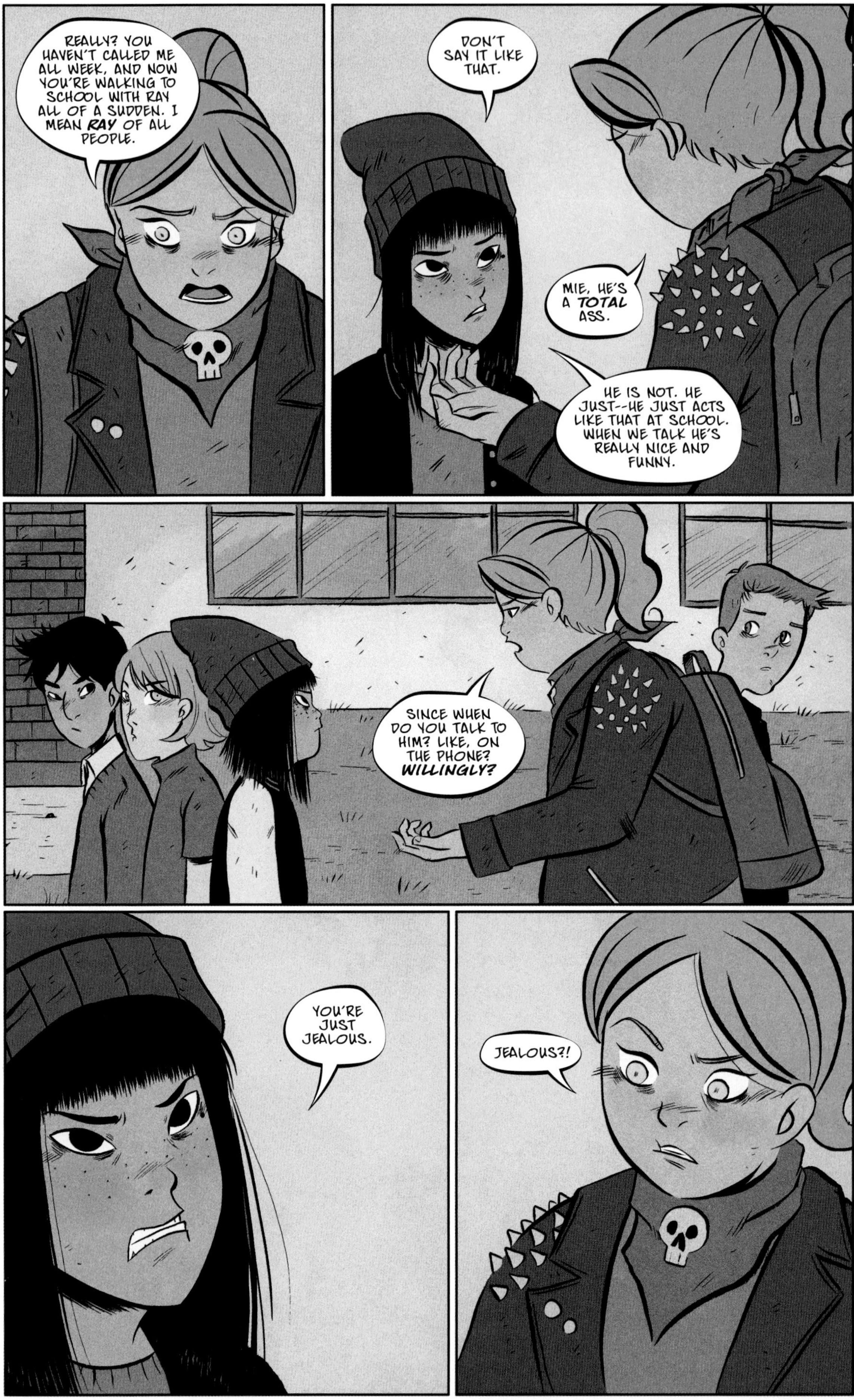
REALLY? YOU HAVEN'T CALLED ME ALL WEEK, AND NOW YOU'RE WALKING TO SCHOOL WITH RAY ALL OF A SUDDEN. I MEAN *RAY* OF ALL PEOPLE.
DON'T SAY IT LIKE THAT.
MIE, HE'S A *TOTAL* ASS.
HE IS NOT. HE JUST--HE JUST ACTS LIKE THAT AT SCHOOL. WHEN WE TALK HE'S REALLY NICE AND FUNNY.
SINCE WHEN DO YOU TALK TO HIM? LIKE, ON THE PHONE? **WILLINGLY?**
YOU'RE JUST JEALOUS.
JEALOUS?!

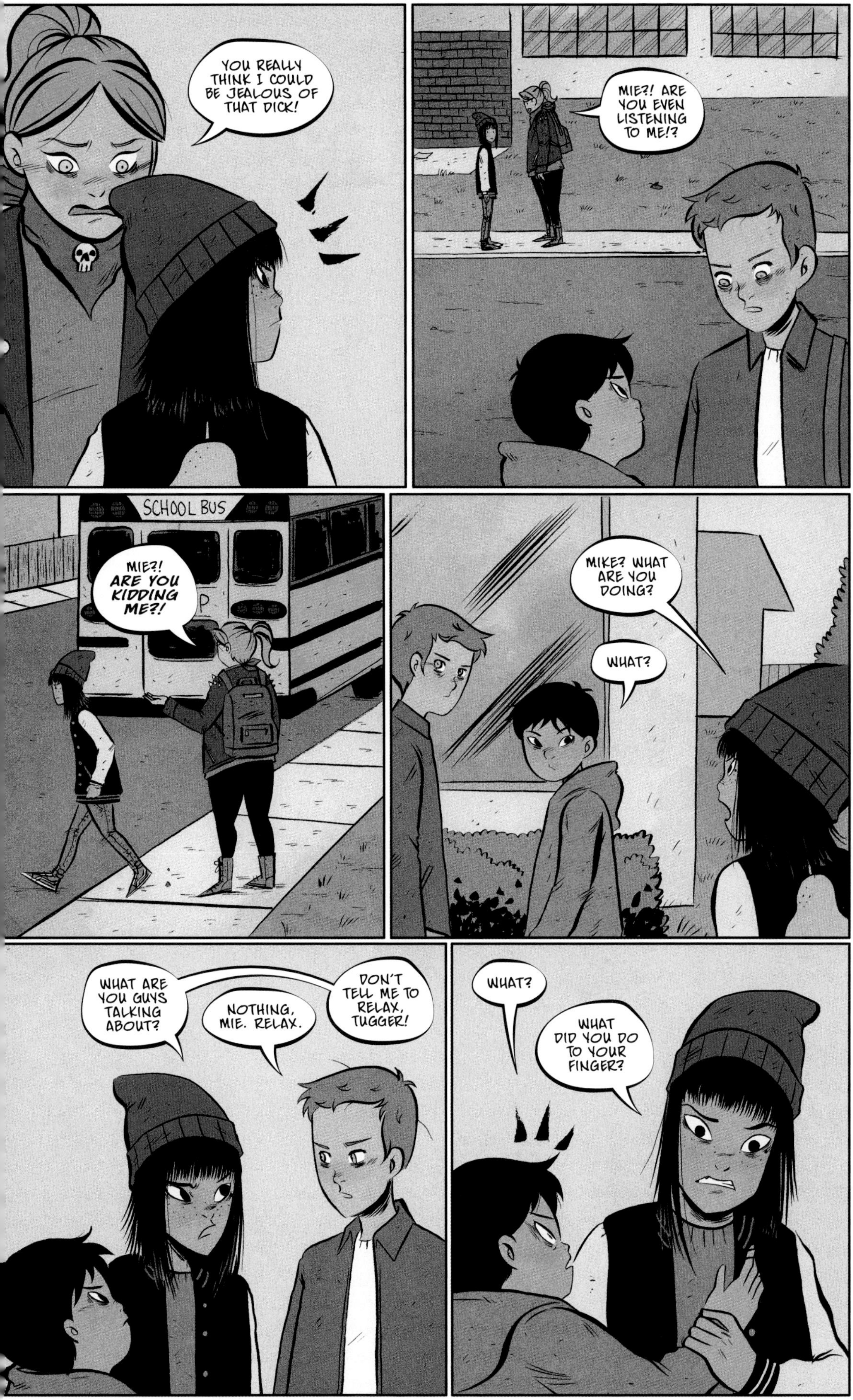
YOU REALLY THINK I COULD BE JEALOUS OF THAT DICK!
MIE?! ARE YOU EVEN LISTENING TO ME!?
SCHOOL BUS
MIE?! ARE YOU KIDDING ME?!
MIKE? WHAT ARE YOU DOING?
WHAT?
WHAT ARE YOU GUYS TALKING ABOUT?
NOTHING, MIE. RELAX.
DON'T TELL ME TO RELAX, TUGGER!
WHAT?
WHAT DID YOU DO TO YOUR FINGER?

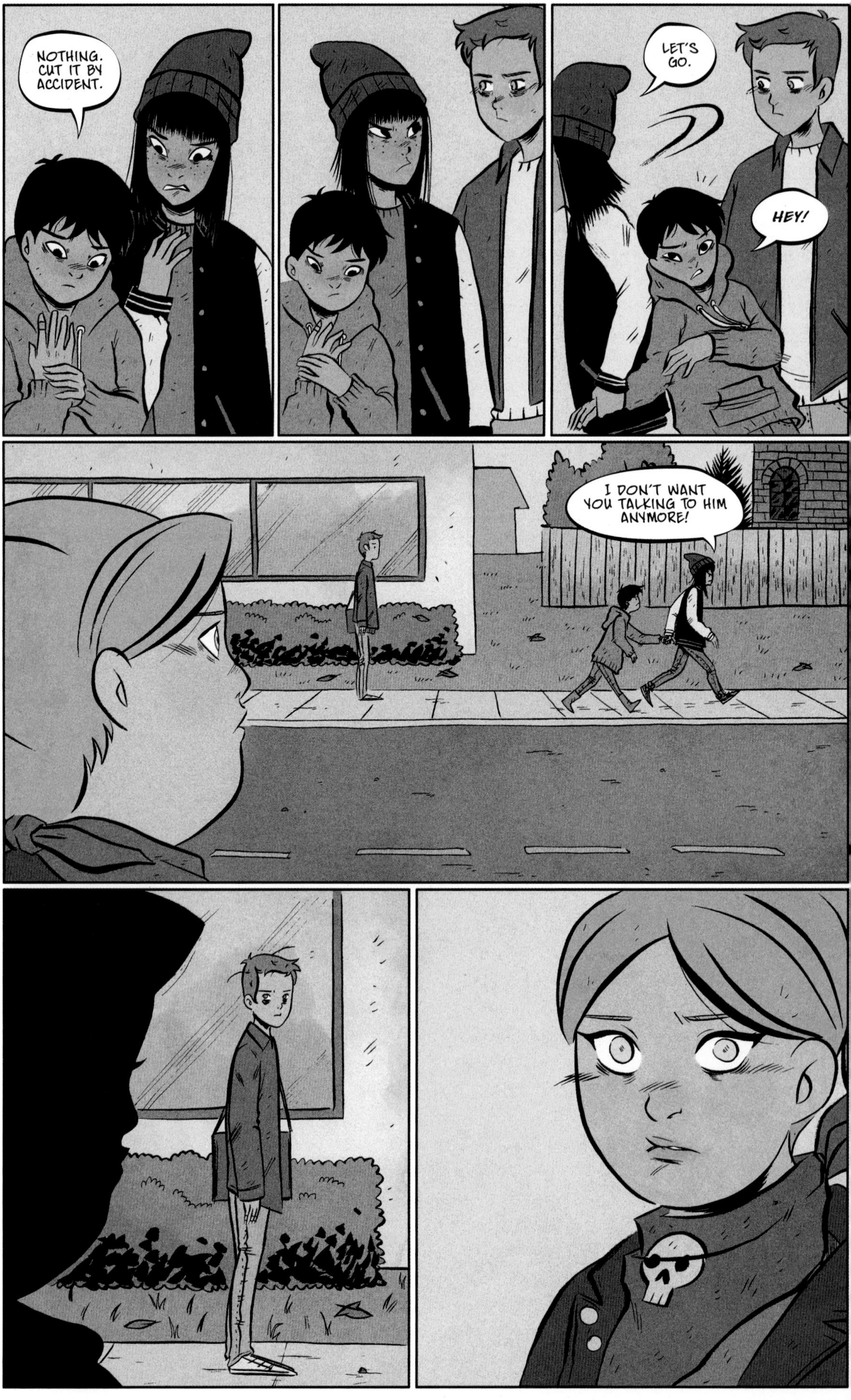
NOTHING. CUT IT BY ACCIDENT.
LET'S GO.
HEY!
I DON'T WANT YOU TALKING TO HIM ANYMORE!

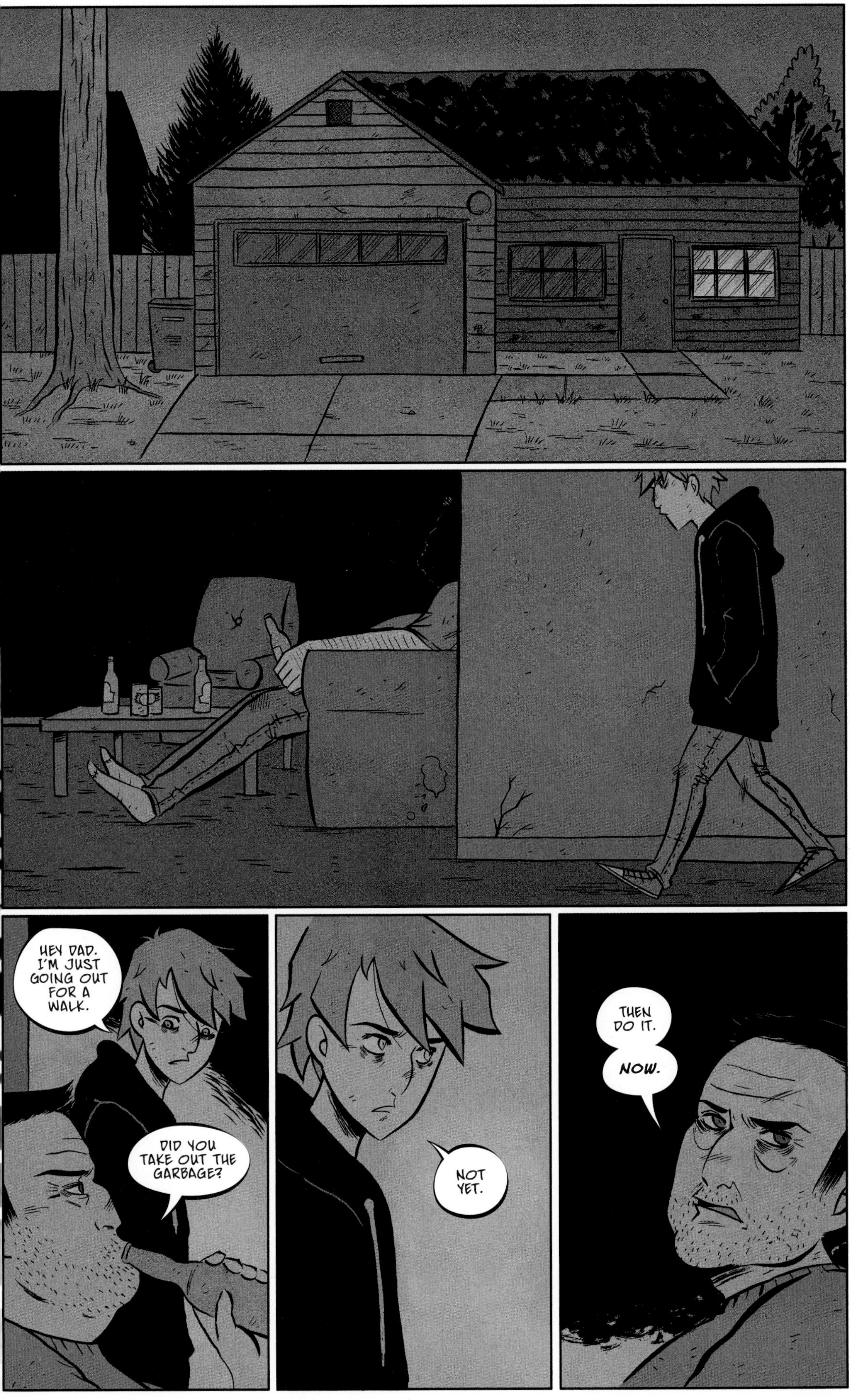
HEY DAD. I'M JUST GOING OUT FOR A WALK.
DID YOU TAKE OUT THE GARBAGE?
NOT YET.
THEN DO IT.
NOW.

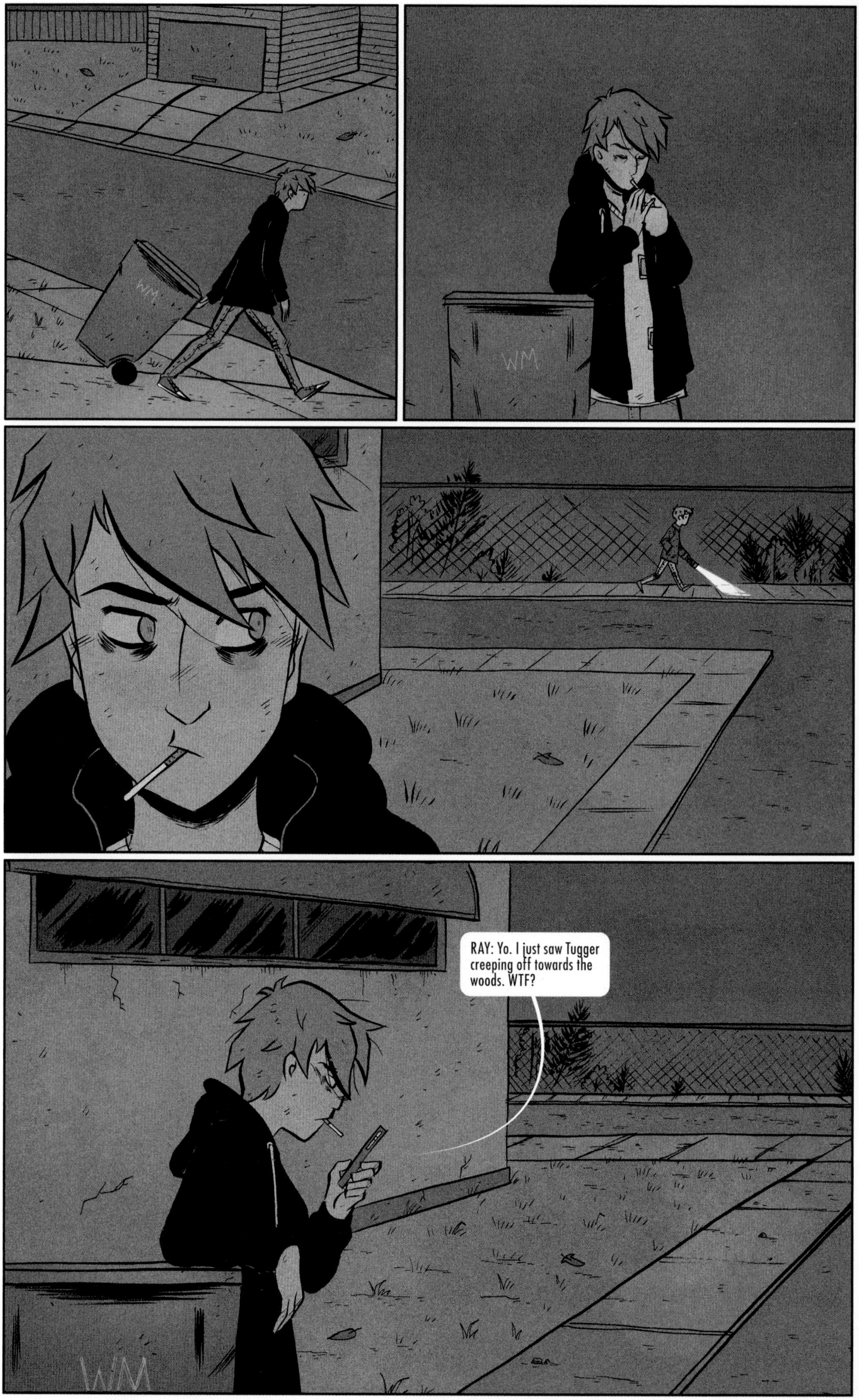
WM
WM
RAY: Yo. I just saw Tugger creeping off towards the woods. WTF?
WM

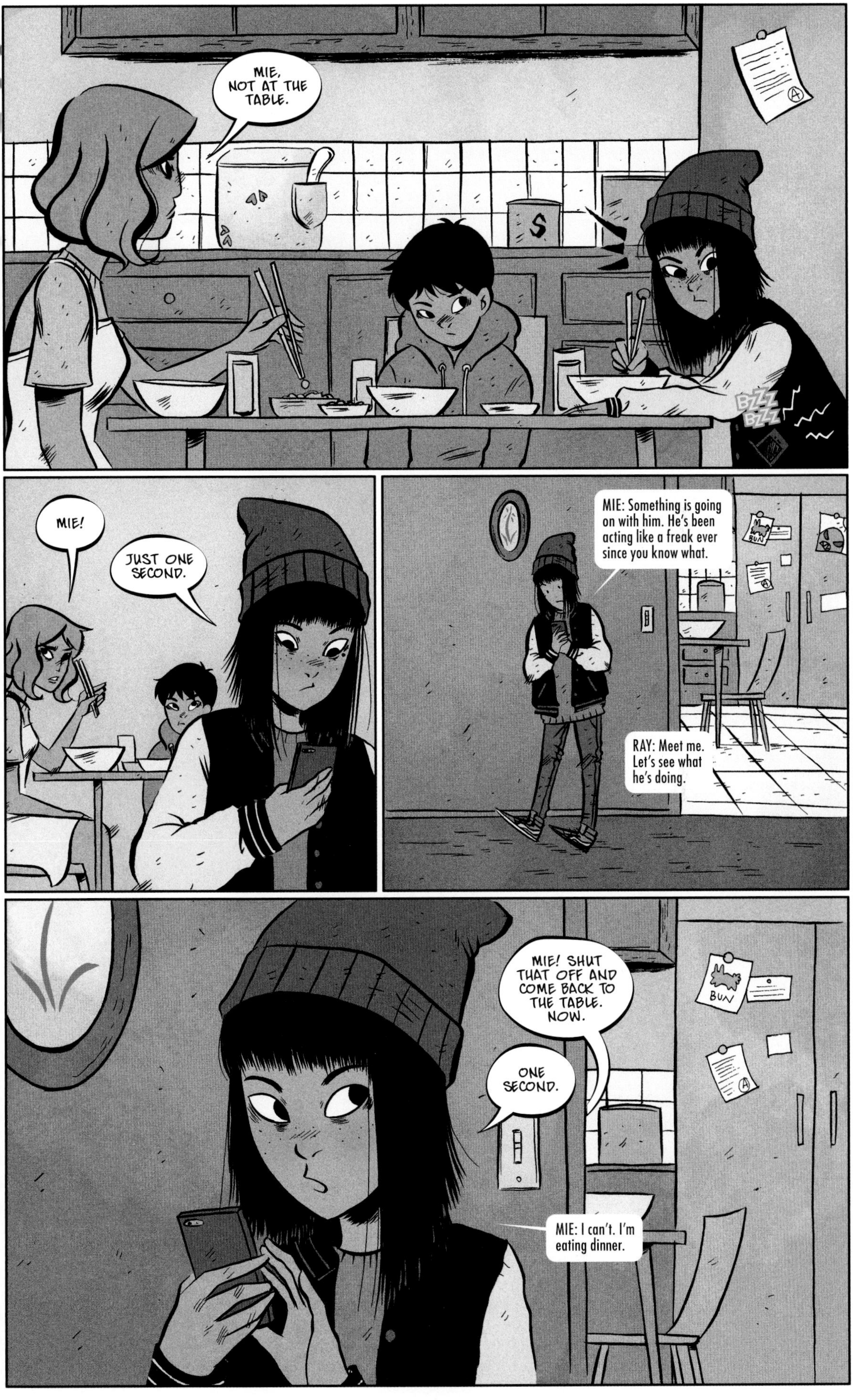
MIE, NOT AT THE TABLE.
BZZZ BZZZ
MIE!
JUST ONE SECOND.
MIE: Something is going on with him. He's been acting like a freak ever since you know what.
RAY: Meet me. Let's see what he's doing.
MIE! SHUT THAT OFF AND COME BACK TO THE TABLE. NOW.
ONE SECOND.
MIE: I can't. I'm eating dinner.

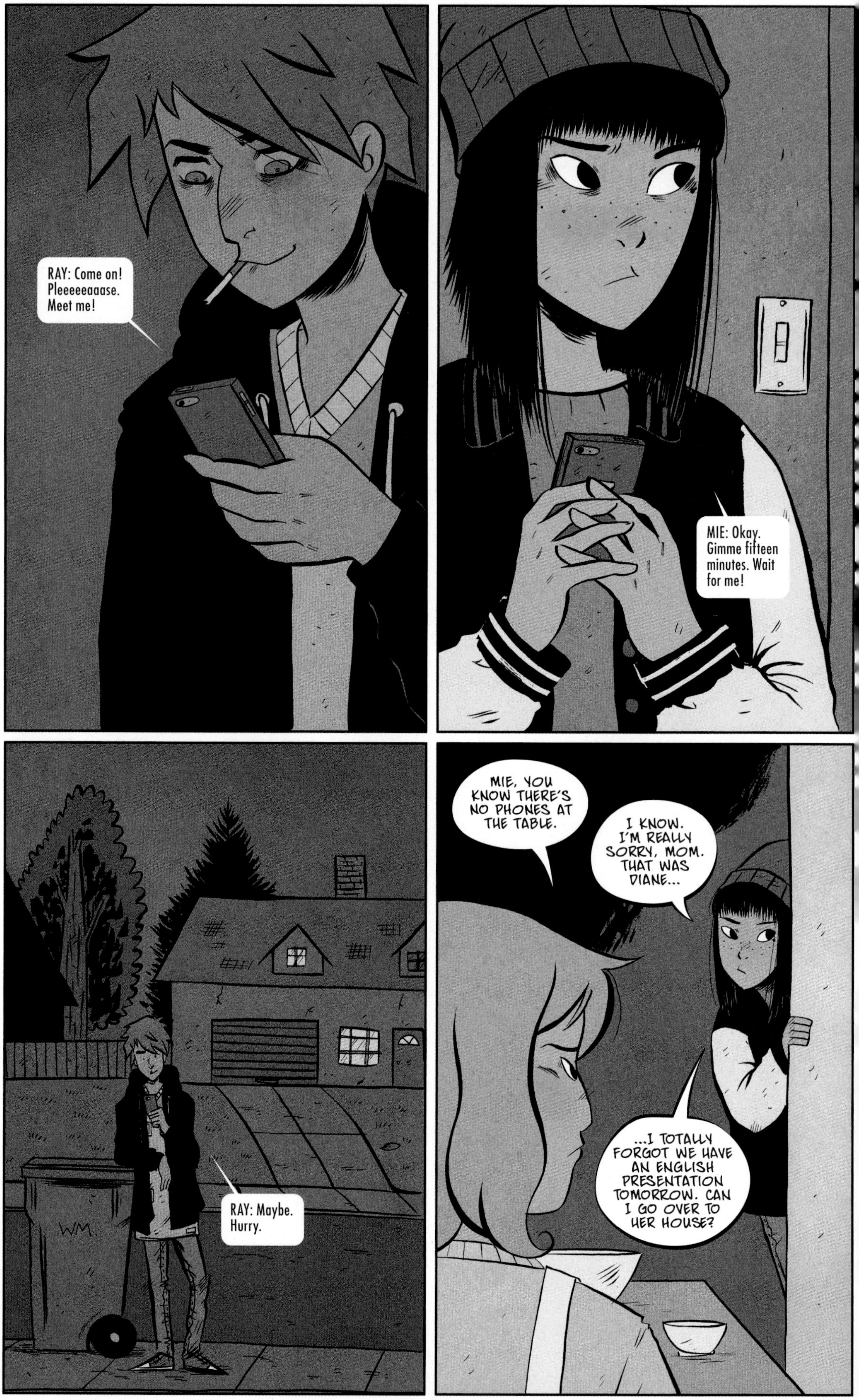
RAY: Come on! Pleeeeeaaase. Meet me!
MIE: Okay. Gimme fifteen minutes. Wait for me!
RAY: Maybe. Hurry.
WM
MIE, YOU KNOW THERE'S NO PHONES AT THE TABLE.
I KNOW. I'M REALLY SORRY, MOM. THAT WAS DIANE...
...I TOTALLY FORGOT WE HAVE AN ENGLISH PRESENTATION TOMORROW. CAN I GO OVER TO HER HOUSE?

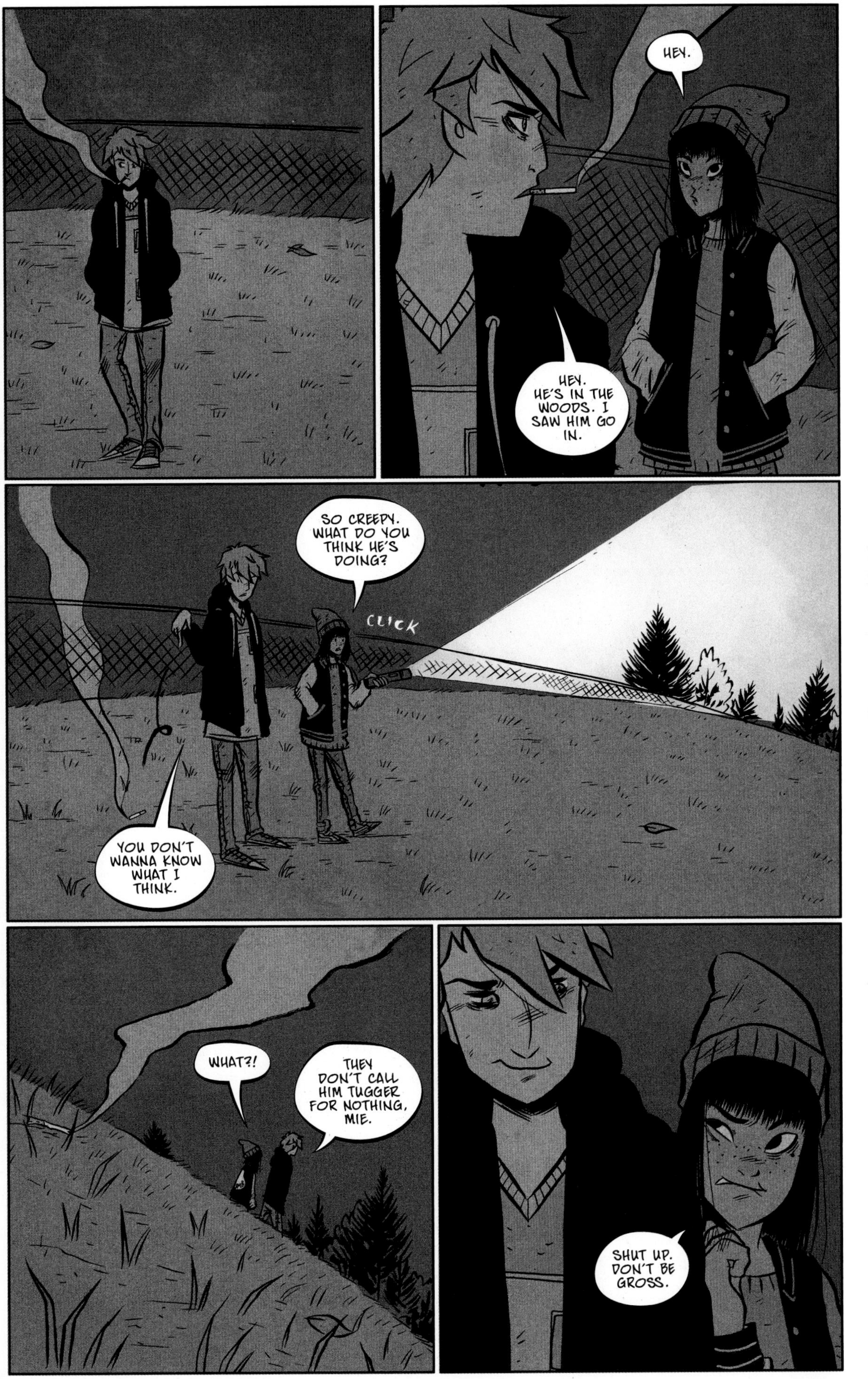
HEY.
HEY. HE'S IN THE WOODS. I SAW HIM GO IN.
SO CREEPY. WHAT DO YOU THINK HE'S DOING?
CLICK
YOU DON'T WANNA KNOW WHAT I THINK.
WHAT?!
THEY DON'T CALL HIM TUGGER FOR NOTHING, MIE.
SHUT UP. DON'T BE GROSS.

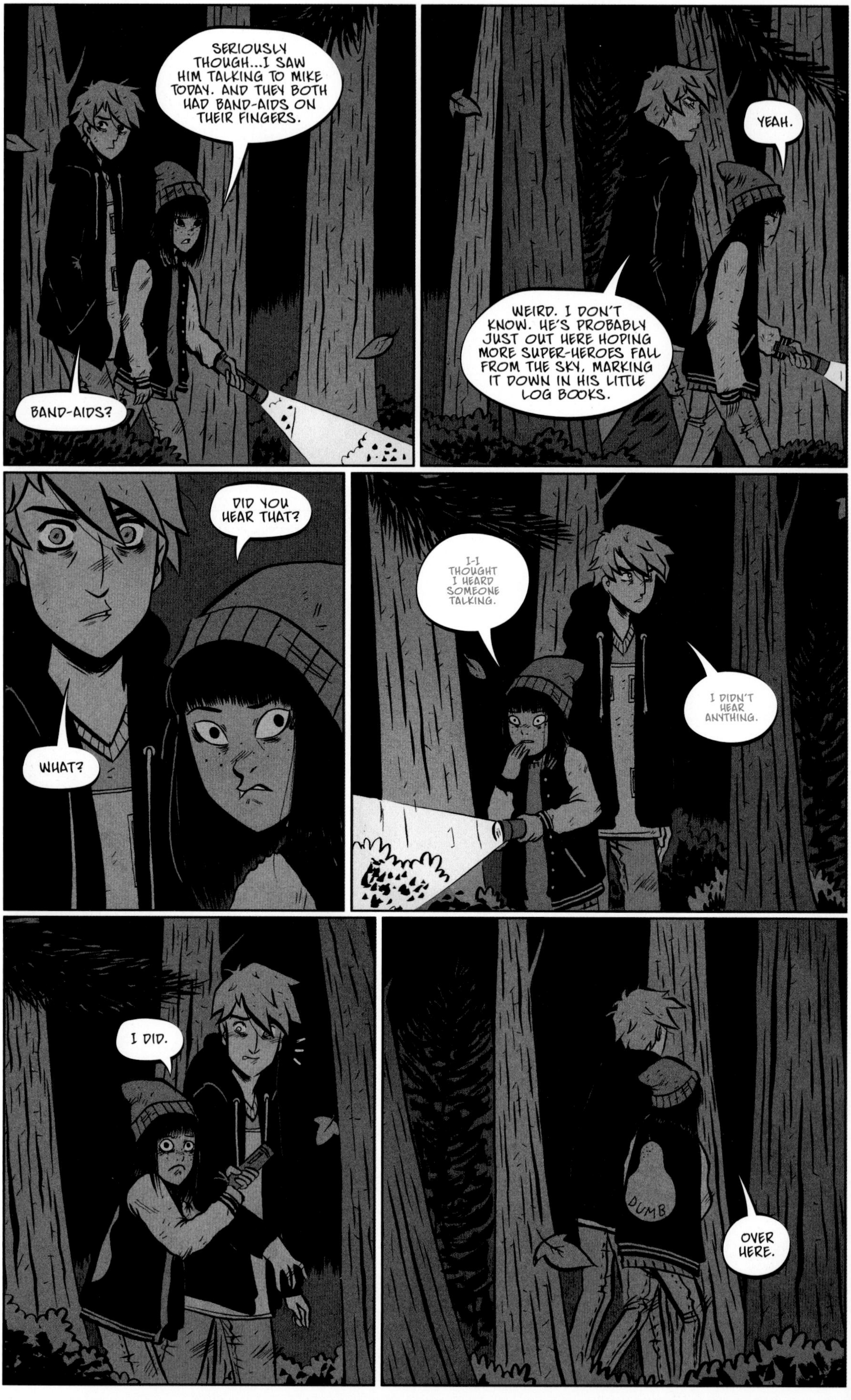
SERIOUSLY THOUGH...I SAW HIM TALKING TO MIKE TODAY. AND THEY BOTH HAD BAND-AIDS ON THEIR FINGERS.
BAND-AIDS?
YEAH.
WEIRD. I DON'T KNOW. HE'S PROBABLY JUST OUT HERE HOPING MORE SUPER-HEROES FALL FROM THE SKY, MARKING IT DOWN IN HIS LITTLE LOG BOOKS.
DID YOU HEAR THAT?
WHAT?
I-I THOUGHT I HEARD SOMEONE TALKING.
I DIDN'T HEAR ANYTHING.
I DID.
DUMB
OVER HERE.

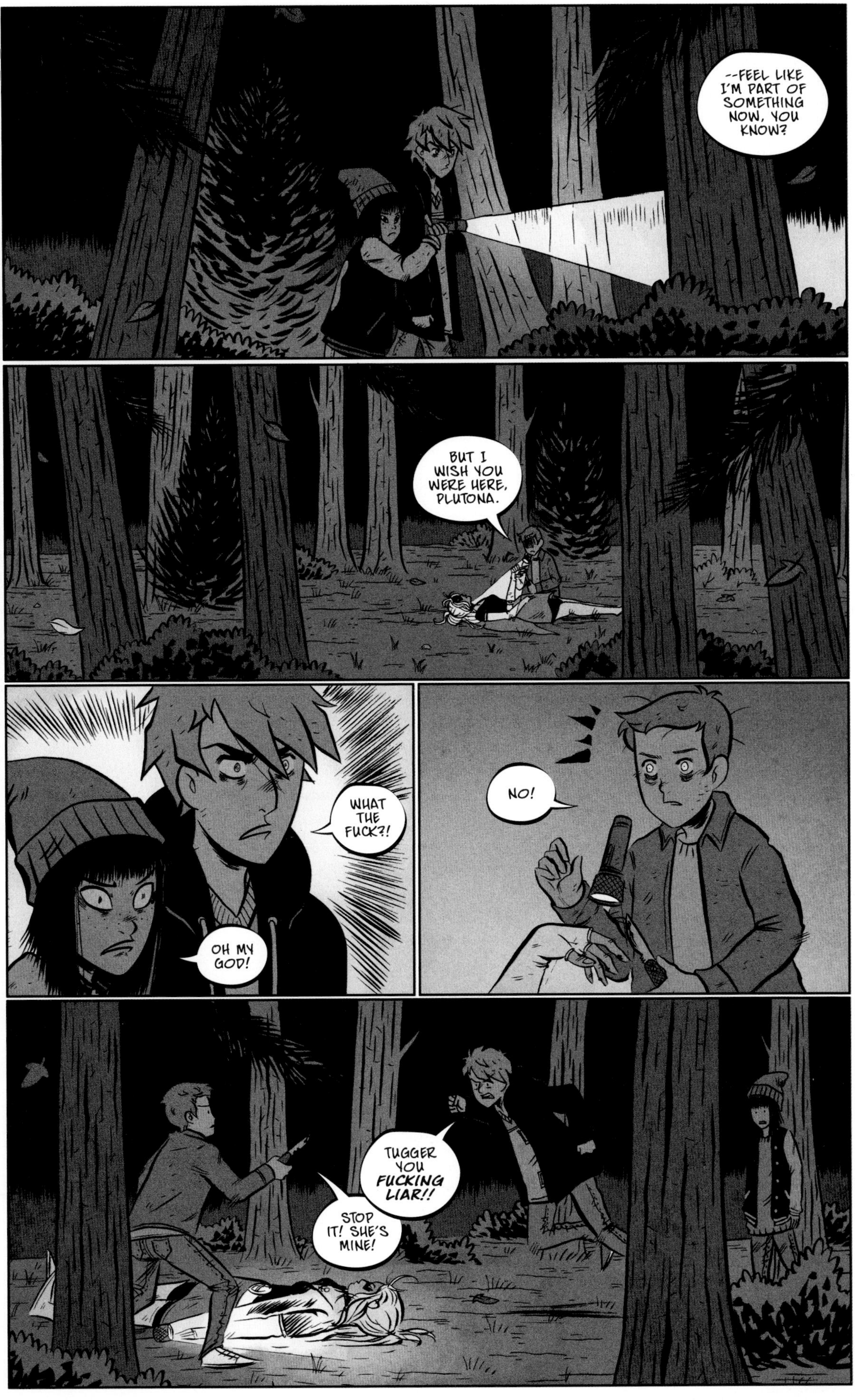
--FEEL LIKE I'M PART OF SOMETHING NOW, YOU KNOW?
BUT I WISH YOU WERE HERE, PLUTONA.
WHAT THE FUCK?!
OH MY GOD!
NO!
TUGGER YOU FUCKING LIAR!!
STOP IT! SHE'S MINE!

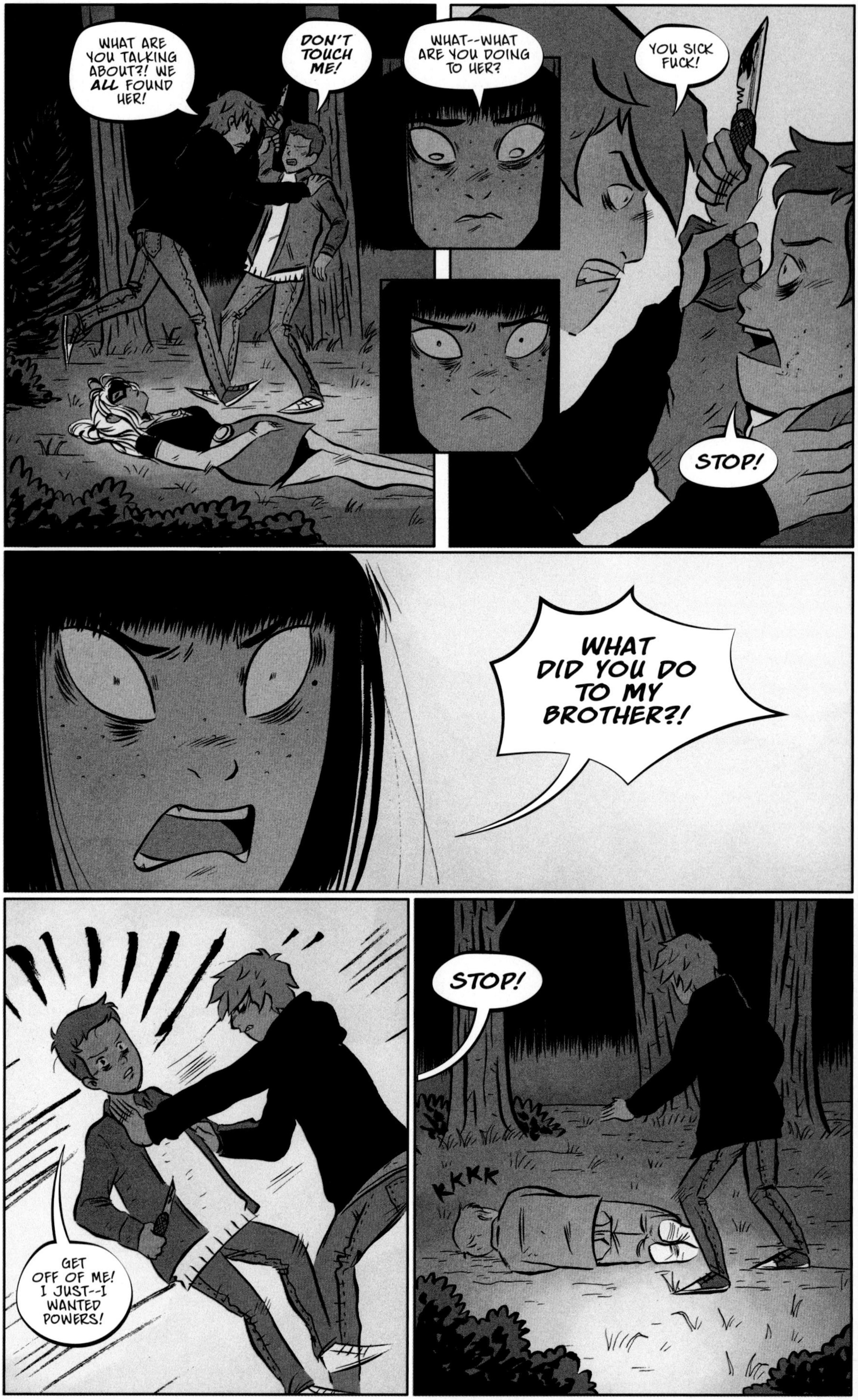

WHAT ARE YOU TALKING ABOUT?! WE ALL FOUND HER!
DON'T TOUCH ME!
WHAT--WHAT ARE YOU DOING TO HER?
YOU SICK FUCK!
STOP!
WHAT DID YOU DO TO MY BROTHER?!
GET OFF OF ME! I JUST--I WANTED POWERS!
STOP!
KKKK

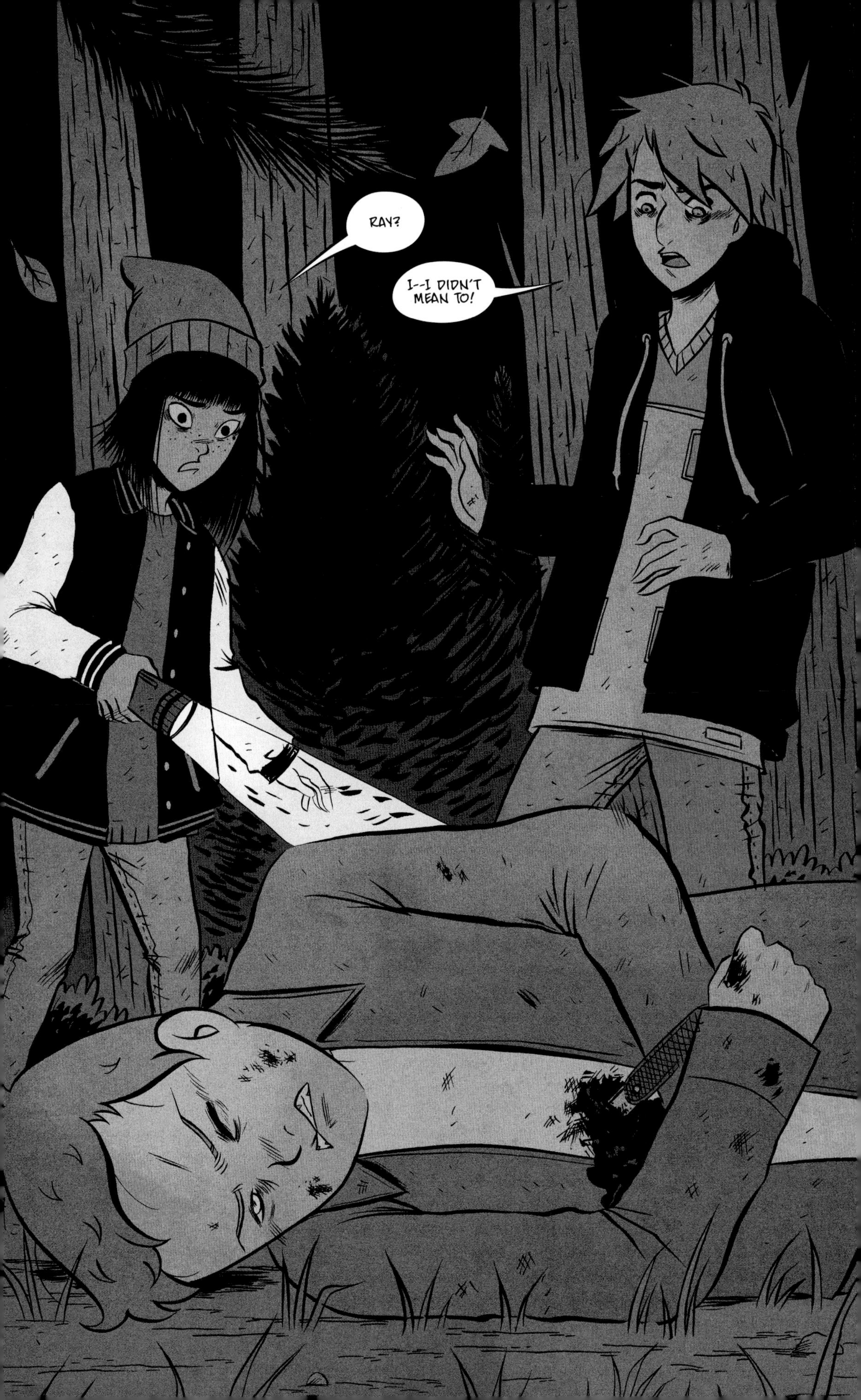
RAY?
I--I DIDN'T MEAN TO!

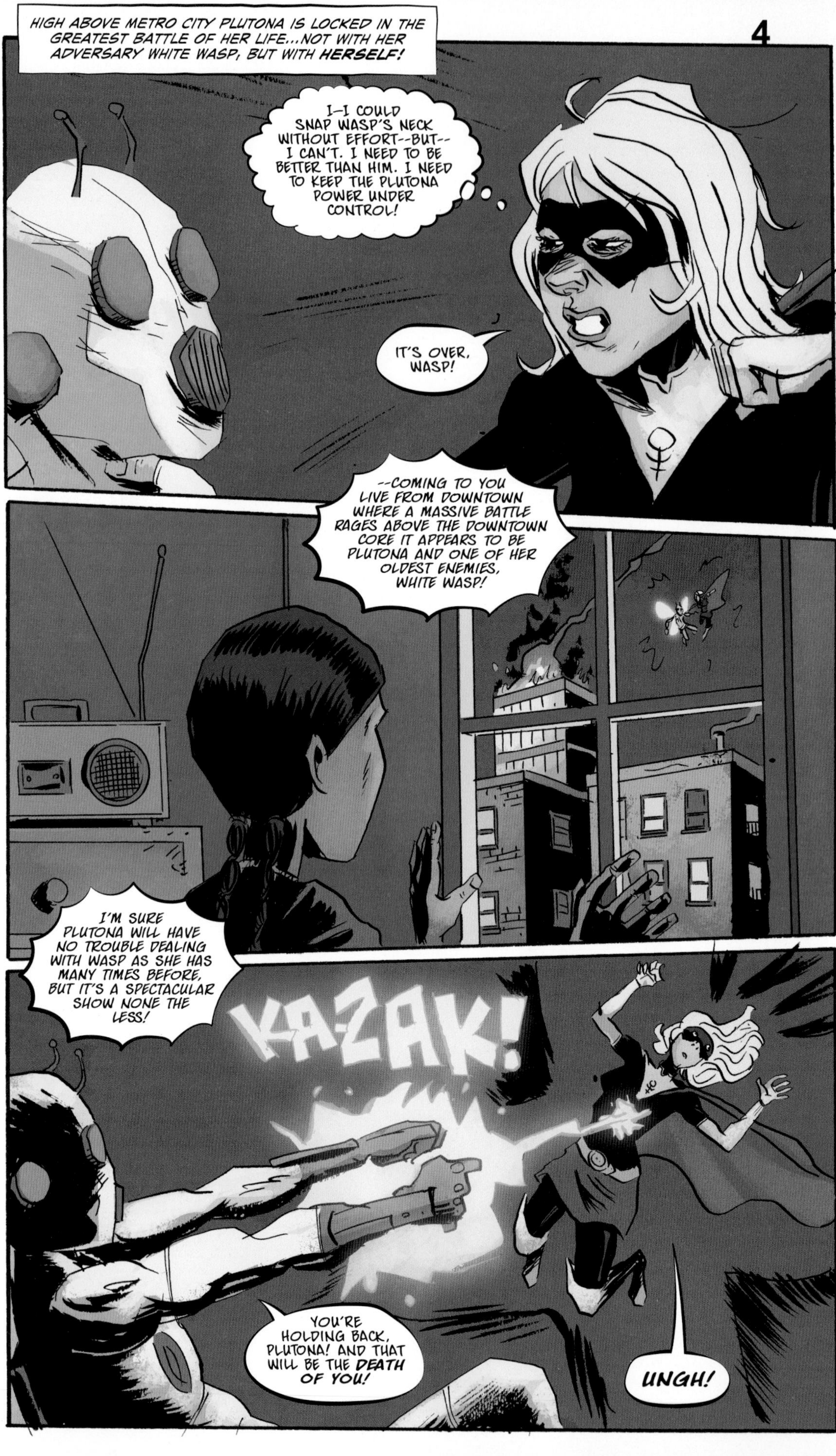
HIGH ABOVE METRO CITY PLUTONA IS LOCKED IN THE GREATEST BATTLE OF HER LIFE...NOT WITH HER ADVERSARY WHITE WASP, BUT WITH ***HERSELF!***
I–I COULD SNAP WASP'S NECK WITHOUT EFFORT--BUT-- I CAN'T. I NEED TO BE BETTER THAN HIM. I NEED TO KEEP THE PLUTONA POWER UNDER CONTROL!
IT'S OVER, WASP!
--COMING TO YOU LIVE FROM DOWNTOWN WHERE A MASSIVE BATTLE RAGES ABOVE THE DOWNTOWN CORE IT APPEARS TO BE PLUTONA AND ONE OF HER OLDEST ENEMIES, WHITE WASP!
I'M SURE PLUTONA WILL HAVE NO TROUBLE DEALING WITH WASP AS SHE HAS MANY TIMES BEFORE, BUT IT'S A SPECTACULAR SHOW NONE THE LESS!
KA-ZAK!
YOU'RE HOLDING BACK, PLUTONA! AND THAT WILL BE THE ***DEATH OF YOU!***
UNGH!

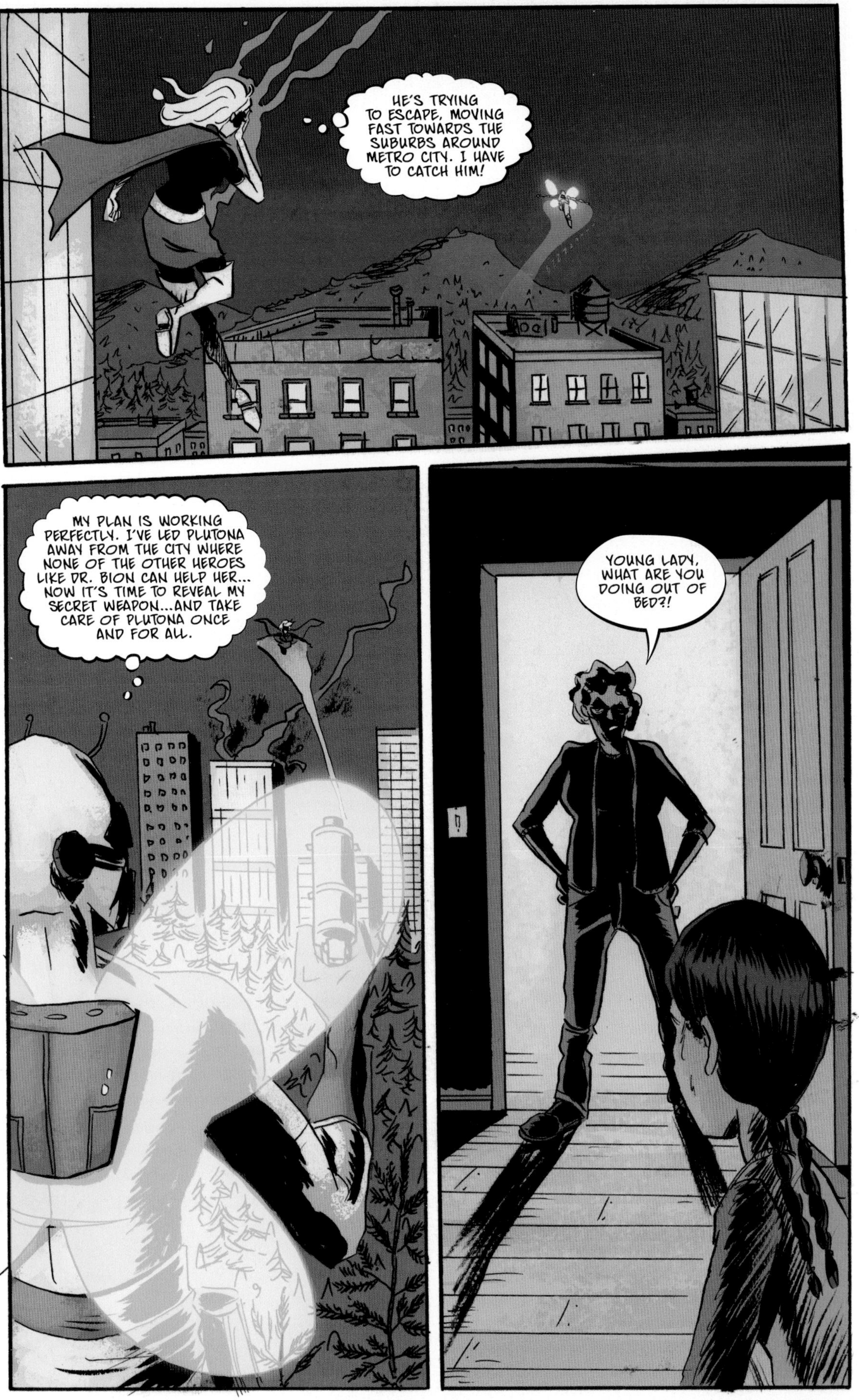
HE'S TRYING TO ESCAPE, MOVING FAST TOWARDS THE SUBURBS AROUND METRO CITY. I HAVE TO CATCH HIM!
MY PLAN IS WORKING PERFECTLY. I'VE LED PLUTONA AWAY FROM THE CITY WHERE NONE OF THE OTHER HEROES LIKE DR. BION CAN HELP HER... NOW IT'S TIME TO REVEAL MY SECRET WEAPON...AND TAKE CARE OF PLUTONA ONCE AND FOR ALL.
YOUNG LADY, WHAT ARE YOU DOING OUT OF BED?!

CHAPTER

5

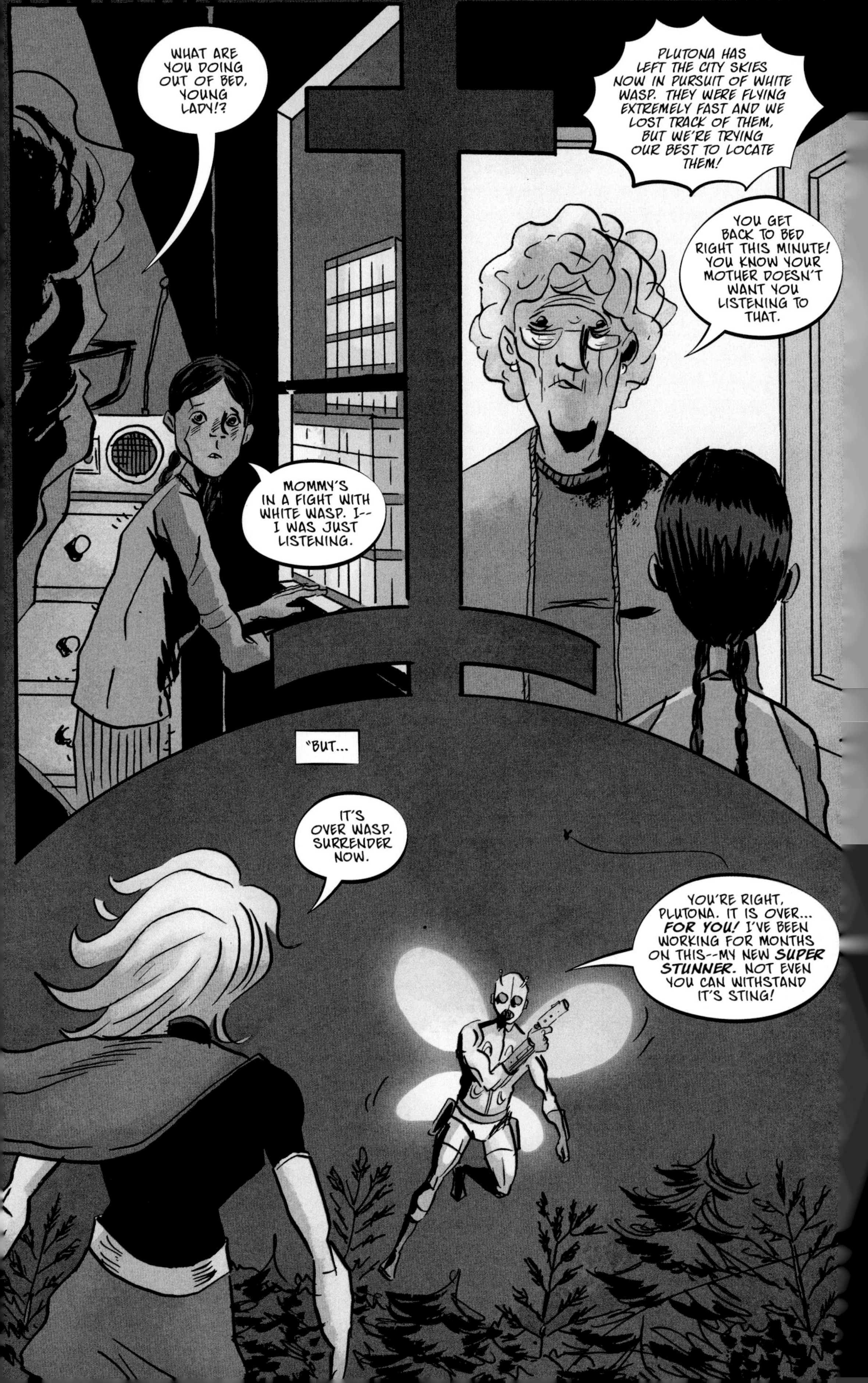
WHAT ARE YOU DOING OUT OF BED, YOUNG LADY!?
MOMMY'S IN A FIGHT WITH WHITE WASP. I-- I WAS JUST LISTENING.
PLUTONA HAS LEFT THE CITY SKIES NOW IN PURSUIT OF WHITE WASP. THEY WERE FLYING EXTREMELY FAST AND WE LOST TRACK OF THEM, BUT WE'RE TRYING OUR BEST TO LOCATE THEM!
YOU GET BACK TO BED RIGHT THIS MINUTE! YOU KNOW YOUR MOTHER DOESN'T WANT YOU LISTENING TO THAT.
"BUT...
IT'S OVER WASP. SURRENDER NOW.
YOU'RE RIGHT, PLUTONA. IT IS OVER... **FOR YOU!** I'VE BEEN WORKING FOR MONTHS ON THIS--MY NEW ***SUPER STUNNER.*** NOT EVEN YOU CAN WITHSTAND IT'S STING!

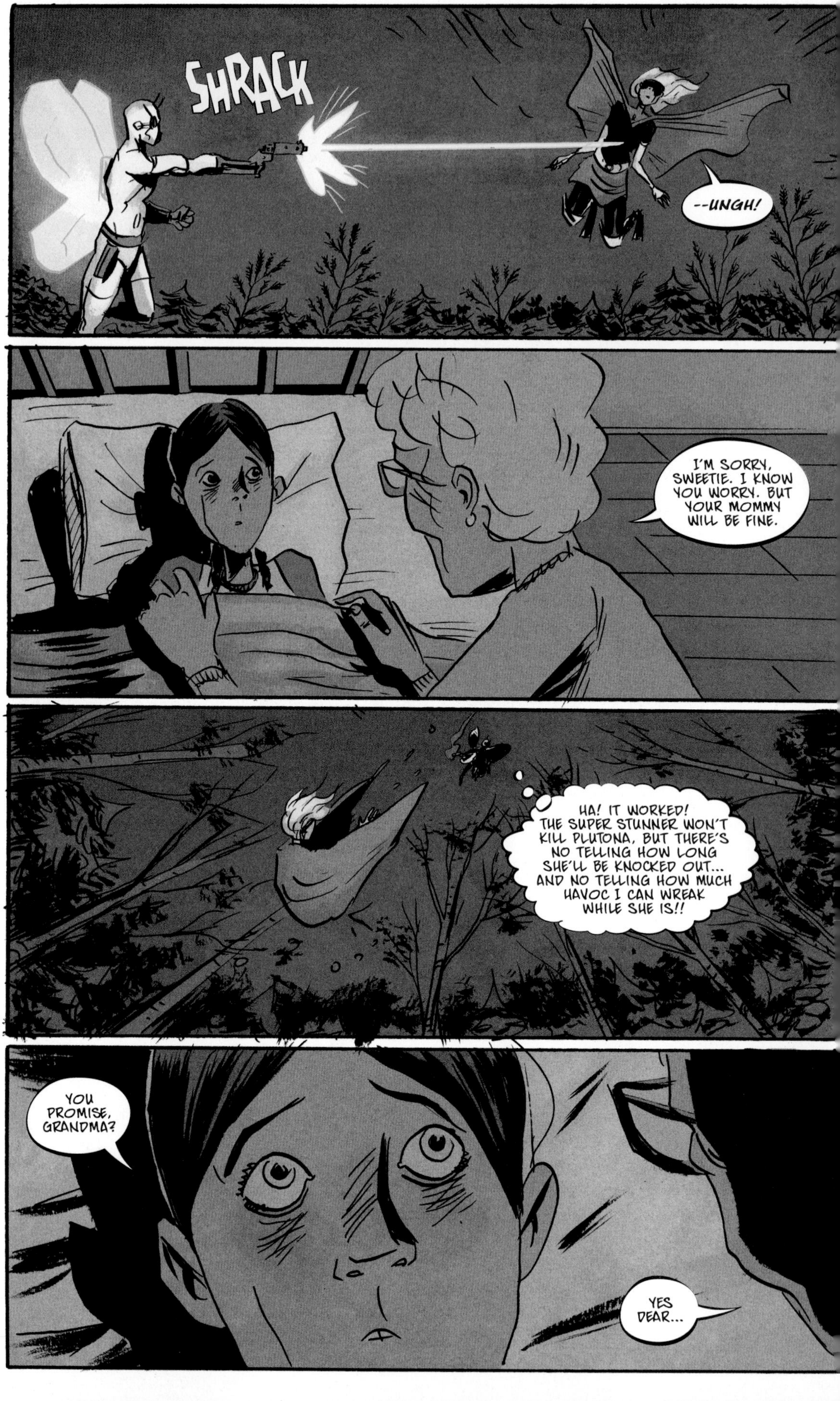
SHRACK
--UNGH!
I'M SORRY, SWEETIE. I KNOW YOU WORRY. BUT YOUR MOMMY WILL BE FINE.
HA! IT WORKED! THE SUPER STUNNER WON'T KILL PLUTONA, BUT THERE'S NO TELLING HOW LONG SHE'LL BE KNOCKED OUT... AND NO TELLING HOW MUCH HAVOC I CAN WREAK WHILE SHE IS!!
YOU PROMISE, GRANDMA?
YES DEAR...

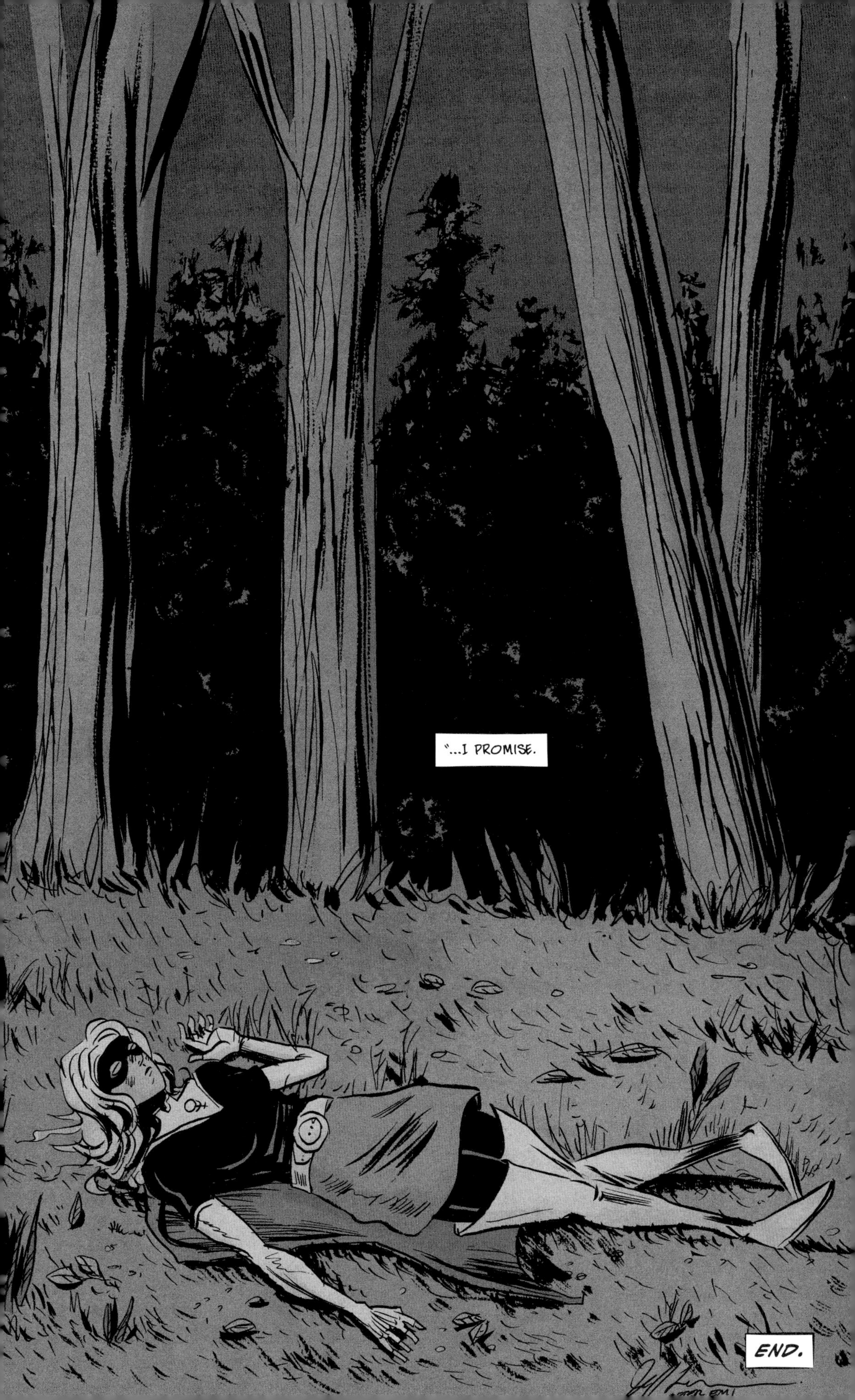
"...I PROMISE.
END.

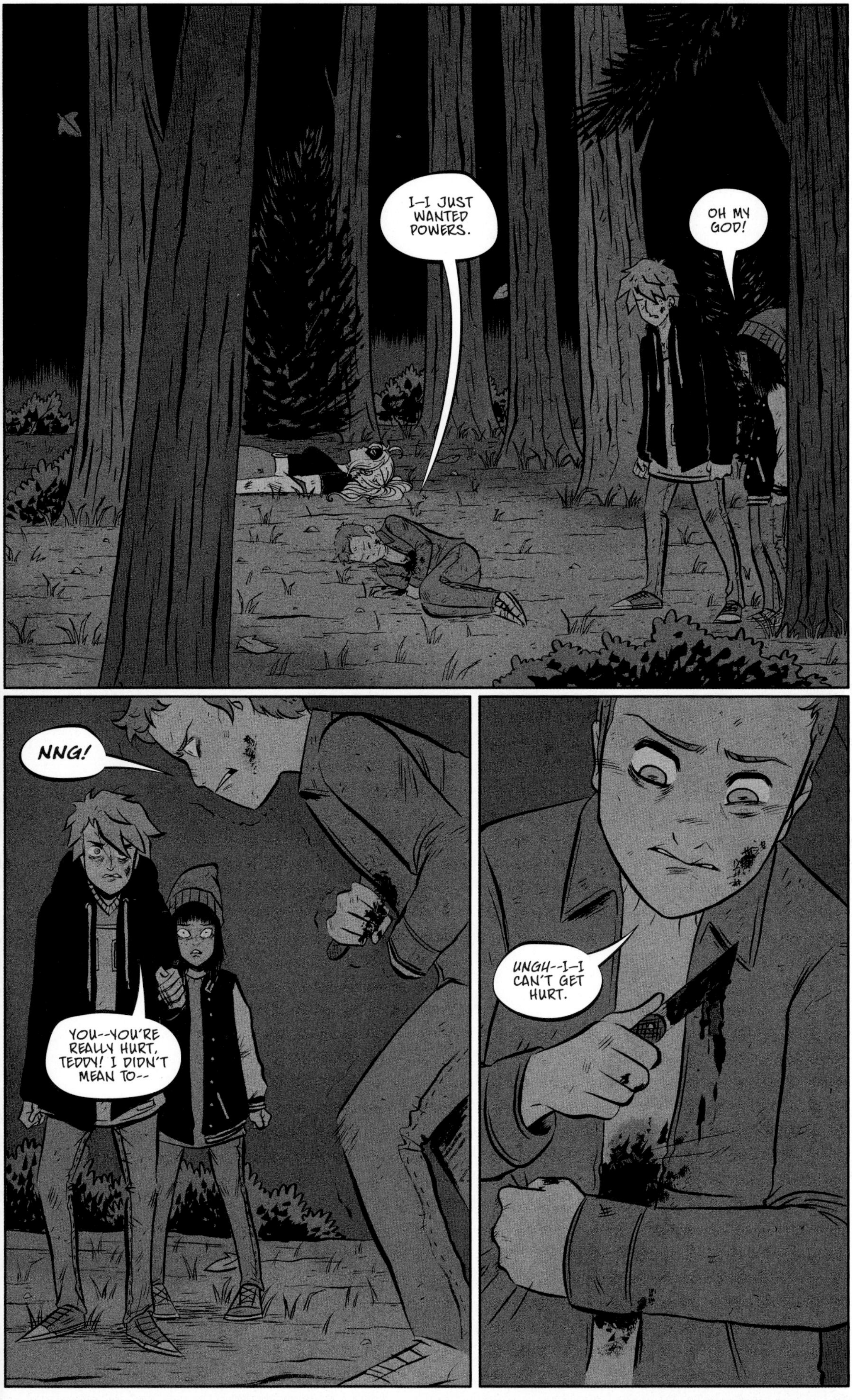
I-I JUST WANTED POWERS.
OH MY GOD!
NNG!
YOU--YOU'RE REALLY HURT, TEDDY! I DIDN'T MEAN TO--
UNGH--I-I CAN'T GET HURT.

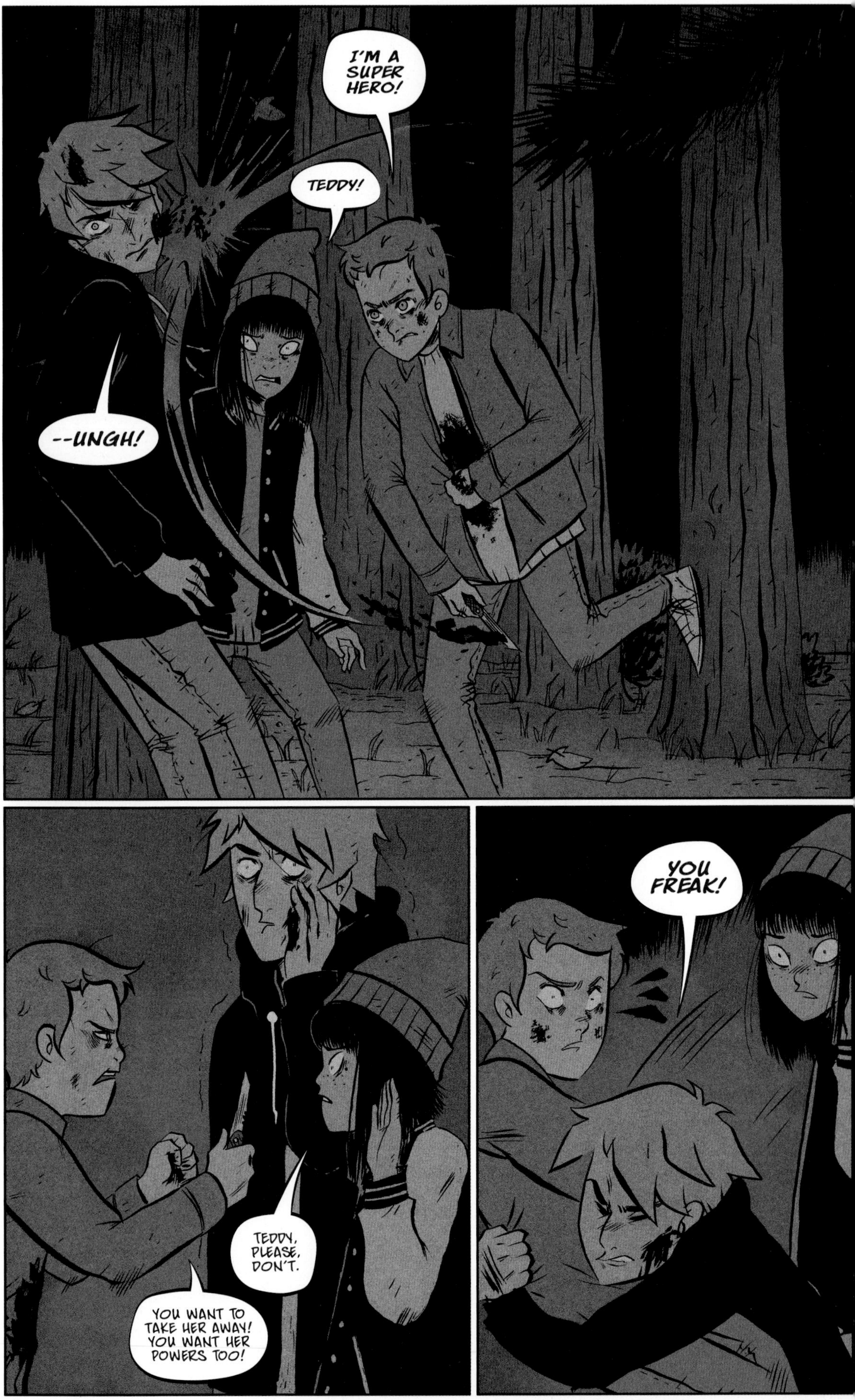
I'M A SUPER HERO!
TEDDY!
--UNGH!
TEDDY, PLEASE, DON'T.
YOU WANT TO TAKE HER AWAY! YOU WANT HER POWERS TOO!
YOU FREAK!

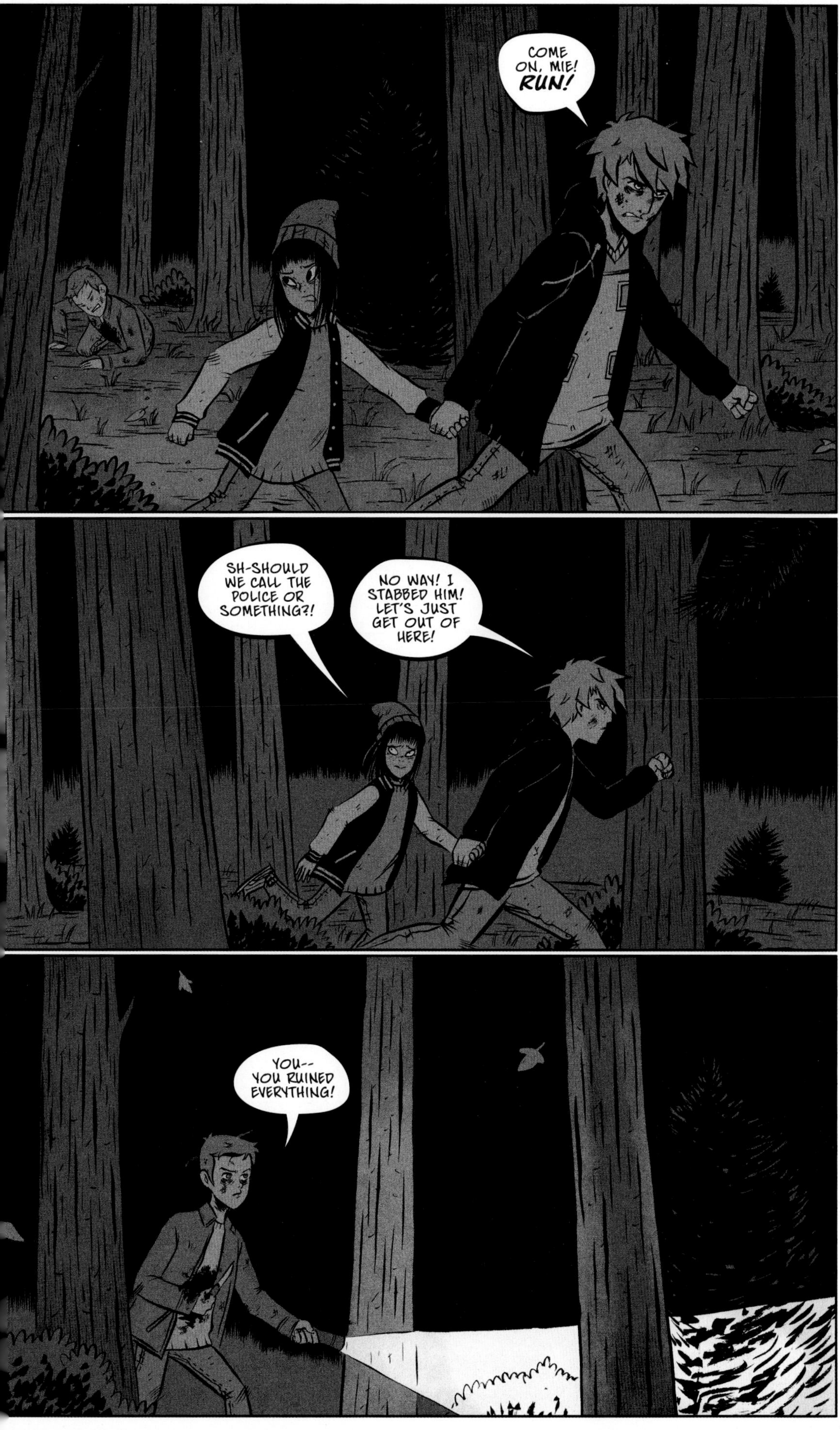
COME ON, MIE! RUN!
SH-SHOULD WE CALL THE POLICE OR SOMETHING?!
NO WAY! I STABBED HIM! LET'S JUST GET OUT OF HERE!
YOU-- YOU RUINED EVERYTHING!

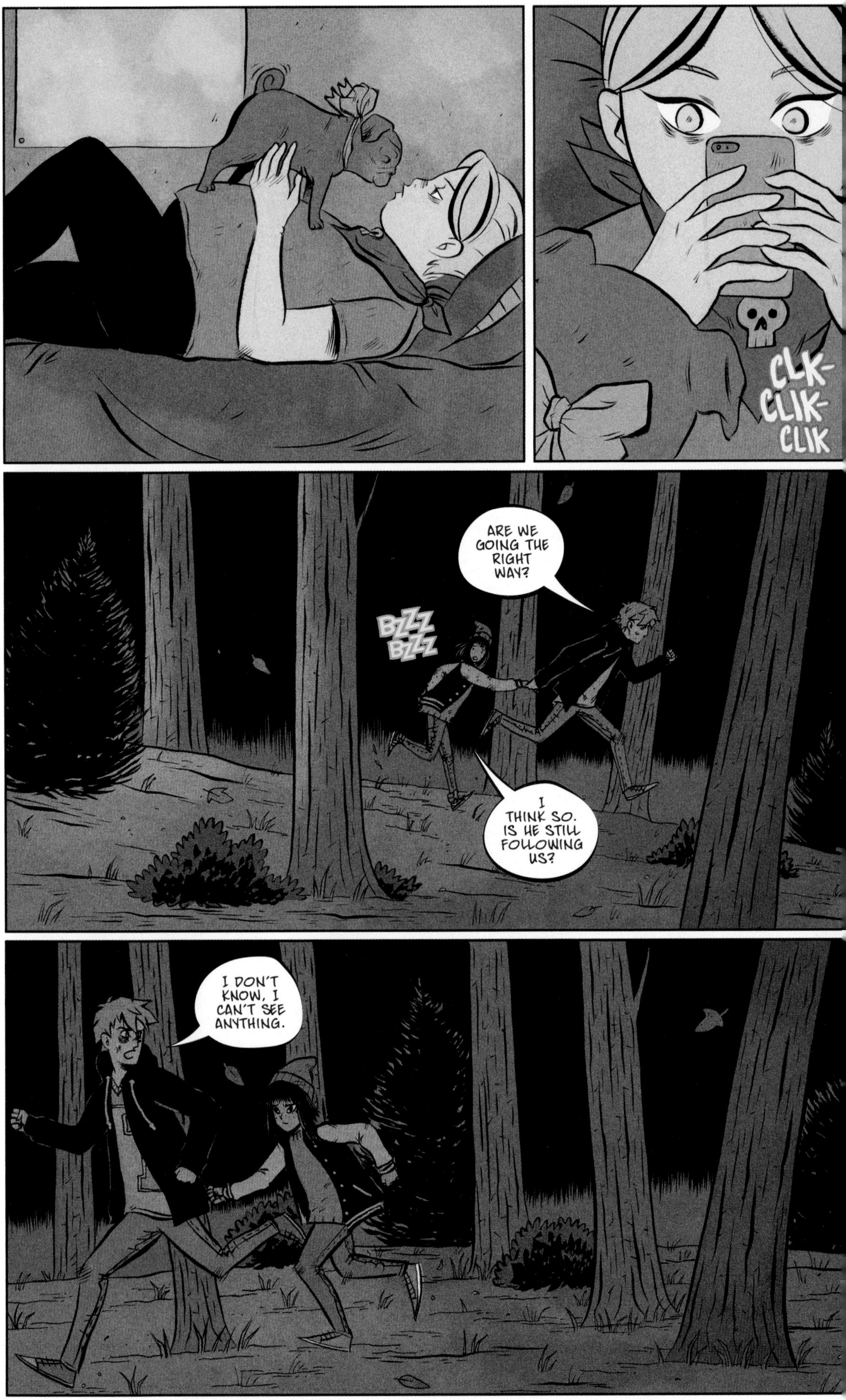
CLK-
CLIK-
CLIK
ARE WE GOING THE RIGHT WAY?
BZZZ BZZZ
I THINK SO. IS HE STILL FOLLOWING US?
I DON'T KNOW, I CAN'T SEE ANYTHING.

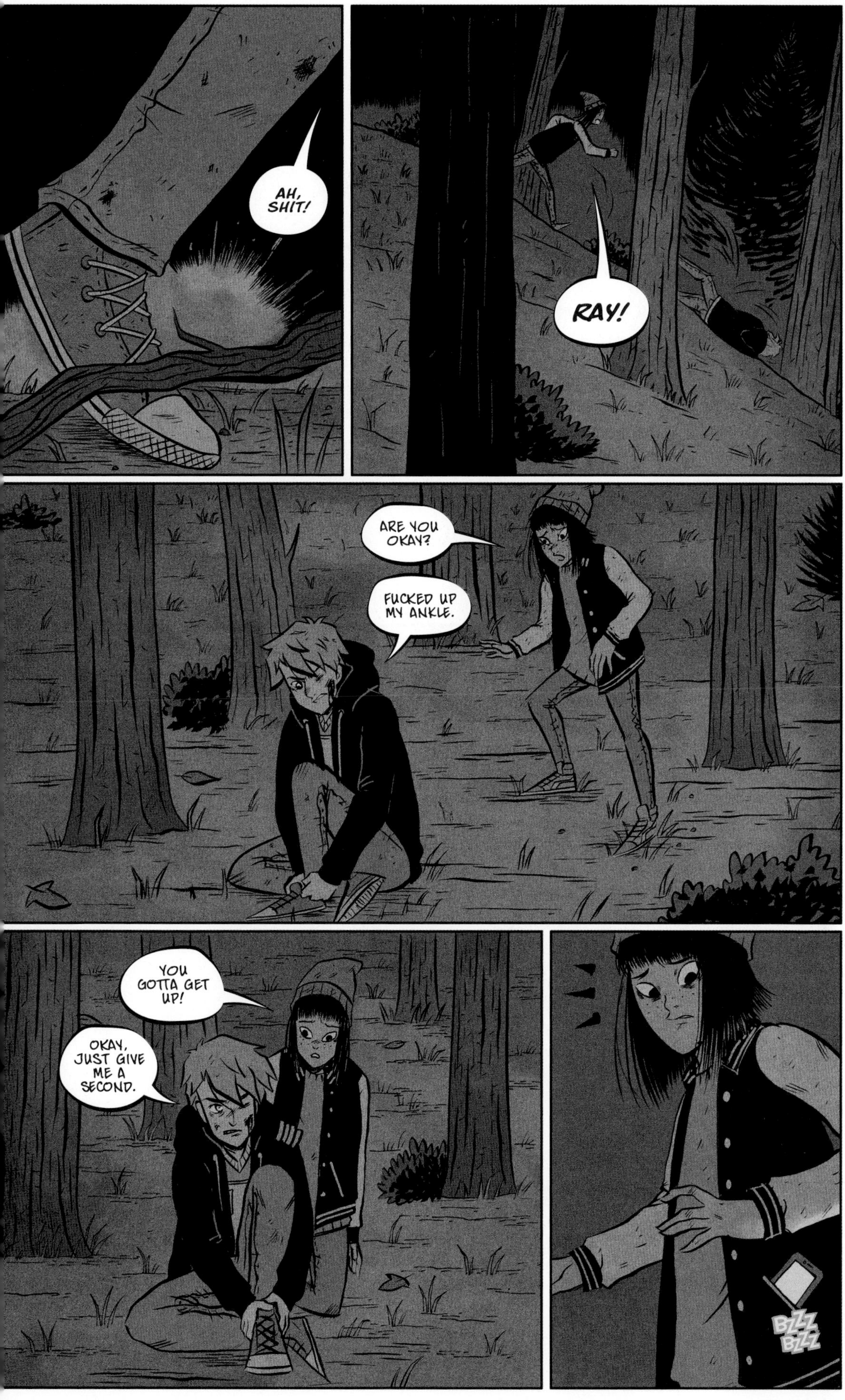
AH, SHIT!
RAY!
ARE YOU OKAY?
FUCKED UP MY ANKLE.
YOU GOTTA GET UP!
OKAY, JUST GIVE ME A SECOND.
BZZZ BZZZ

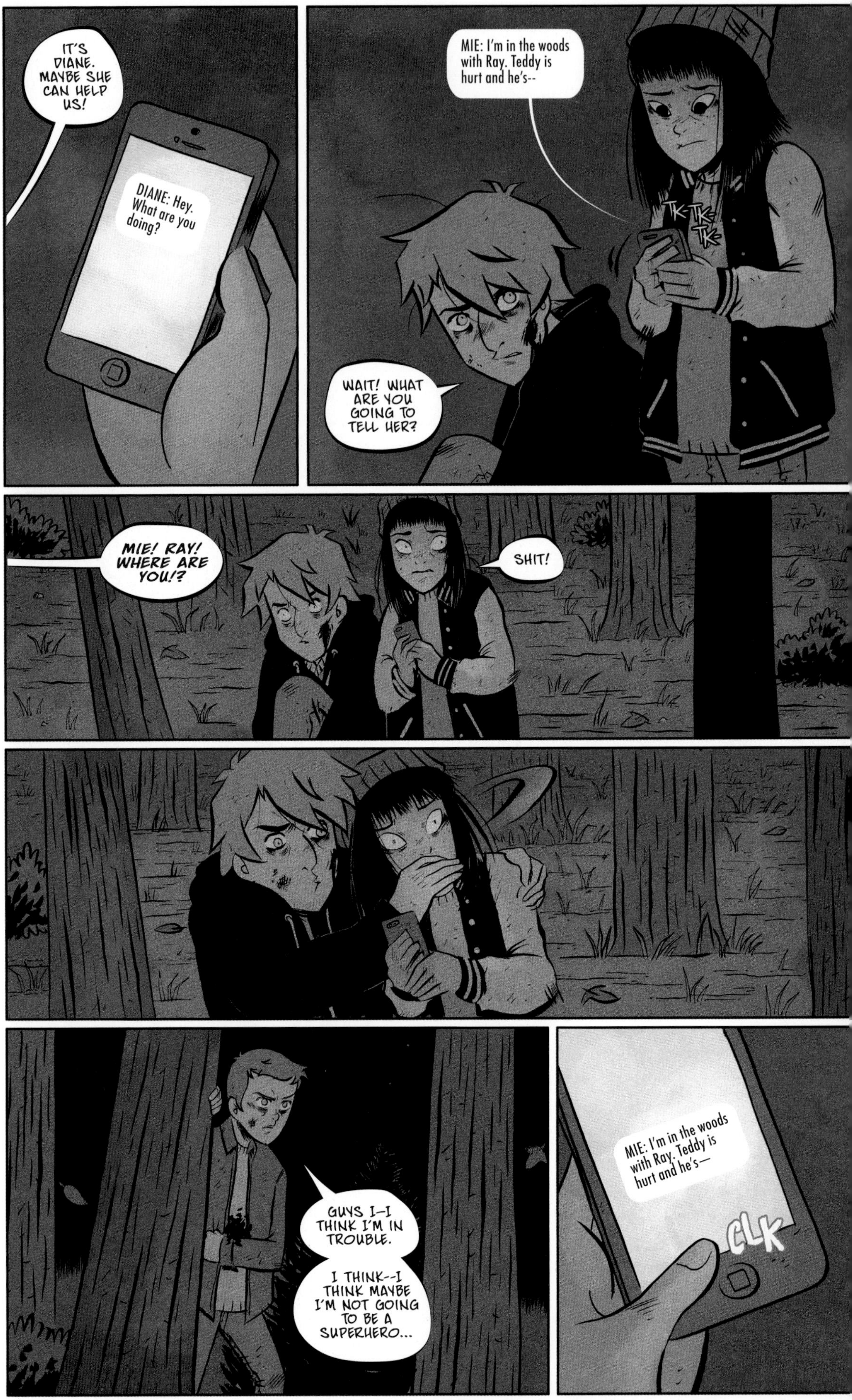

IT'S DIANE. MAYBE SHE CAN HELP US!
DIANE: Hey. What are you doing?
MIE: I'm in the woods with Ray. Teddy is hurt and he's--
TK-TK-TK-
WAIT! WHAT ARE YOU GOING TO TELL HER?
MIE! RAY! WHERE ARE YOU!?
SHIT!
GUYS I--I THINK I'M IN TROUBLE.
I THINK--I THINK MAYBE I'M NOT GOING TO BE A SUPERHERO...
MIE: I'm in the woods with Ray. Teddy is hurt and he's—
CLK

BZZ--BZZ
DIANE: I'm sorry about today I just—
MIE: I'm in the woods with Ray. Teddy is hurt and he's—
GUYS?! I-- I CAN'T LET YOU TELL ANYONE WHAT I DID. THEY WON'T LET ME KEEP HER!
TEDDY?
WHA-?!

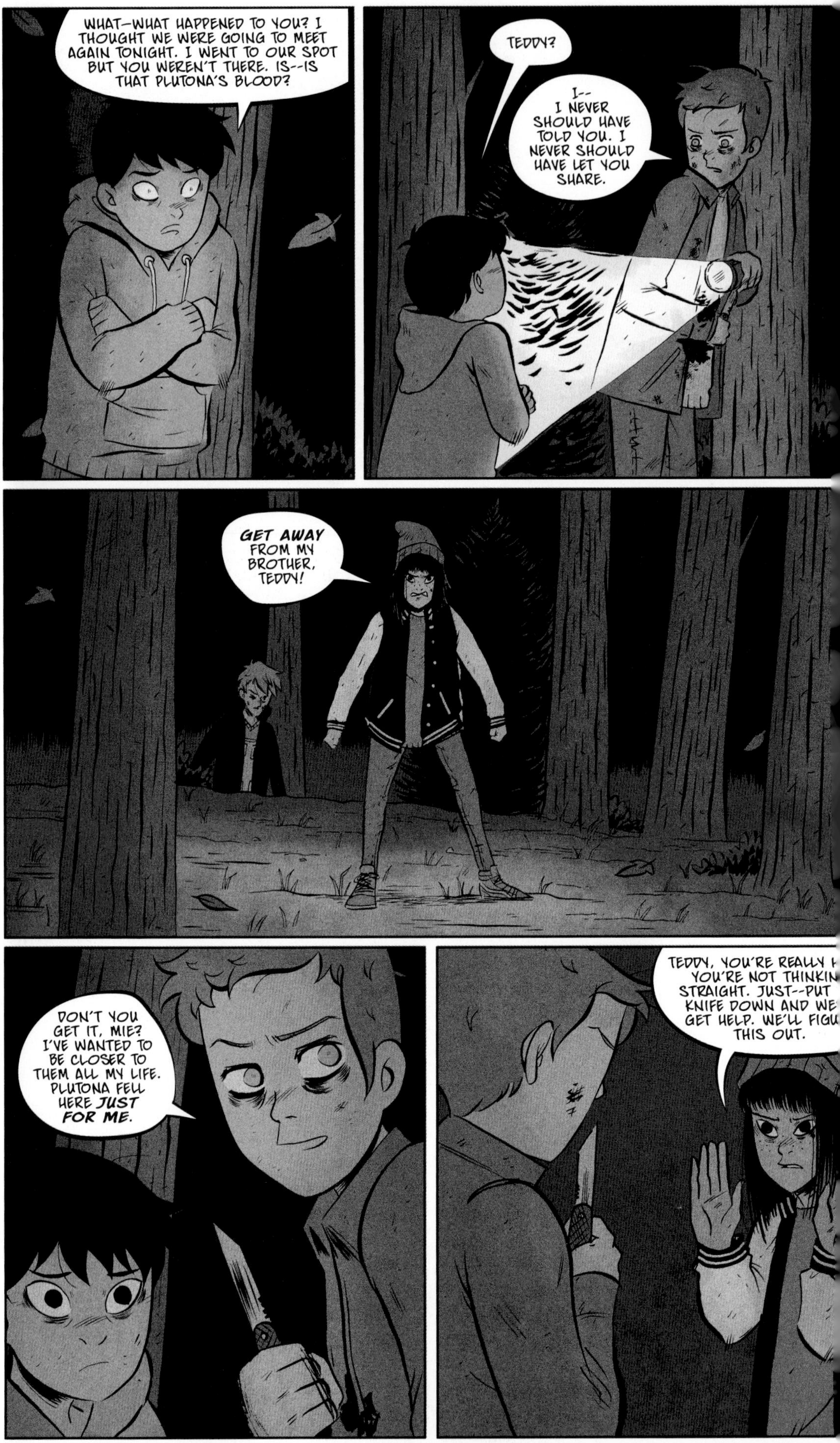
WHAT—WHAT HAPPENED TO YOU? I THOUGHT WE WERE GOING TO MEET AGAIN TONIGHT. I WENT TO OUR SPOT BUT YOU WEREN'T THERE. IS--IS THAT PLUTONA'S BLOOD?
TEDDY?
I-- I NEVER SHOULD HAVE TOLD YOU. I NEVER SHOULD HAVE LET YOU SHARE.
GET AWAY FROM MY BROTHER, TEDDY!
DON'T YOU GET IT, MIE? I'VE WANTED TO BE CLOSER TO THEM ALL MY LIFE. PLUTONA FELL HERE **JUST FOR ME**.
TEDDY, YOU'RE REALLY
YOU'RE NOT THINKIN
STRAIGHT. JUST--PUT
KNIFE DOWN AND WE
GET HELP. WE'LL FIGU
THIS OUT.

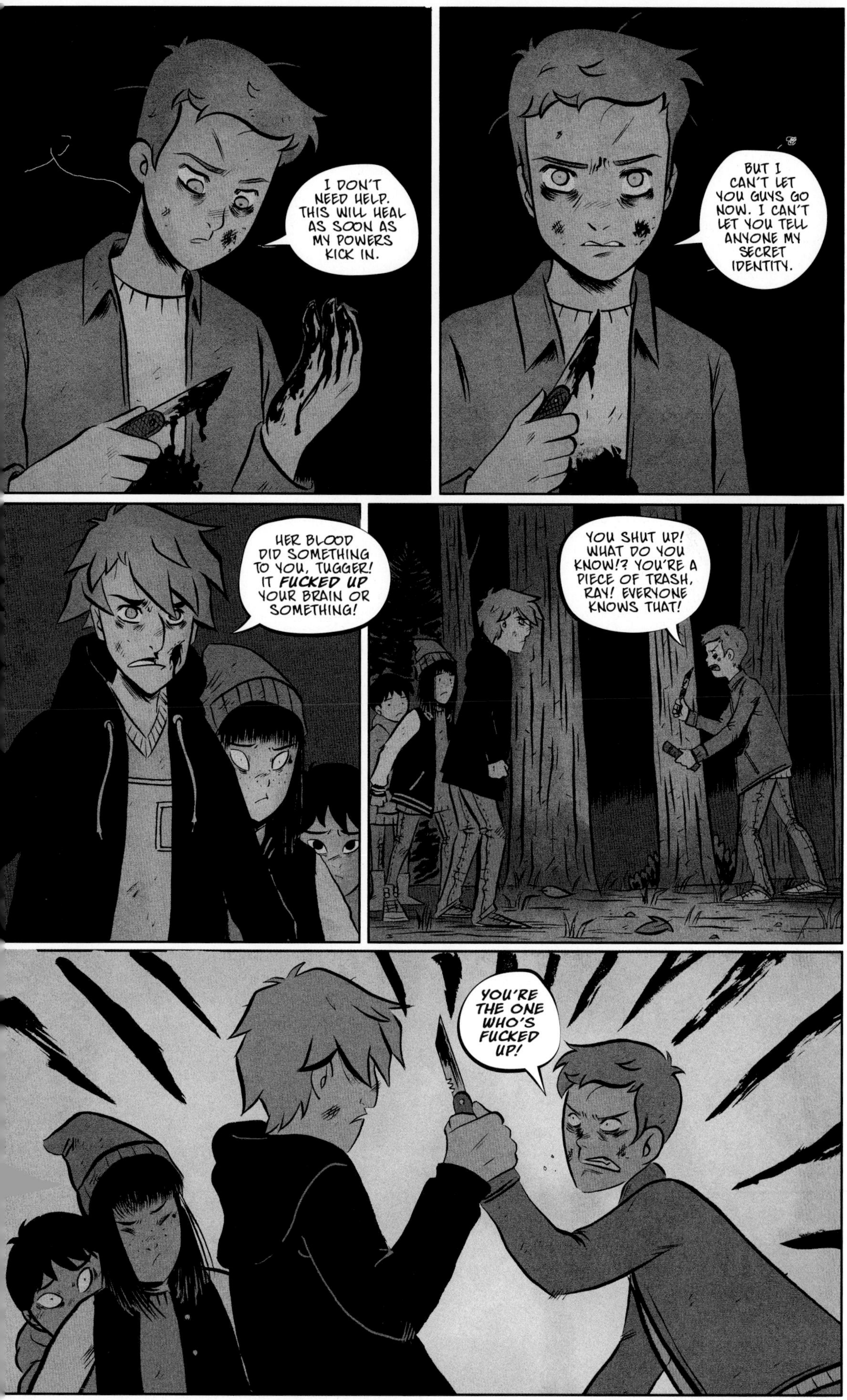
I DON'T NEED HELP. THIS WILL HEAL AS SOON AS MY POWERS KICK IN.
BUT I CAN'T LET YOU GUYS GO NOW. I CAN'T LET YOU TELL ANYONE MY SECRET IDENTITY.
HER BLOOD DID SOMETHING TO YOU, TUGGER! IT **FUCKED UP** YOUR BRAIN OR SOMETHING!
YOU SHUT UP! WHAT DO YOU KNOW!? YOU'RE A PIECE OF TRASH, RAY! EVERYONE KNOWS THAT!
YOU'RE THE ONE WHO'S FUCKED UP!

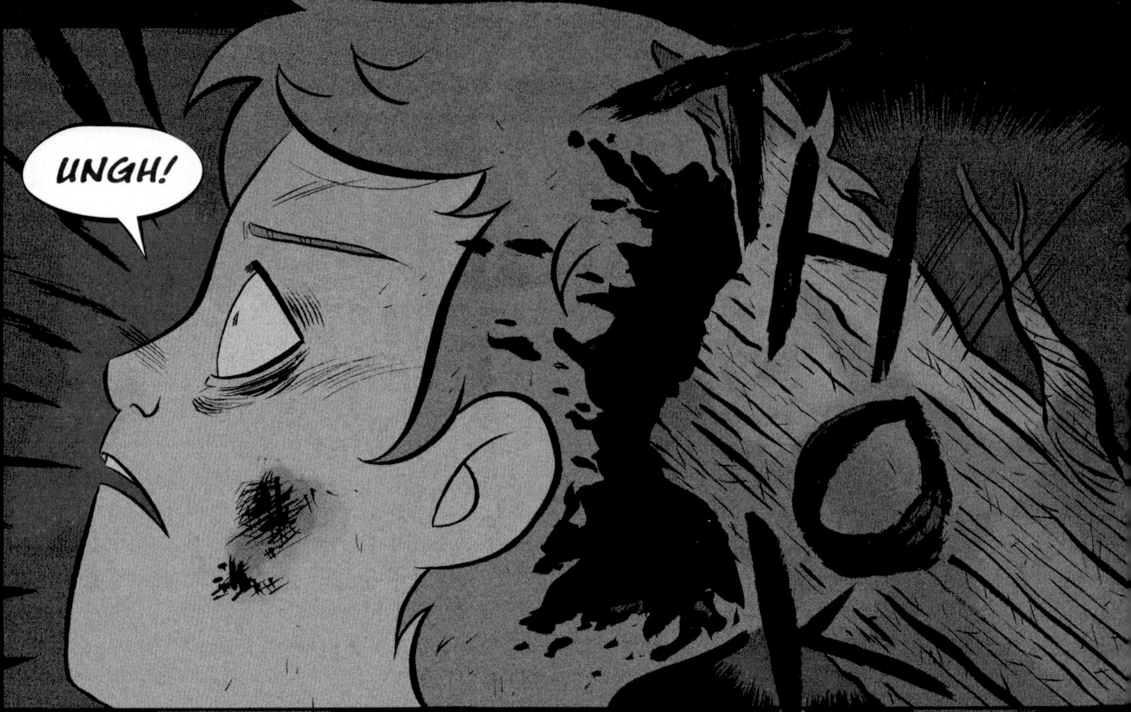
UNGH!

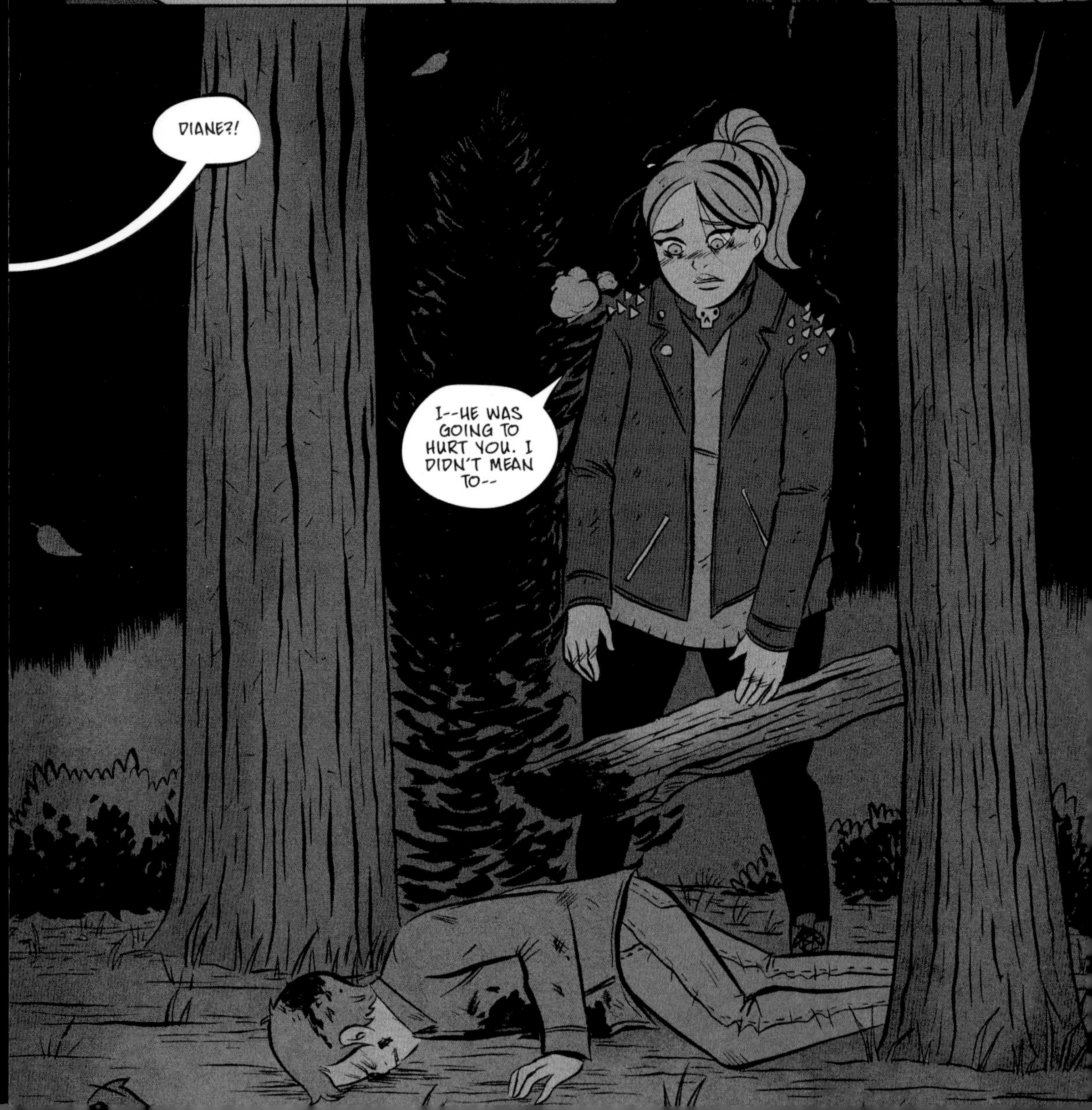
DIANE?!
I--HE WAS GOING TO HURT YOU. I DIDN'T MEAN TO--

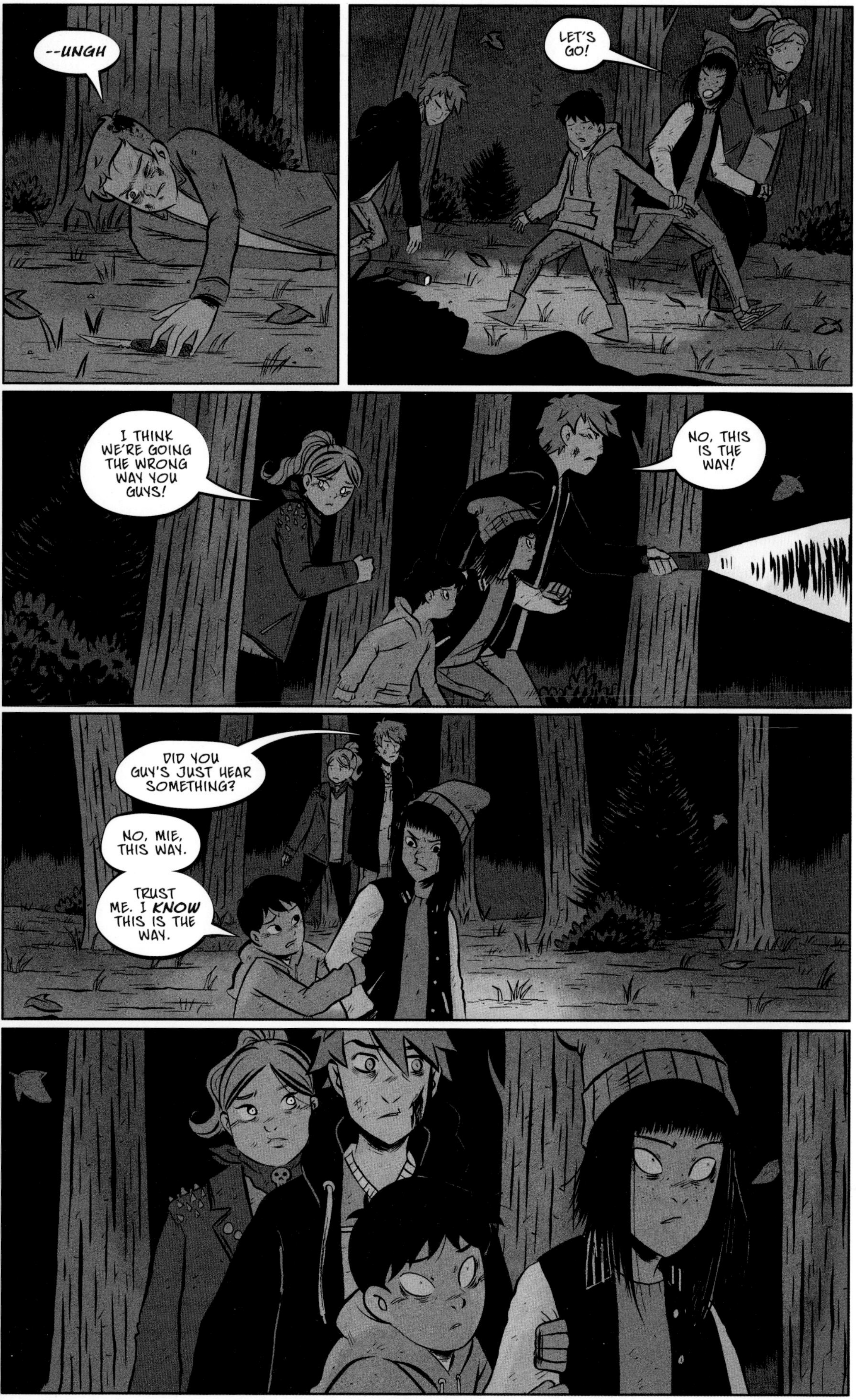
--UNGH
LET'S GO!
I THINK WE'RE GOING THE WRONG WAY YOU GUYS!
NO, THIS IS THE WAY!
DID YOU GUY'S JUST HEAR SOMETHING?
NO, MIE, THIS WAY.
TRUST ME. I **KNOW** THIS IS THE WAY.

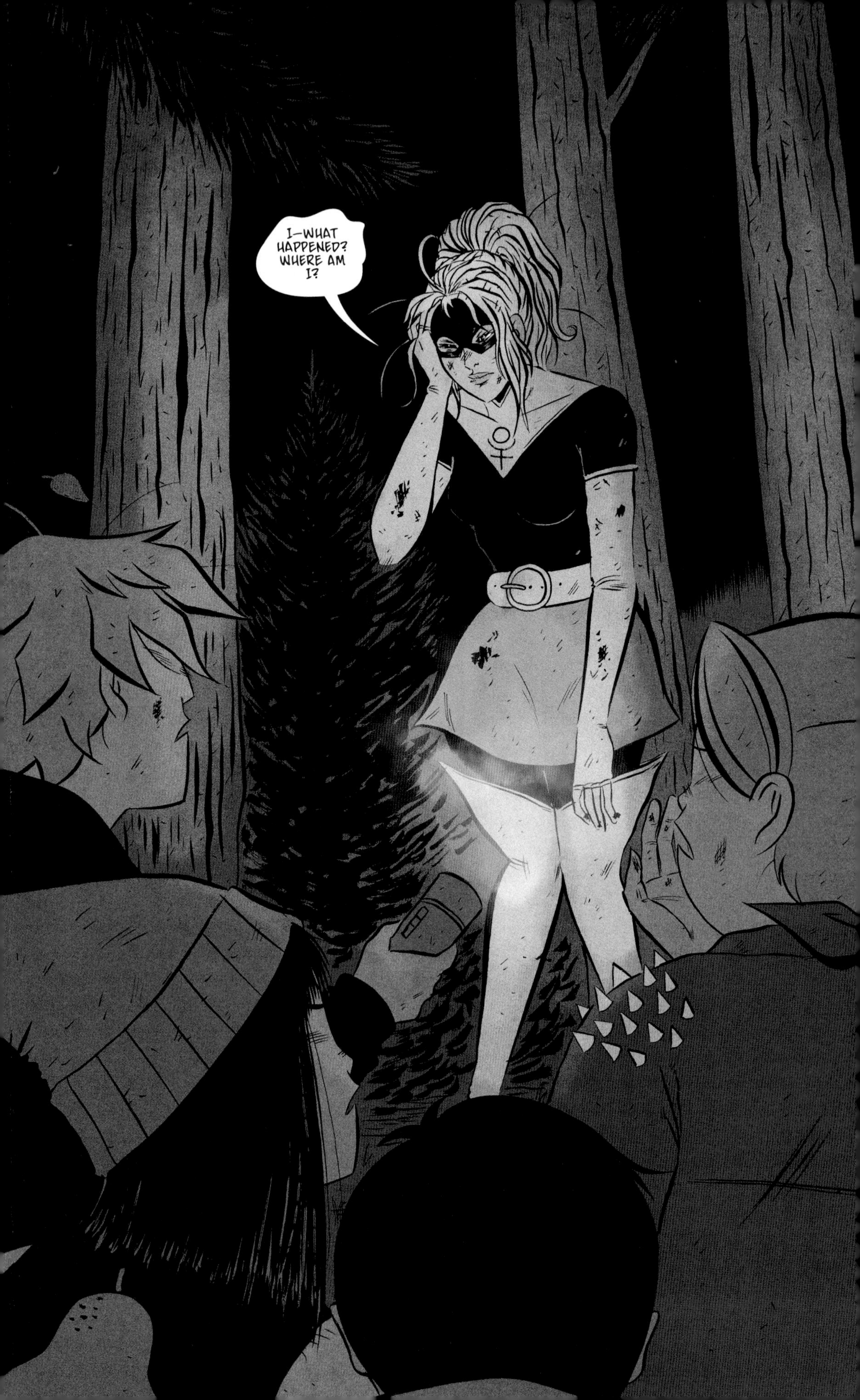
I—WHAT HAPPENED? WHERE AM I?

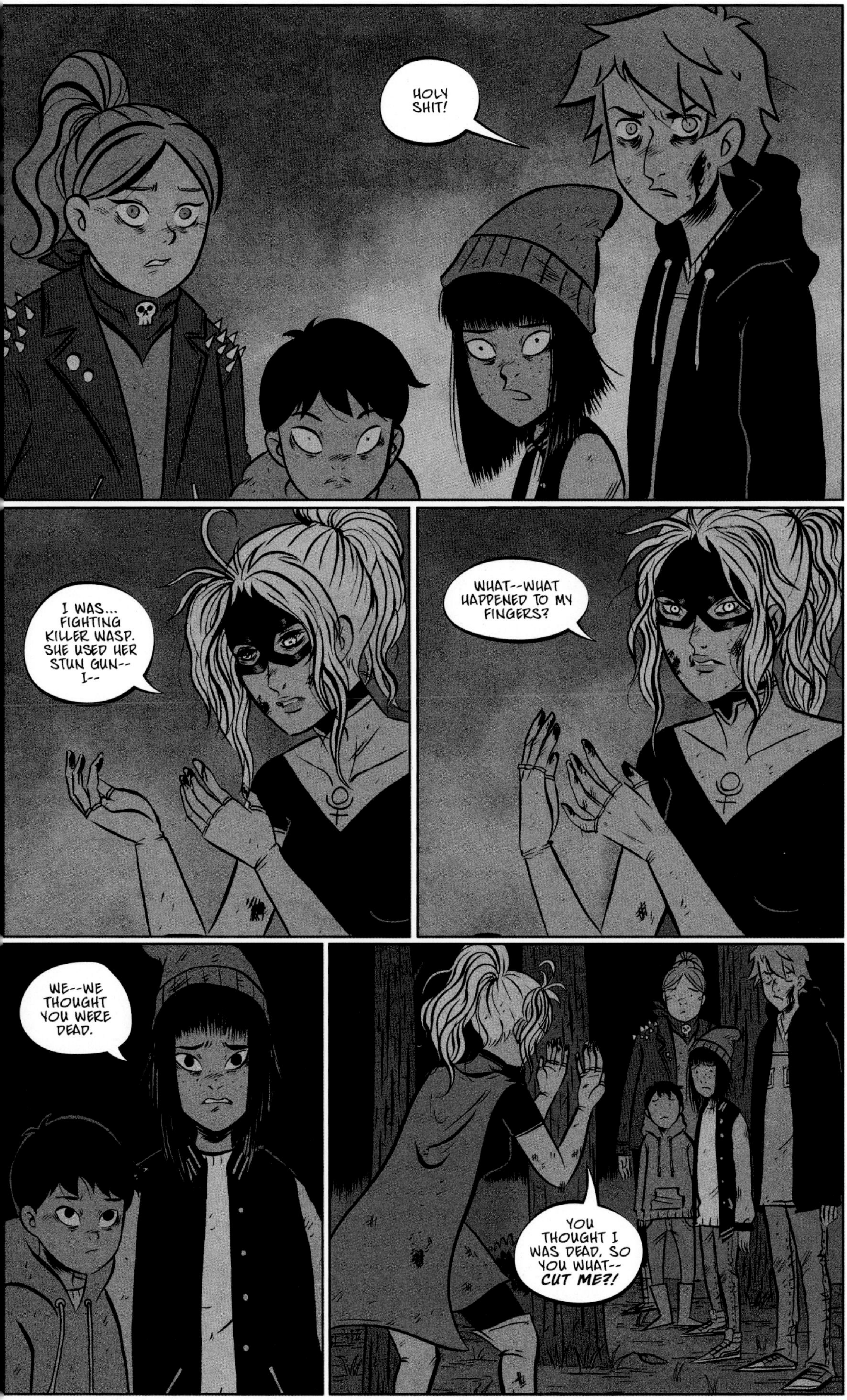
HOLY SHIT!
I WAS... FIGHTING KILLER WASP. SHE USED HER STUN GUN-- I--
WHAT--WHAT HAPPENED TO MY FINGERS?
WE--WE THOUGHT YOU WERE DEAD.
YOU THOUGHT I WAS DEAD, SO YOU WHAT-- CUT ME?!

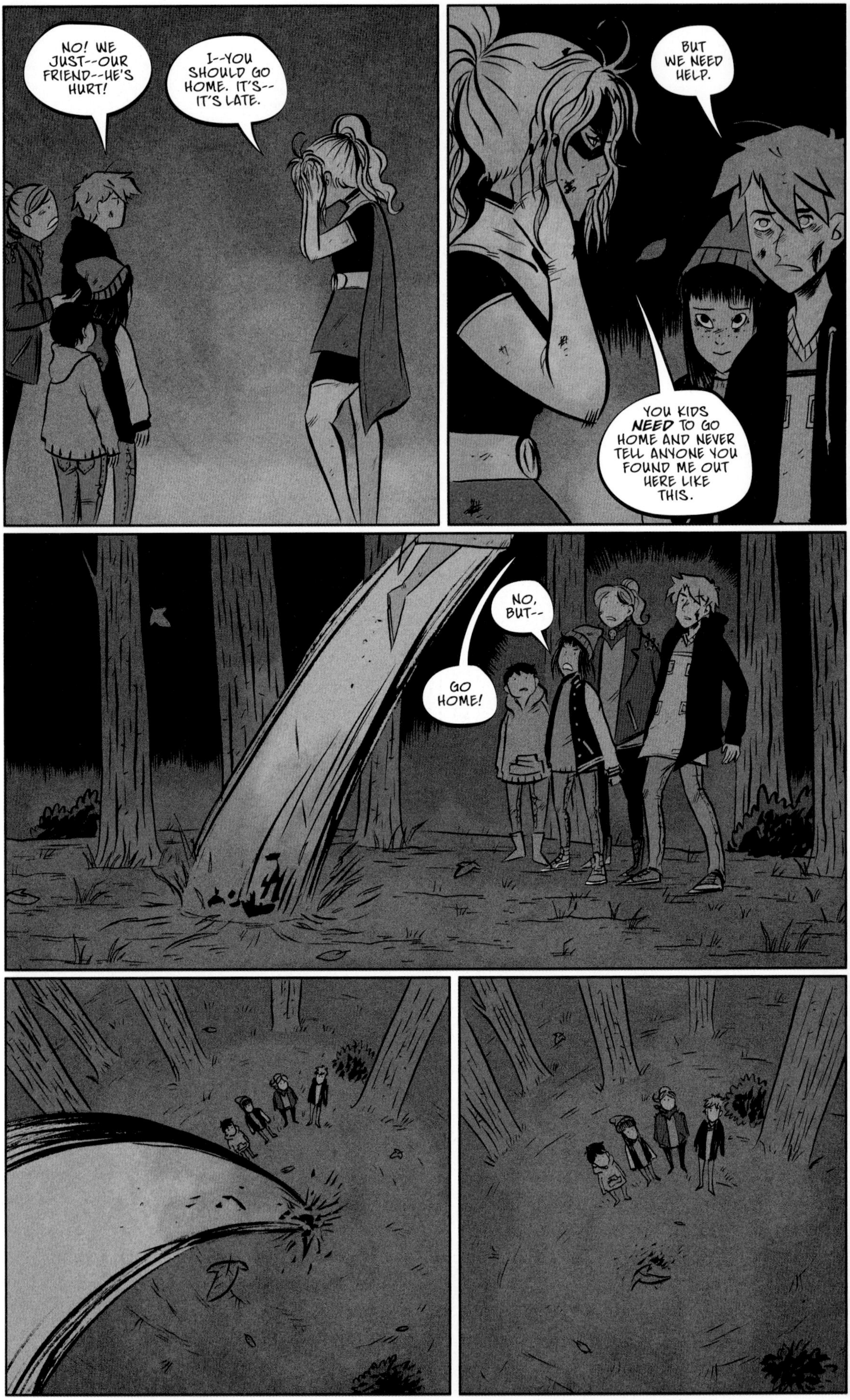
NO! WE JUST--OUR FRIEND--HE'S HURT!
I--YOU SHOULD GO HOME. IT'S--IT'S LATE.
BUT WE NEED HELP.
YOU KIDS **NEED** TO GO HOME AND NEVER TELL ANYONE YOU FOUND ME OUT HERE LIKE THIS.
NO, BUT--
GO HOME!

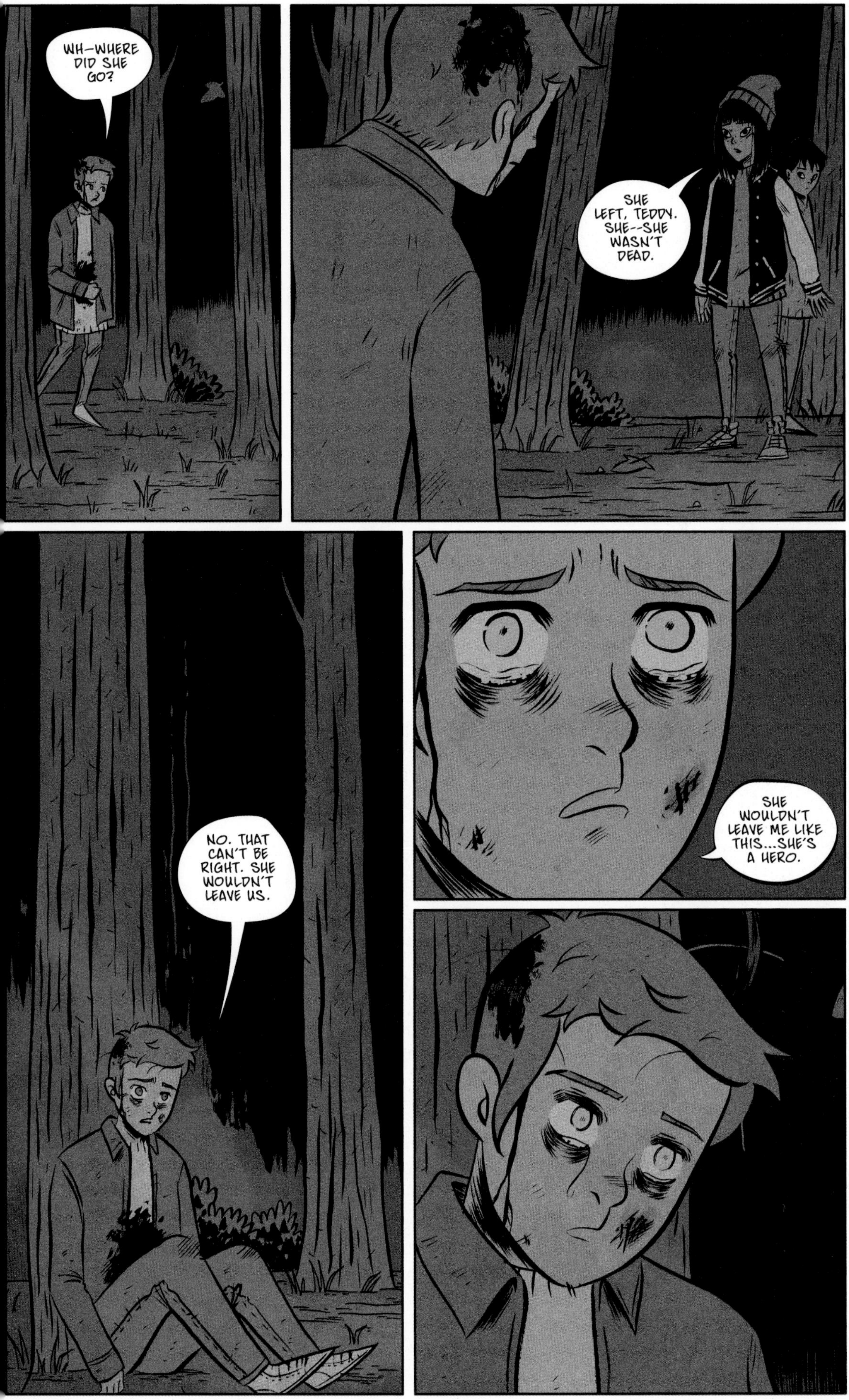
WH—WHERE DID SHE GO?
SHE LEFT, TEDDY. SHE--SHE WASN'T DEAD.
NO. THAT CAN'T BE RIGHT. SHE WOULDN'T LEAVE US.
SHE WOULDN'T LEAVE ME LIKE THIS...SHE'S A HERO.

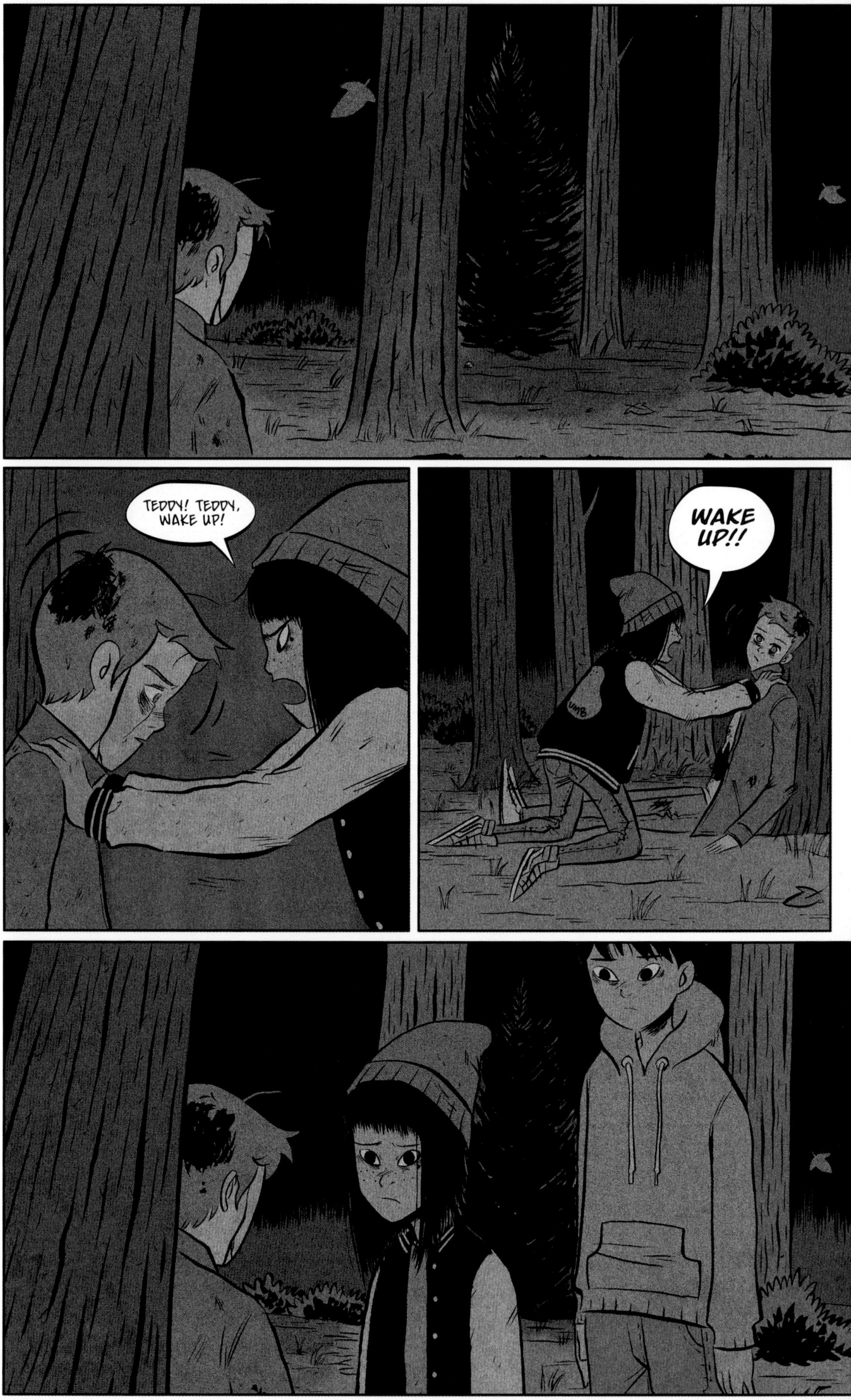
TEDDY! TEDDY, WAKE UP!
WAKE UP!!

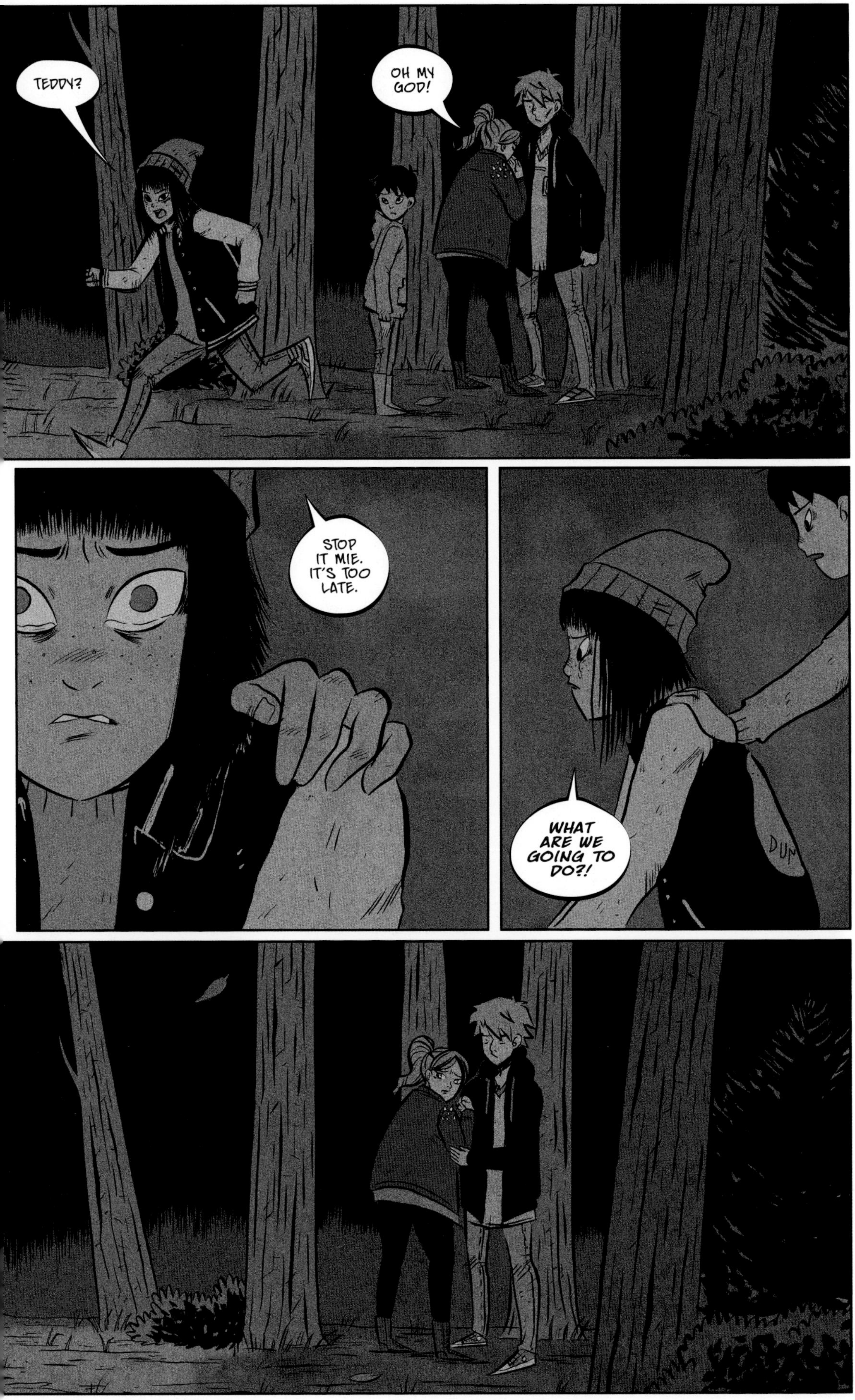
TEDDY?
OH MY GOD!
STOP IT MIE. IT'S TOO LATE.
WHAT ARE WE GOING TO DO?!

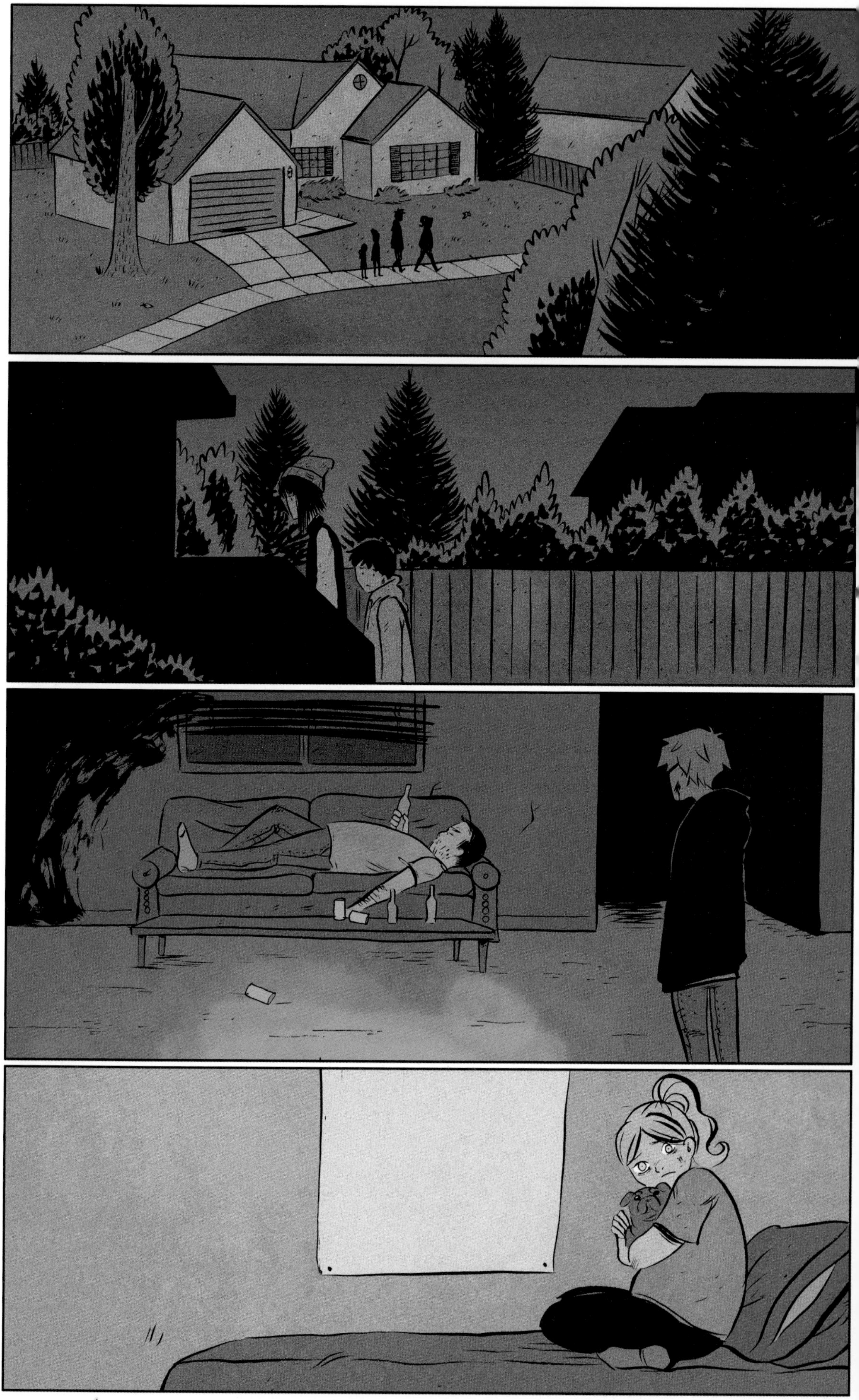

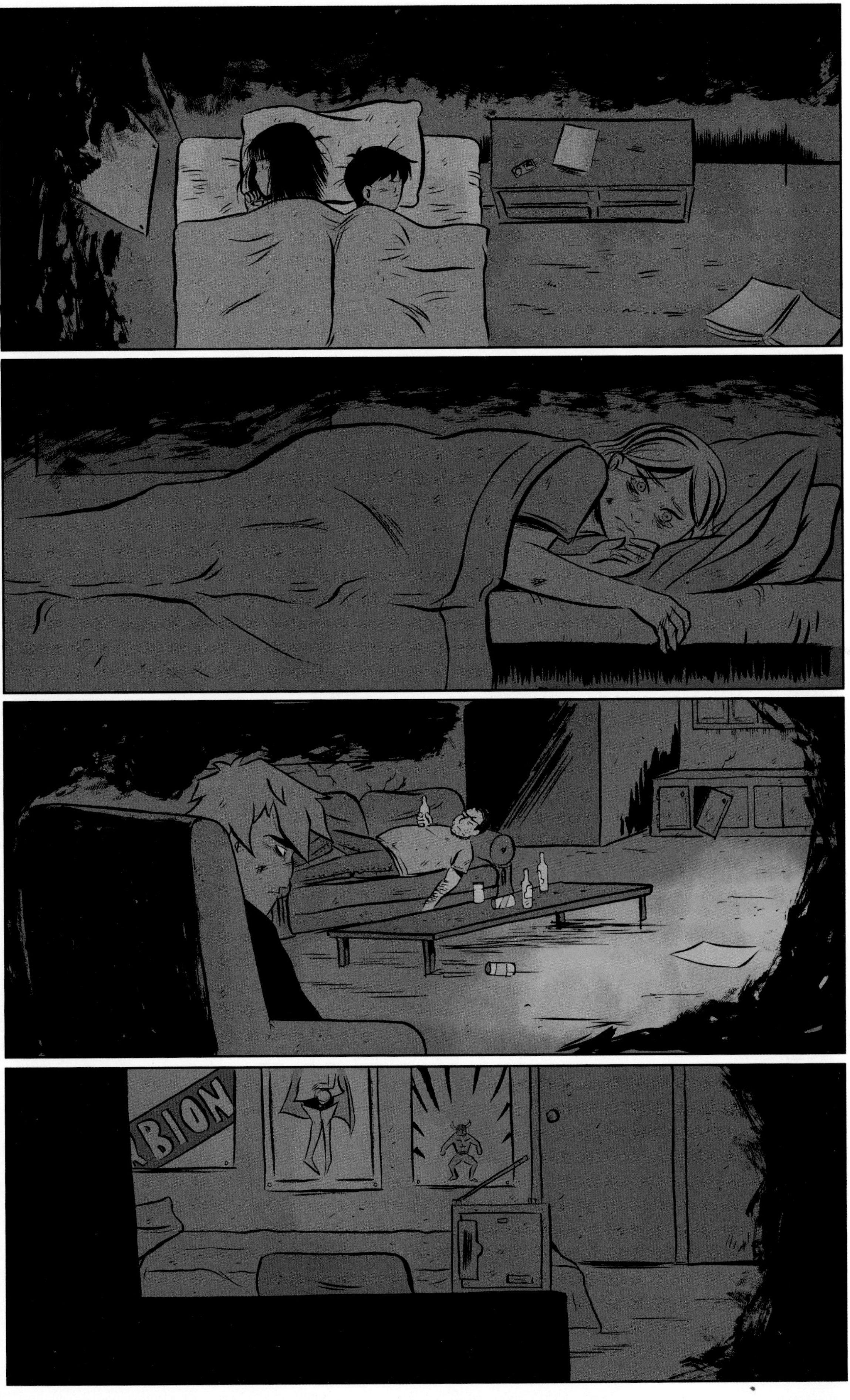
ABION

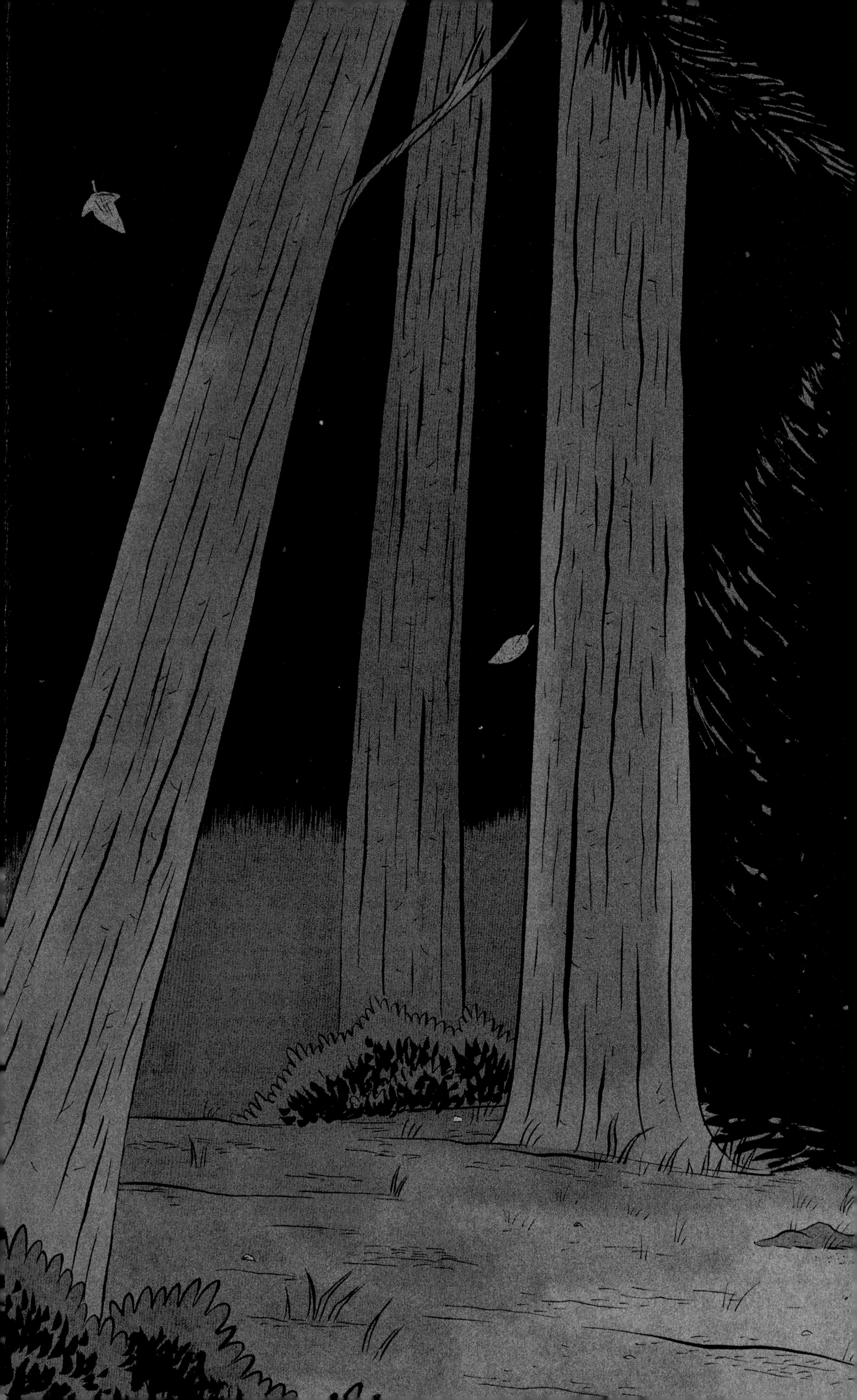

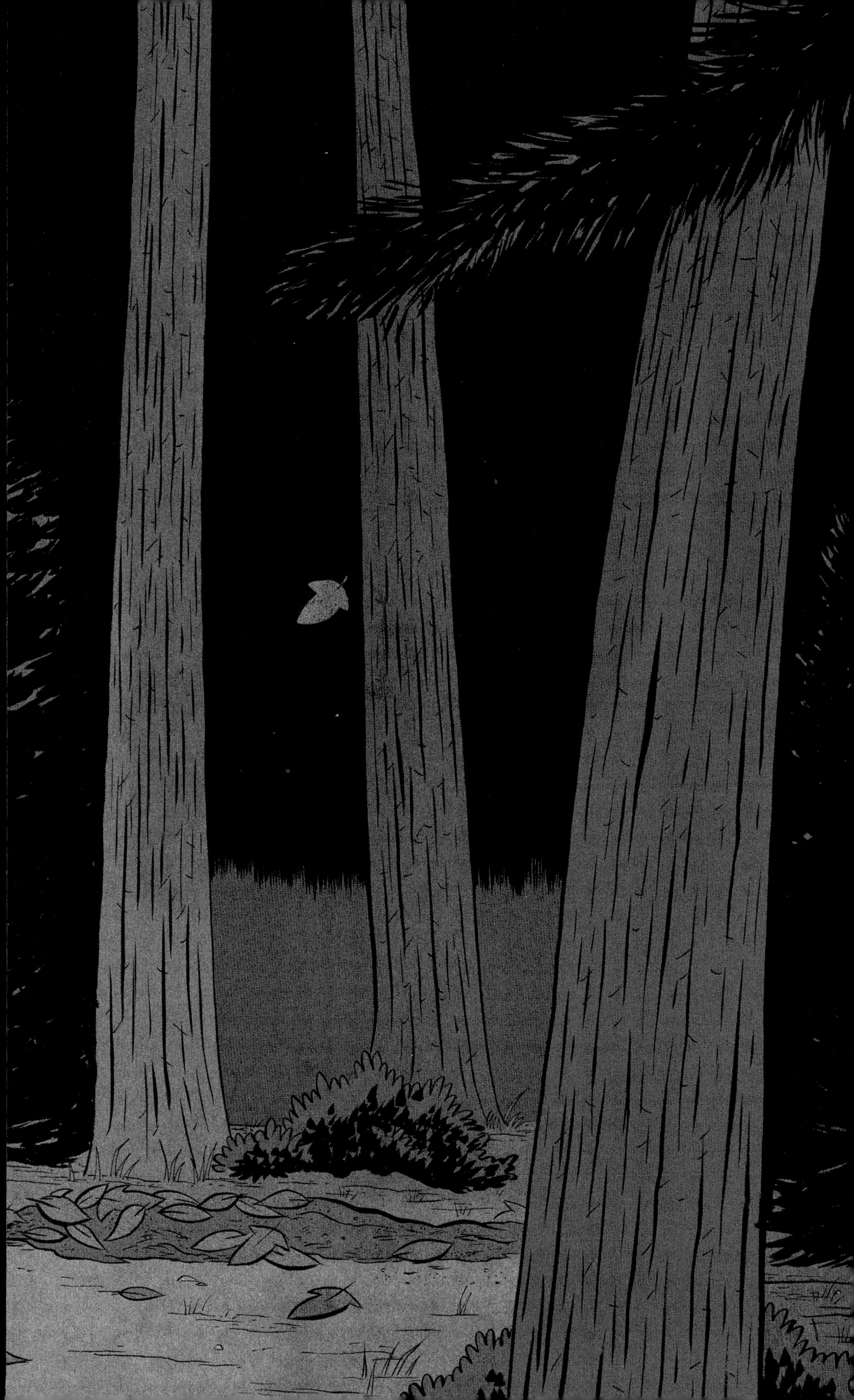

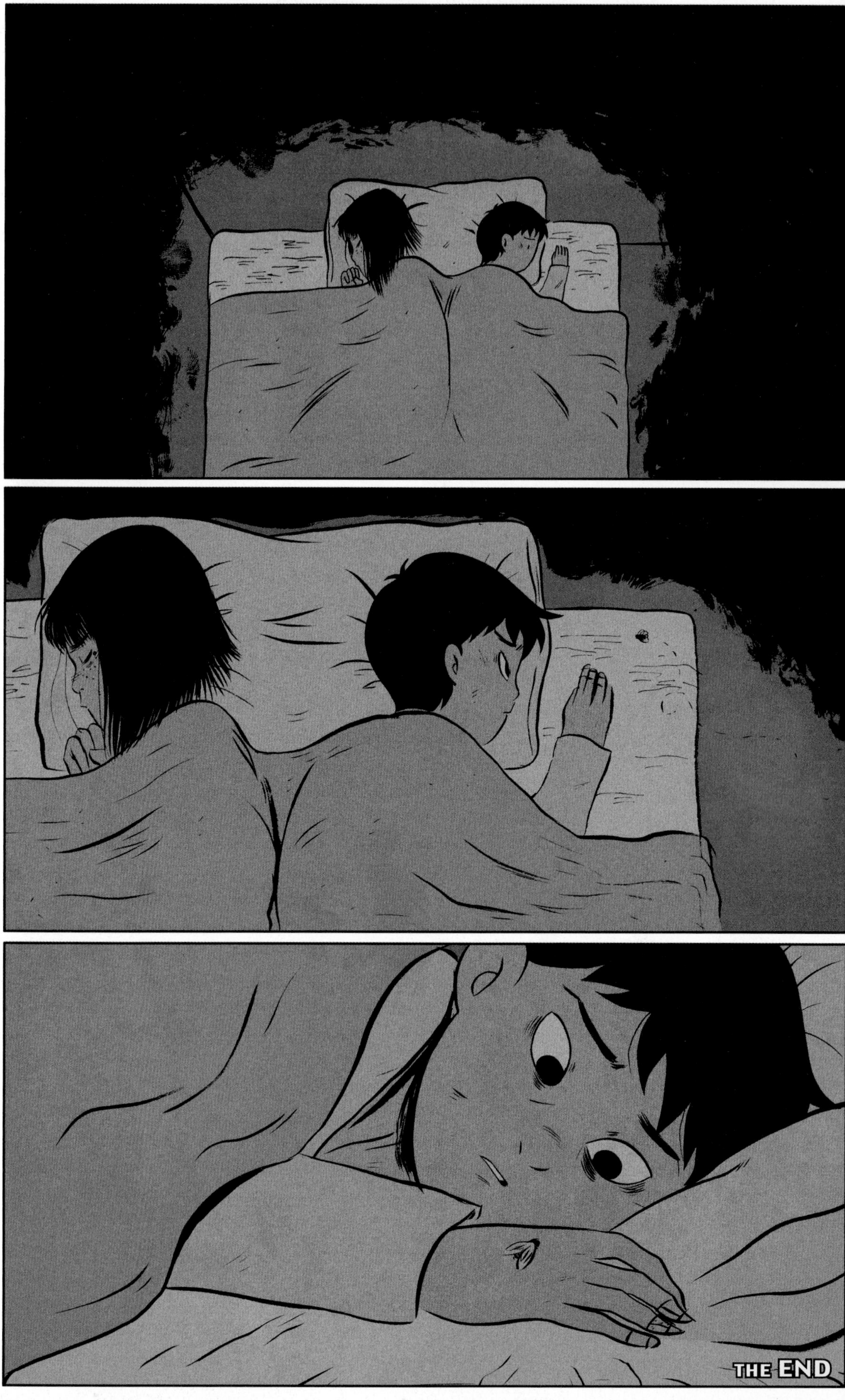
THE END

GALLERY

ORIGINAL SERIES COVERS (#1-5)

EMERALD CITY COMIC CON 2015 PRINT

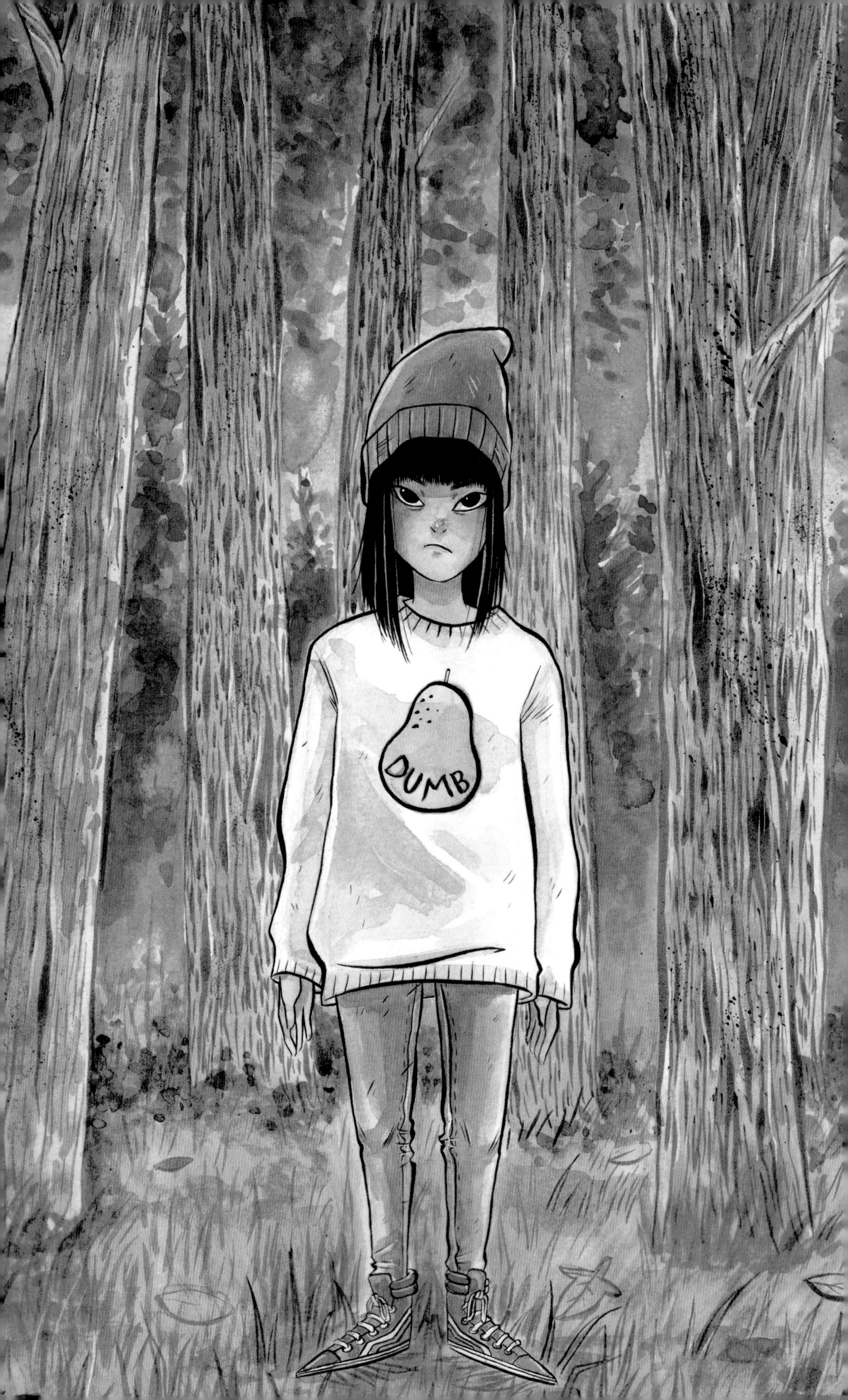
DUMB

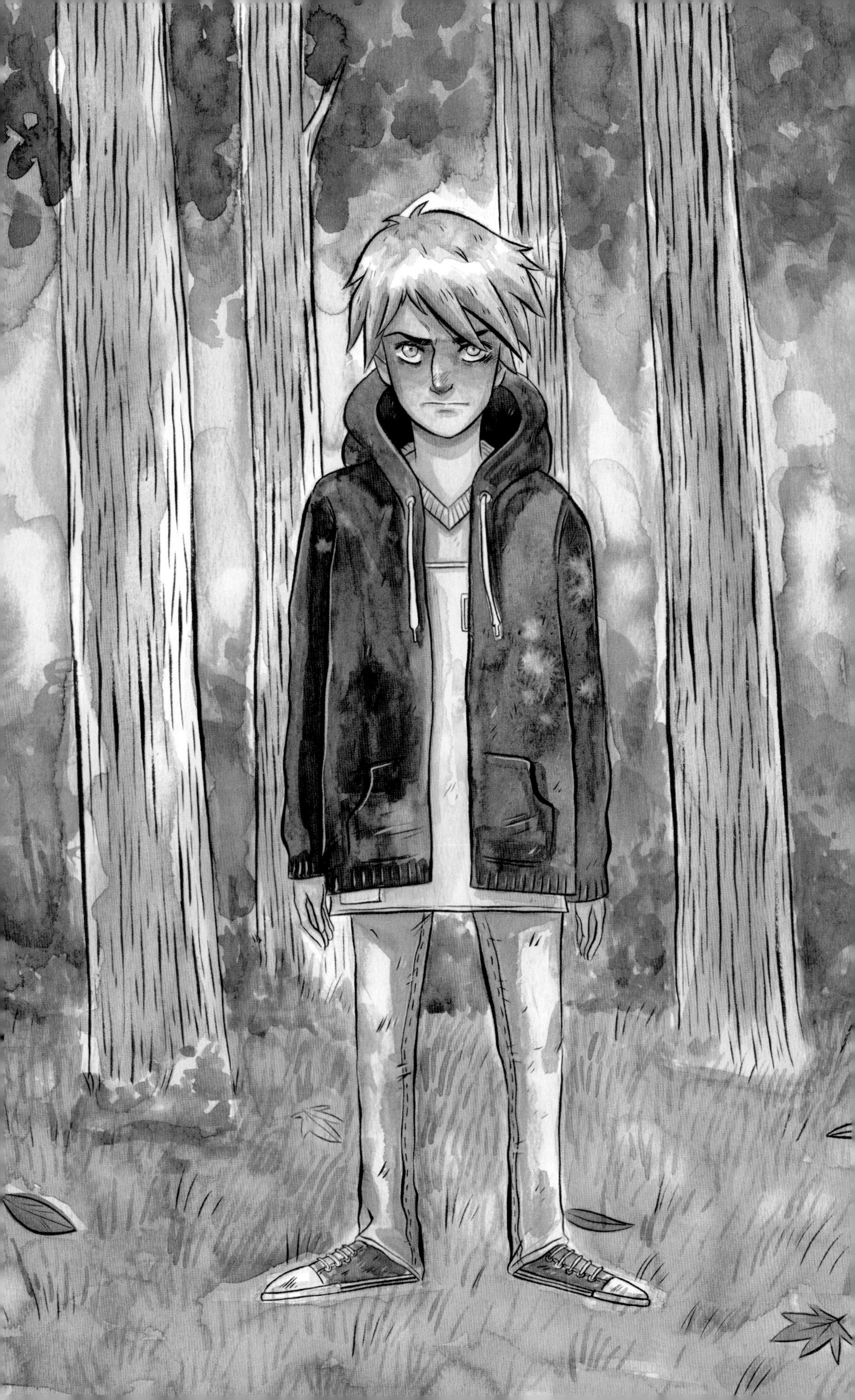

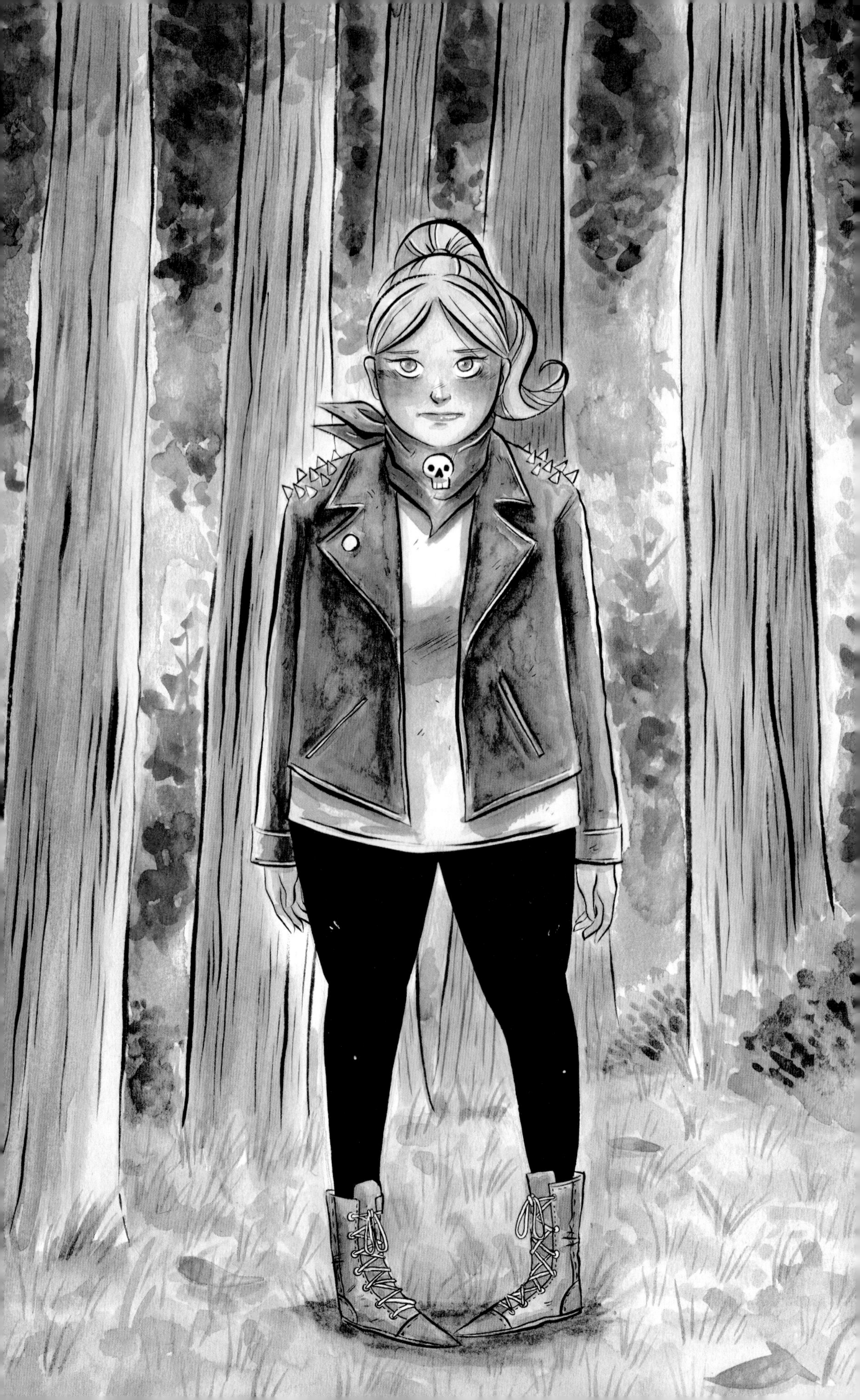

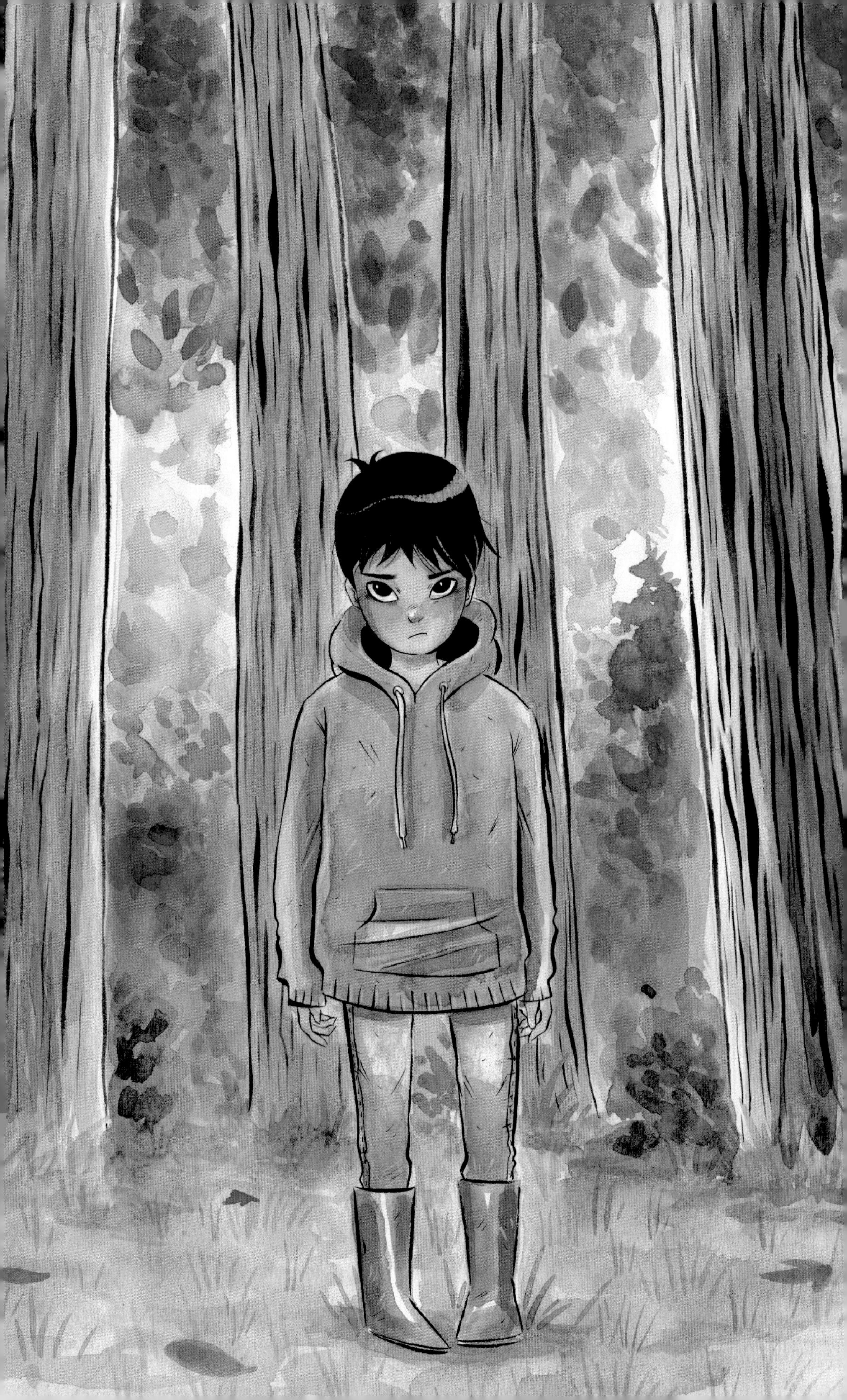

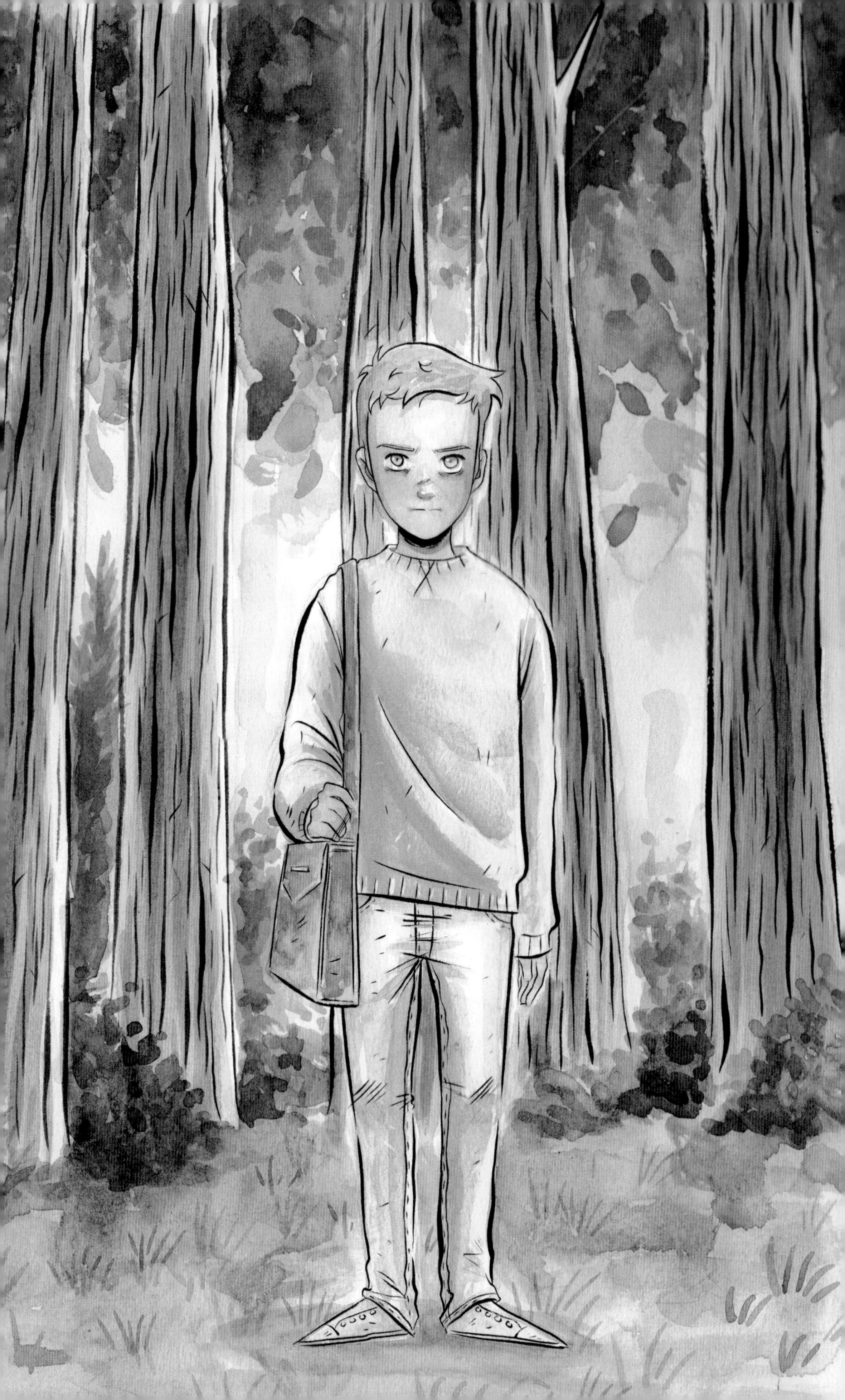

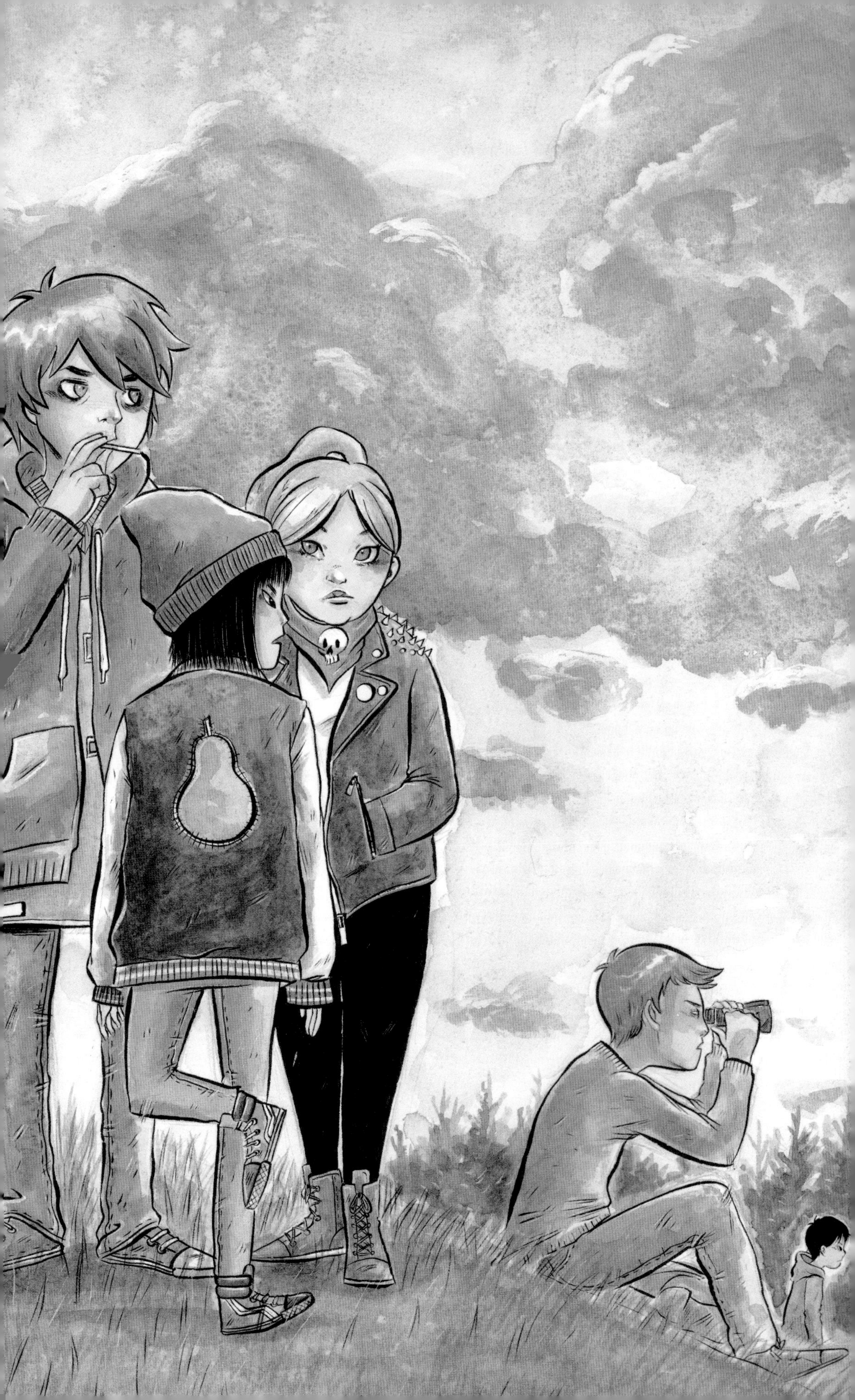

PROCESS

MIE'S OUTFITS (COOL-ASS THREADS)

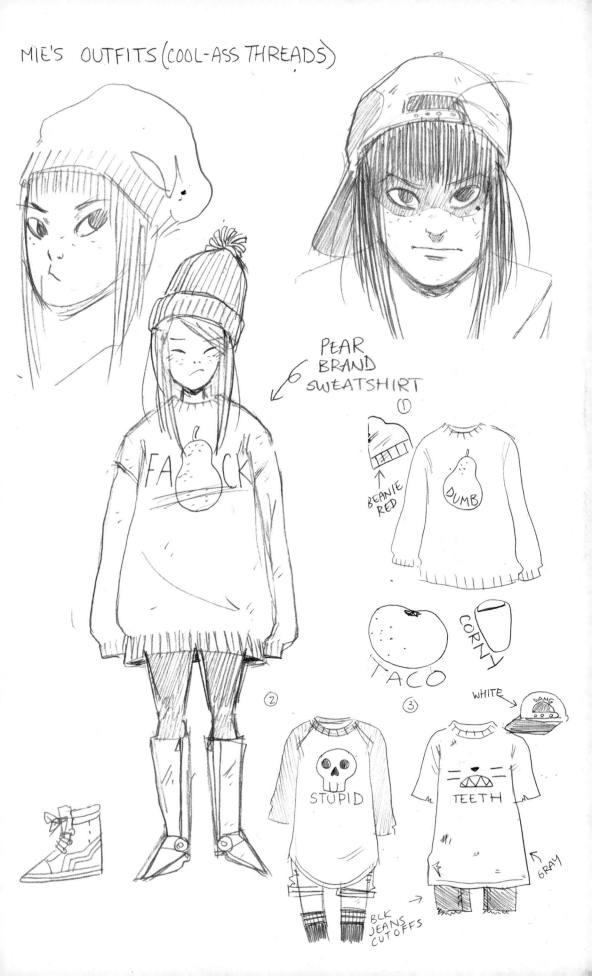

PEAR BRAND SWEATSHIRT

①
BEANIE RED

DUMB

② FA 🍐 CK

TACO
CORNY

③

STUPID

BCK JEANS CUTOFFS

TEETH

WHITE → DANG

GRAY

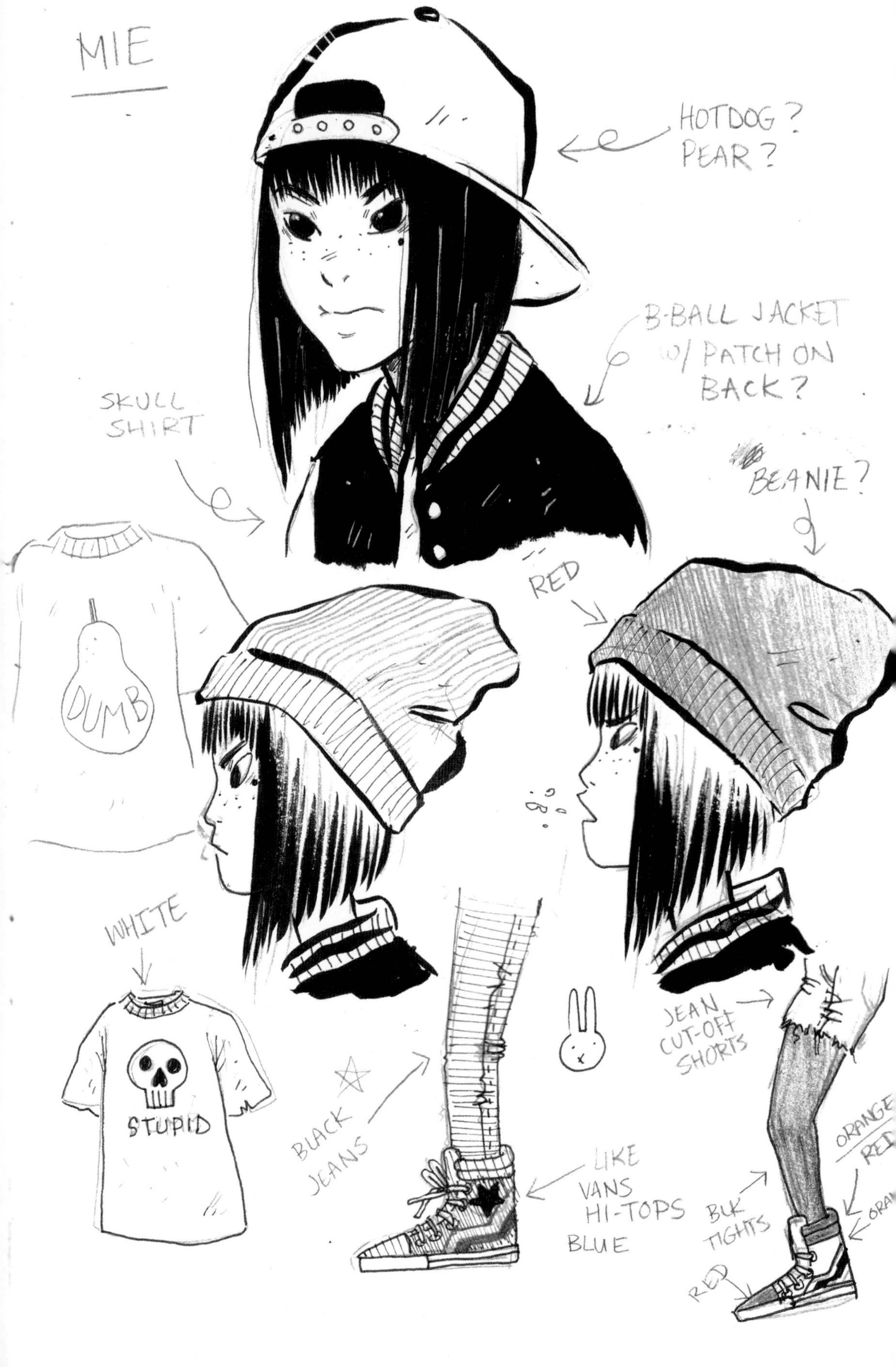

MIE
HOTDOG?
PEAR?
B-BALL JACKET
W/ PATCH ON
BACK?
SKULL
SHIRT
BEANIE?
RED
DUMB
WHITE
STUPID
BLACK
JEANS
LIKE
VANS
HI-TOPS
BLUE
JEAN
CUT-OFF
SHORTS
ORANGE
BLK
TIGHTS
RED

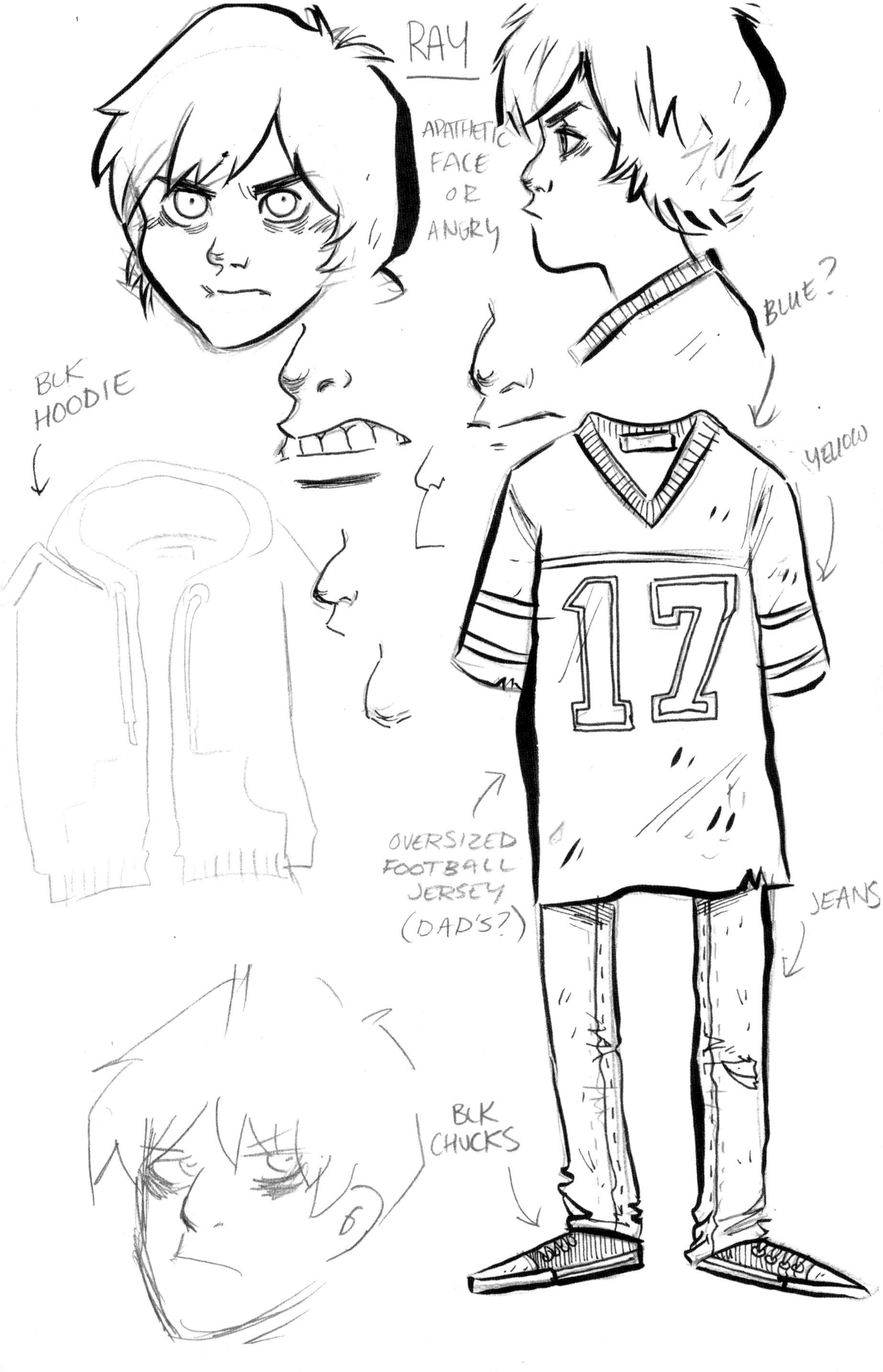
RAY
APATHETIC FACE OR ANGRY
BLUE?
YELLOW
BLK HOODIE
17
OVERSIZED FOOTBALL JERSEY (DAD'S?)
JEANS
BLK CHUCKS

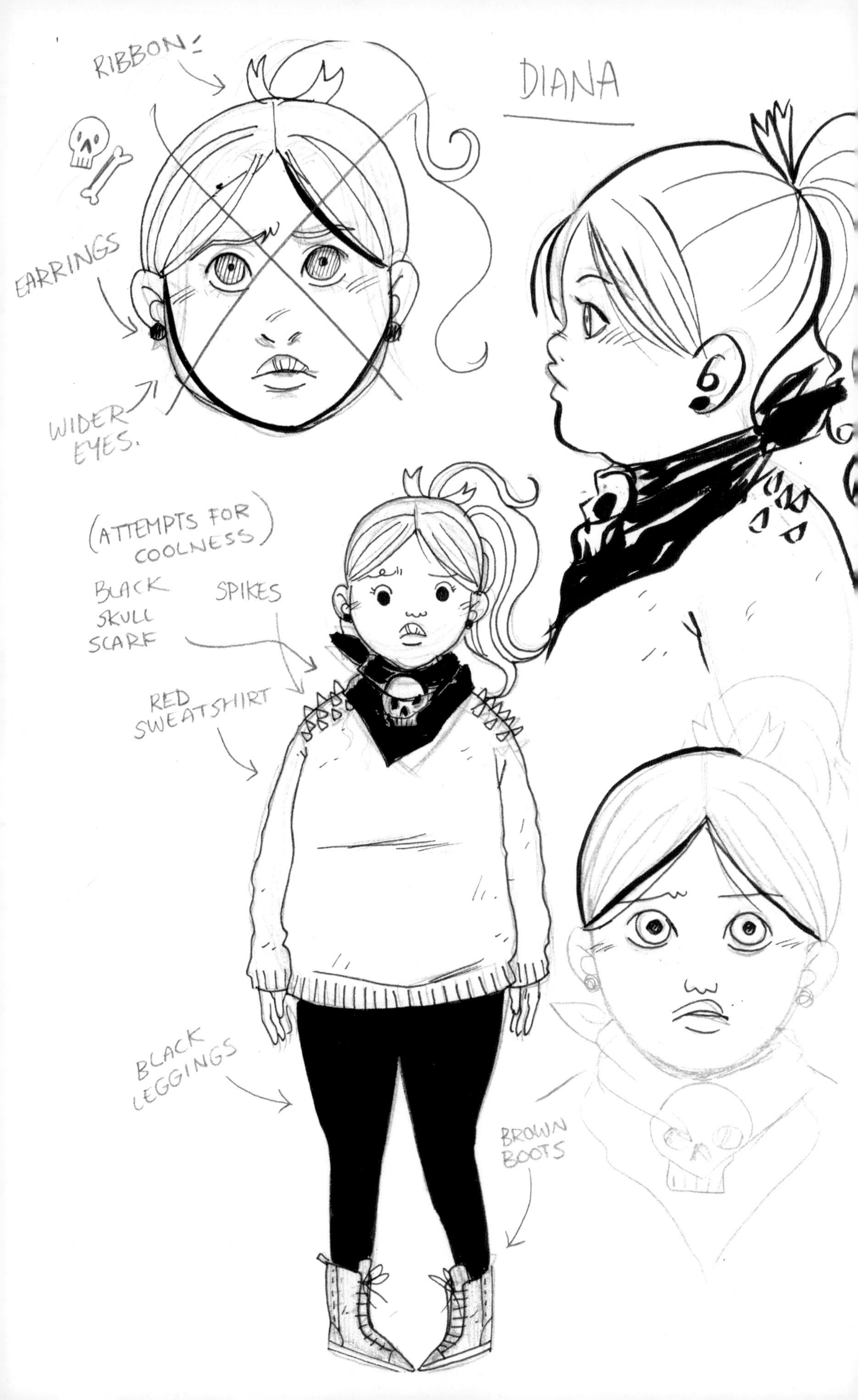
DIANA
RIBBON!
EARRINGS
WIDER EYES.
(ATTEMPTS FOR COOLNESS)
BLACK SKULL SCARF
SPIKES
RED SWEATSHIRT
BLACK LEGGINGS
BROWN BOOTS

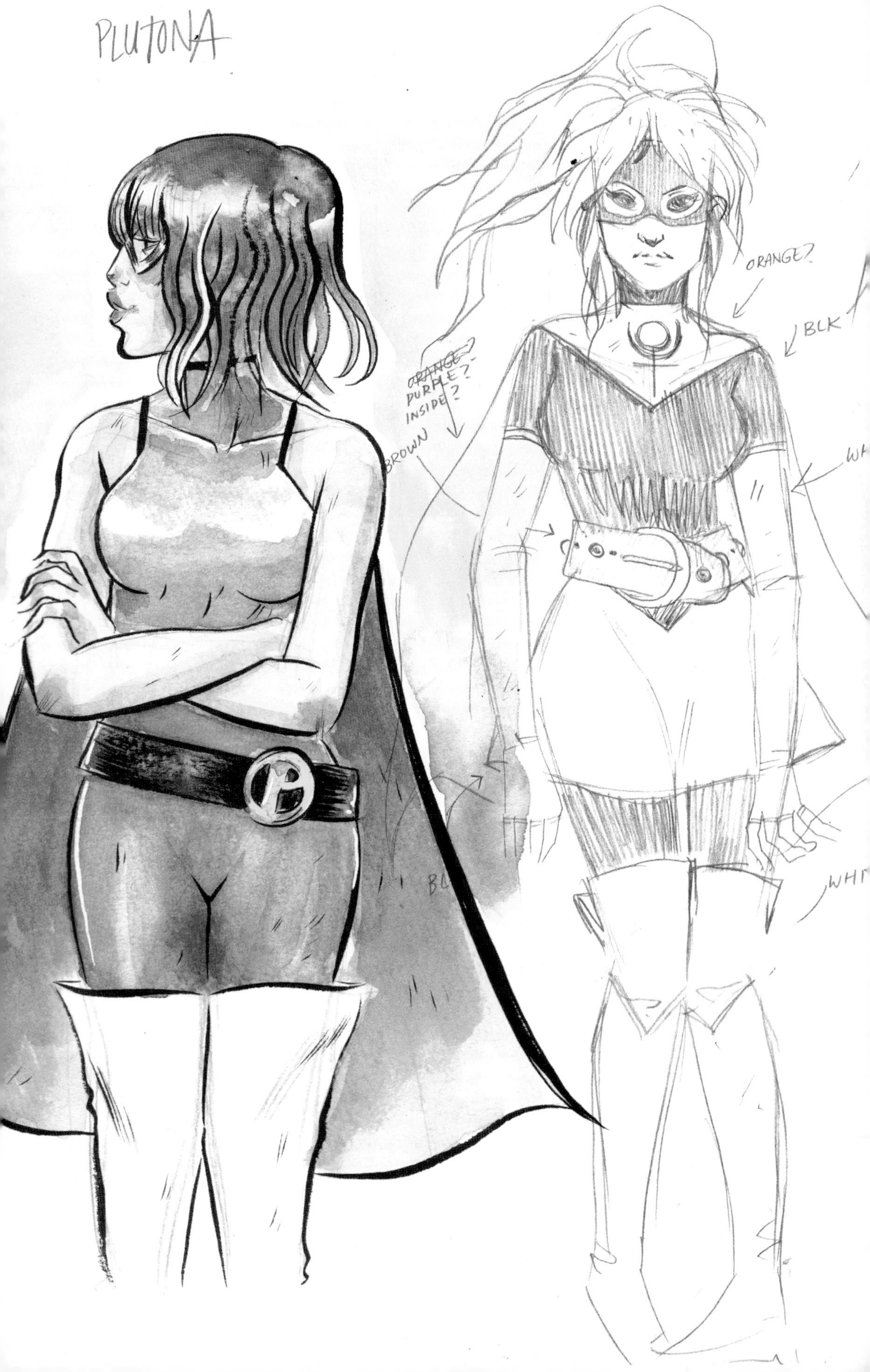
PLUTONA
ORANGE?
BLK
PURPLE?
INSIDE?
BROWN

PIN-UPS

IN ORDER:

DUSTIN **NGUYEN**

RON **CHAN**

SIMON **GANE**

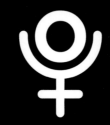

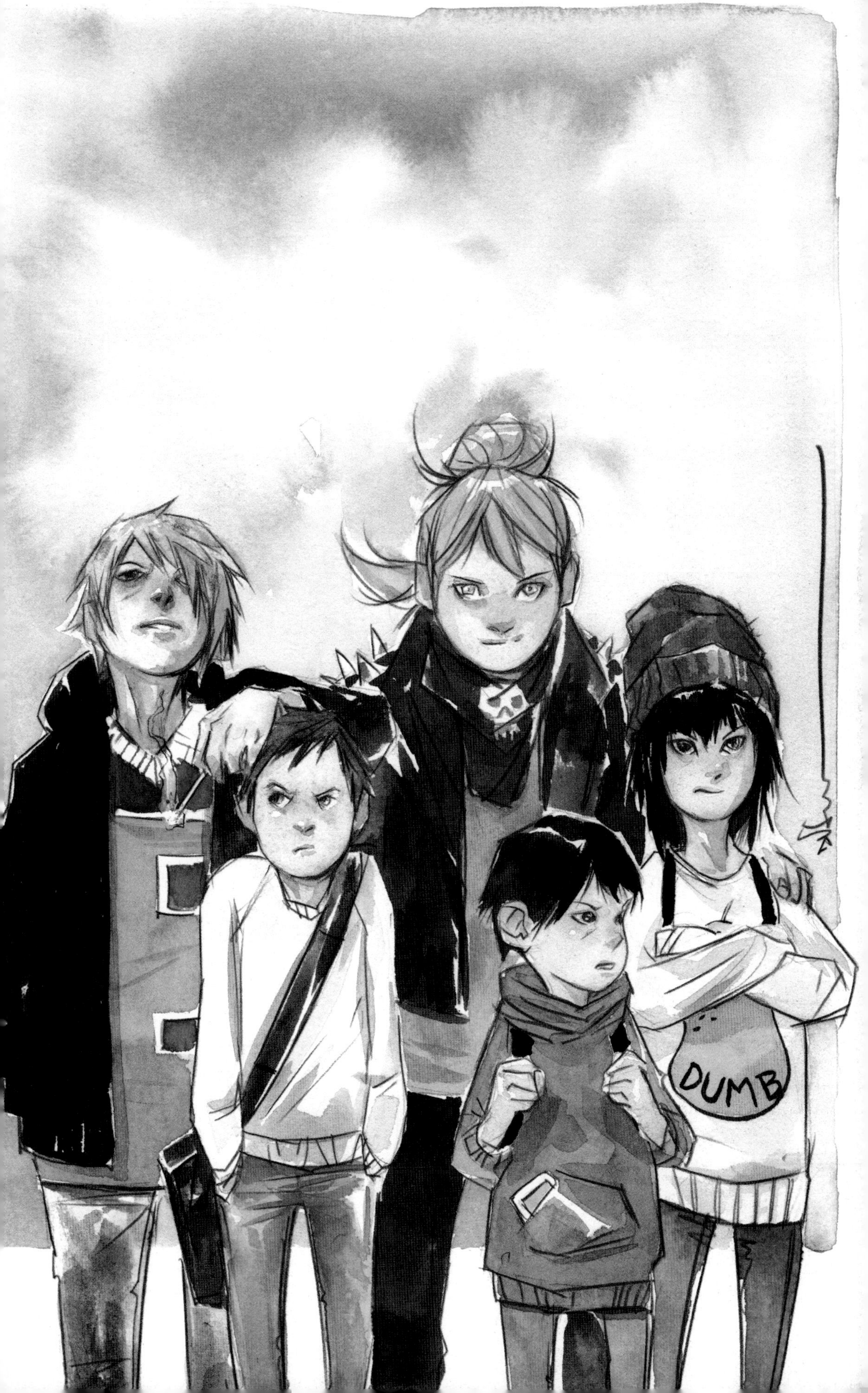
DUMB

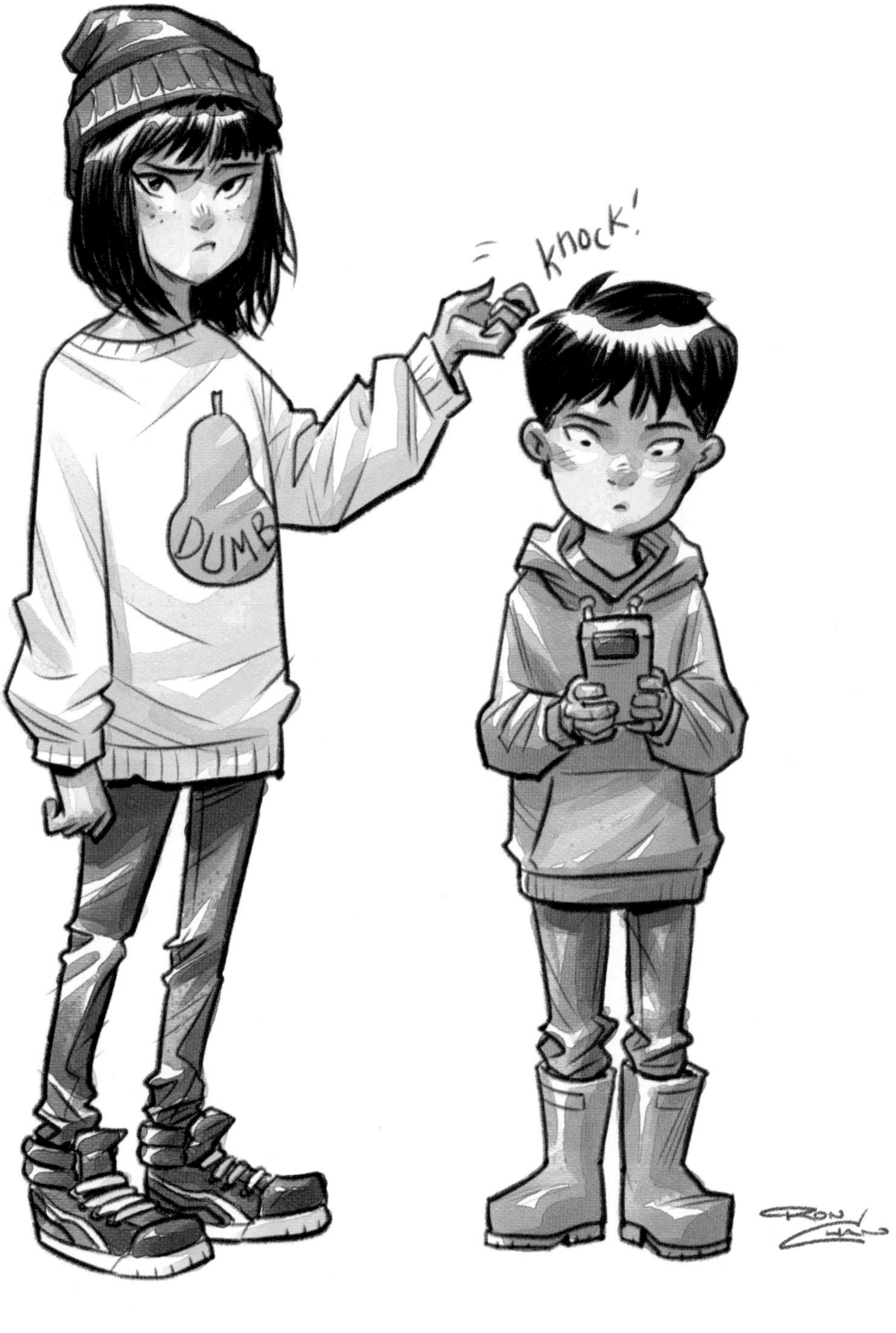
knock!
DUMB

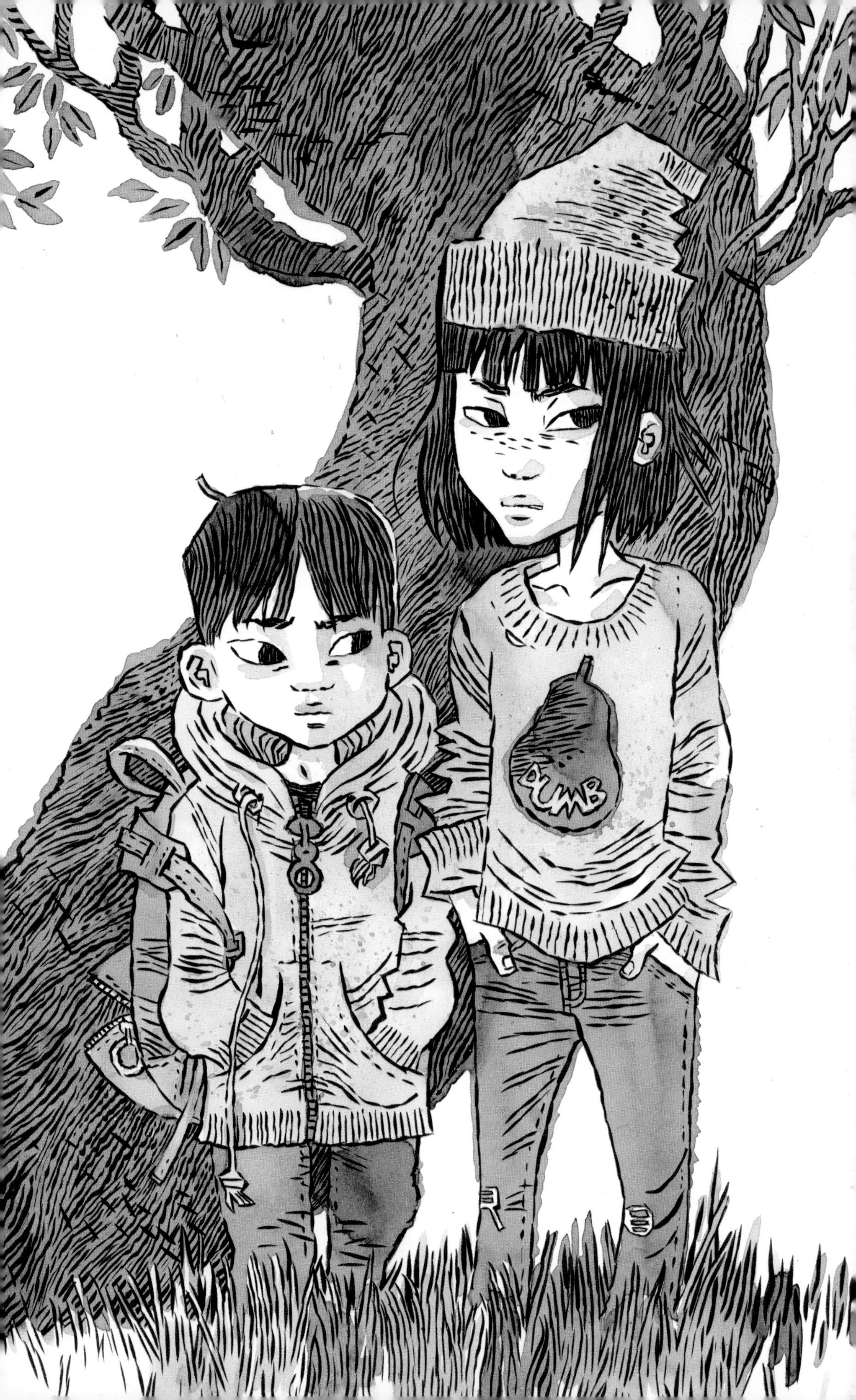
DUMB

JEFF **LEMIRE**

New York Times bestselling author **Jeff Lemire** is the writer and artist of acclaimed literary graphic novels such as **Essex County**, **The Underwater Welder**, **Sweet Tooth**, and **Trillium**. He is co-creator and writer of the bestselling sci-fi series **Descender** with **Dustin Nguyen**, and of **Plutona** with **Emi Lenox**, as well as co-creator and artist on **AD: After Death**.

Lemire's list of accolades includes nominations for 8 Eisner awards, 7 Harvey Awards, 8 Shuster Awards with many of his properties currently in development at major studios for film and TV.

His forthcoming novel *Roughneck* will be published by Simon and Schuster in early 2017.

EMI **LENOX**

Based out of the magical land of Portland, Oregon, **Emi Lenox** is a gal who enjoys drawing comics. She is assisted by Henry the Dog and Kittin the cat.

Her other original published works include **Emitown Volume 1** and **2**. Her work can be seen in other people's works such as **Sweet Tooth**, **Nowhere Men**, **Madman**, **CBLDF's Liberty Annual** to name a few.

She enjoys fruit candies and thai iced teas and she'll never turn down a delicious bloody mary. Black Mage for life.

JORDIE **BELLAIRE**

Jordie Bellaire is an Eisner award winning colorist who has worked on many titles with many publishers. Her credits include *Pretty Deadly*, *Nowhere Men*, *Moon Knight*, *Injection*, *Autumnlands*, *They're Not Like Us*, *X-Files*, *Vision* and others.

She lives in Ireland with her famous cat, Buffy.

STEVE **WANDS**

is a letterer working on top titles at Image Comics, DC, Vertigo, BOOM! Studios, Random House, and Kodansha Comics (to name a few). He also designs, inks, and illustrates for those, and other, companies. When not working he spends time with his wife and sons in New Jersey. Oh, and he drinks a lot of coffee.

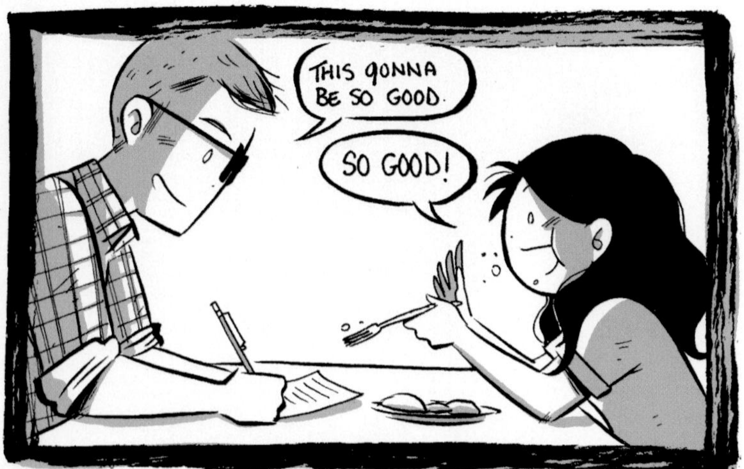
THIS GONNA BE SO GOOD.
SO GOOD!

MET UP WITH JEFF FOR BREAKFAST AND WORKED ON PLUTONA STUFF. I AM SO EXCITED FOR PLUTONA! IT'S SO FUN TO WORK ON A PROJECT WITH A FRIEND TOO. THIS IS THE LIFE.